Springer Series on Agent Technology

Series Editors: T. Ishida N. Jennings K. Sycara

Springer
Berlin
Heidelberg
New York
Barcelona
Hong Kong
London
Milan
Paris
Singapore
Tokyo

Mark d'Inverno
Michael Luck

Understanding
Agent Systems

With 35 Figures and 11 Tables

 Springer

Mark d'Inverno
Cavendish School of Computer Science
University of Westminster
115 New Cavendish Street
London, W1M 8JS
UK
E-mail: dinverm@wmin.ac.uk

Michael Luck
Electronics and Computer Science
University of Southampton
Southampton, SO17 1BJ
UK
E-mail: mml@ecs.soton.ac.uk

Library of Congress Cataloging-in-Publication Data applied for

Die Deutsche Bibliothek – CIP-Einheitsaufnahme

Understanding agent systems/Mark d'Inverno; Michael Luck –
Berlin; Heidelberg; New York; Barcelona; Hong Kong; London;
Milan; Paris; Singapore; Tokyo: Springer, 2001
  (Springer series on agent technology)
  ISBN 3-540-41975-6

ACM Subject Classification (1998): I.2, C.2.4, F.3.1, D.2.1

ISBN 3-540-41975-6 Springer-Verlag Berlin Heidelberg New York

Springer-Verlag Berlin Heidelberg New York
a member of BertelsmannSpringer Science+Business Media GmbH

http://www.springer.de

© Springer-Verlag Berlin Heidelberg 2001
Printed in Germany

Typesetting: Camera-ready by the editors
Cover Design: design + production, Heidelberg
Printed on acid-free paper   SPIN 10781836 – 06/3142SR – 5 4 3 2 1 0

Preface

Around ten years ago, when we were both PhD students, working on different but related aspects of artificial intelligence, we shared an office in the furthest corner of the Department of Computer Science at University College London. Our friendship began then, but our professional collaboration only really got going when we both left, one of us moving the few yards to the University of Westminster and the other further afield to the University of Warwick and later the University of Southampton. Nevertheless, we can trace back many of our inspirations to those days at UCL, in discussions with Derek Long, John Campbell, Maria Fox and John Wolstencroft, who all contributed to our initial enthusiasm for working in this area.

On leaving UCL, however, we tried to bring our research interests together in the newly emerging area of agent-based systems, but found difficulties in communication with each other over basic terms and concepts, simply due to the immaturity of the field. In other words, the problems we had in finding a base on which to develop our ideas set us on a long path, over a number of years, resulting in our construction and refinement of a conceptual framework within which to define, analyse and explore different aspects of agents and multi-agents systems. This is the work reported in this book.

Chapter 1 reviews the *agent landscape*, outlining the key concepts of agent-based systems and some of the difficulties that have arisen, particularly in relation to definition and characterisation of agents. It makes reference to numerous reviews and definitions and shows just how varied the attitudes towards agents are. The chapter ends with an introduction to the methodology used in the book: the need for a formal framework, the choice of the Z specification language, and the style of presentation that is used throughout.

Chapter 2 is perhaps the most fundamental chapter in the book, providing full details of the SMART agent framework that underpins everything else. It begins with the introduction of the primitive notions used, and moves on to define the different kinds of entity that exist in our four-tiered agent hierarchy, considering both action and perception along the way. Here agents are distinguished from both objects and autonomous agents in a clear and detailed fashion, both intuitively and mathematically.

The relationships between agents are the subject of Chapter 3, arising as a natural consequence of the basic definitions of agents from the previous chapter. In particular, goal adoption is seen as the critical mechanism underlying multi-agent systems, with the notions of engagement of one agent by another and the cooperation of two autonomous agents resulting directly from it. These relationships are analysed further to arrive at a more sophisticated taxonomy of inter-agent relationships. Chapter 4 complements this by describing the ways in which these relationships can be created and destroyed. One of our key motivations is to remain connected to issues of implementation, requiring just such an operational account as well as the declarative one of Chapter 3.

In Chapter 5, the SMART framework is further developed to include different dimensions of agents that are necessary for their effective operation in multi-agent systems in dynamic and open environments. In particular, the chapter considers various aspects of agent modelling as well as the incorporation of plans for more complex action and interaction. One key result here is the construction of a taxonomy of plan and agent categories that are useful for agents to better understand their environments and to take greater advantage of them.

The remaining chapters are concerned with the development of case studies to illustrate the application of the SMART framework to a range of diverse systems and theories. Chapter 6 shows how the contract net protocol is easily captured within the framework; Chapter 7 demonstrates its applicability to a BDI architecture, AgentSpeak(L); and Chapter 8 shows how it can be used to reformulate, and identify limiting assumptions in, a rather different theoretical model, Social Power Theory, and its computational counterpart, Social Dependence Networks.

Finally, Chapter 9 reviews the overall contribution of the book, and evaluates the applicability and generality of SMART. In all this, each chapter provides an intuitive conceptual description of the basic concepts, and augments it with a formal specification in Z. Both of these aspects are intended to be self contained, with adequate explanation to make sense of the formalisation in most cases, even for those without prior knowledge of the Z language.

The work described here is the result of a number of years of joint work, and is reported in several journal and conference papers published in that time [27, 28, 29, 30, 31, 32, 33, 34, 35, 36, 61, 80, 81, 82, 83, 84, 85]. We would like to take this opportunity to thank the anonymous referees who have provided useful comments and feedback for those articles, and also to make special mention of Alfred Hofmann at Springer who has seen this book through to completion.

Perhaps more important has been the support we have had from colleagues, family and friends, at work and home, who provided an environment that encouraged us in our research. Particular thanks should go to Paul Howells, Nick Jennings, Mike Joy, Sara Kalvala, Muthu Muthukrishnan, Mark Priestly, Maarten de Rijke and Steve Winter, who provided support from within our own institutions.

Colleagues at other institutions have also helped greatly with discussion, debate and sometimes disagreement over our work in particular, and agent-based systems in general. Thanks to Cristiano Castelfranchi, Alex Coddington, Rosaria Conte, Jon Crowcroft, Rogier van Eijk, Michael Fisher, Stan Franklin, Mike Georgeff, Suran Goonatilake, Koen Hindriks, Wiebe van der Hoek, David Kinny, John-Jules Meyer, Jörg Müller, Simon Parsons, Anand Rao, Mike Wooldridge, and Chengqi Zhang.

Many of our students and research fellows also helped along the way by identifying errors, problems, and generally causing our presentation to be enhanced: Ronald Ashri, Kevin Bryson, Sorabain de Lioncourt, Nathan Griffiths, Fabiola Lopez y Lopez, Simon Miles, Alex Poylisher and Craig Tunstall.

Thanks also to Abha, Jo and Leo, Jeremy and Monica (and Francesca and Martina), Dan and Franky, Lucy, Catherine, John and Philippa, Guido and Betty, Rachel, Orly, Rona, Erzsebet, Sharon and Ben (and Daniel, Jonathan and Francesca) Marcia, Val, Debbie, Christine, Carla, Dolly and Candy (and Tiger and Hector), Phil and Geddy (and Michael and Daisy), Gi and Philly (and Beany, Tatti, Oscar and Flo), Andy and Mel (and Thomas and Max), Neil and Susi (and Alex and Olly), Tim and Lisa, Dave and Jo, Karen and Jason, Val and Bill, Emma, Ali and Dave, Chris and Secha, Jenny, Nicki and Tony, Nicki and Giles, Chris and Sylvia, Tony and Leslie, Polly and Antonia, Lisa Rigg, Mike Freeman, Mike Bacon, Dicks, Hutch, Gib, Lawso, Banksy, Pog, the Lab Bar, Weekenders C.C. and Choral Clench, all of whom have distracted us so easily.

Finally, special thanks to Claire, and to both sets of parents.

London and Southampton   *Michael Luck*
February 2001   *Mark d'Inverno*

Contents

List of Figures

List of Tables

1. The Agent Landscape

1.1 Introduction

Over the last decade or so, the notions underlying agent-based systems have become almost commonplace, yet were virtually unknown in earlier years. Not only have agent-based systems moved into the mainstream, they have spread beyond a niche area of interest in artificial intelligence, and have come to be a significant and generic computing technology. The dramatic and sustained growth of interest is demonstrated by the increasing number of major conferences and workshops in this very dynamic field, covering a depth and breadth of research that testifies to an impressive level of maturity for such a relatively young area.

Some of the reasons for the growth in popularity of the field (apart from the obvious intuitive appeal of the agent metaphor) can be seen in the progress made in complementary technologies [79], of which perhaps the most dramatic has been the emergence of the World Wide Web. The distribution of information and associated technologies lend themselves almost ideally to use by, in and for multi-agent systems, while the problems that arise as a consequence suggest no solution quite as much as agents. The dual aspect of this interaction with the World Wide Web has thus been a major driving force. Other contributing factors include advances in distributed object technology that have provided an infrastructure without which the development of large-scale agent systems would become much more difficult and less effective. For example, the CORBA distributed computing platform [99] and the more recent Jini networking infrastructure [1], to handle low-level interoperation of heterogeneous distributed components, are both valuable technologies that can underpin the development of agent systems without the need for re-invention of fundamental techniques.

The contradiction of agent-based systems is that there is still an effort to provide a sound conceptual foundation despite the onward march of applications development. Indeed, while there are still disagreements over the nature of agents themselves, significant commercial and industrial research and development efforts have been underway for some time [13, 21, 101, 102], and are set to grow further.

A recurrent theme that is raised in one form or another at many agent conferences and workshops is the lack of agreement over what it is that actually constitutes an agent. It is difficult to know if this is a help or hindrance, but the truth is that it is probably both. On the one hand, the immediately engaging concepts and images that spring to mind when the term is mentioned are a prime reason for the popularisation of agent systems in the broader (and even public) community, and for the extremely rapid growth and development of the field. Indeed the elasticity in terminology and definition of agent concepts has led to the adoption of common terms for a broad range of research activity, providing an inclusive and encompassing set of interacting and cross-fertilising sub-fields. This is partly responsible for the richness of the area, and for the variety of approaches and applications. On the other hand, however, the lack of a common understanding leads to difficulties in communication, a lack of precision (and sometimes even confusion) in nomenclature, vast overuse and abuse of the terminology, and a proliferation of systems adopting the agent label without obvious justification for doing so. The discussion is valuable and important, for without a common language, there can be significant barriers to solid progress, but it is problematic to find a way to converge on such a language without constraining or excluding areas in the current spectrum of activity.

This book seeks to address the aforementioned problems by providing a sound conceptual framework with which to understand and organise the landscape of agent-based systems. The approach is not to constrain the use of terminology through rigid definition, but to provide an encompassing infrastructure that may be used to understand the nature of different systems. The benefit of this is that the richness of the agent metaphor is preserved throughout its diverse uses, while the distinct identities of different perspectives are highlighted and used to direct and focus research and development according to the particular objectives of a sub-area.

1.2 Agents

1.2.1 Terminology

In artificial intelligence, the introduction of the notion of agents is partly due to the difficulties that have arisen when attempting to solve problems without regard to a real external environment or to the entity involved in that problem-solving process. Thus, though the solutions constructed to address these problems are in themselves important, they can be limited and inflexible in not coping well in real-world situations. In response, agents have been proposed as *situated* and *embodied* problem-solvers that are capable of functioning effectively and efficiently in complex environments. This means that the agent receives input from its environment through some sensory device, and acts so as to affect that environment in some way through effectors. Such a simple but powerful concept has been adopted with remarkable speed and vigour by many branches of computer science because of its usefulness and broad applicability.

Indeed, there is now a plethora of different labels for agents ranging from the generic *autonomous agents* [70], *software agents* [52], and *intelligent agents* [137] to the more specific *interface agents* [77], *virtual agents* [2], *information agents* [75], *mobile agents* [15, 131], and so on. The diverse range of applications for which agents are being touted include operating systems interfaces [41], processing satellite imaging data [126], electricity distribution management [69], air-traffic control [72] business process management [67], electronic commerce [57] and computer games [56], to name a few.

The richness of the agent metaphor that leads to such different uses of the term is both a strength and a weakness. Its strength lies in the fact that it can be applied in very many different ways in many situations for different purposes. The weakness, however, is that the term *agent* is now used so frequently that there is no commonly accepted notion of what it is that constitutes an agent. Given the range of areas in which the notions and terms are applied, this lack of consensus over meaning is not surprising. As Shoham [111] points out, the number of diverse uses of the term *agent* are so many that it is almost meaningless without reference to a particular concept of agent. Similarly, Connah and Wavish [18] state that the term agent has "almost as many meanings as there are instances of its use" and that this causes "considerable confusion".

That there is no agreement on what it is that makes something an agent is now generally recognised, and it is standard, therefore, for many researchers to provide their own definition. In a relatively early collection of papers, for example, several different views emerge. Smith [116] takes an agent to be a "persistent software entity dedicated to a specific purpose." Selker [110] views agents as "computer programs that simulate a human relationship by doing something that another person could do for you." More loosely, Riecken [105] refers to "integrated reasoning processes" as agents. Others take agents to be computer programs that behave in a manner analogous to human agents, such as travel agents or insurance agents [42] or software entities capable of autonomous goal-oriented behaviour in a heterogeneous computing environment [59], while some avoid the issue completely and leave the interpretation of their agents to the reader. Many such other agent definitions can be found in the excellent review by Franklin and Graesser [47], in advance of proposing their own definition.

Typically, however, agents are *characterised* along certain dimensions, rather than defined precisely. For example, in the now foundational survey of the field by Wooldridge and Jennings[137], a *weak notion* of agency is identified that involves *autonomy* or the ability to function without intervention, *social ability* by which agents interact with other agents, *reactivity* allowing agents to perceive and respond to a changing environment, and *pro-activeness* through which agents behave in a goal-directed fashion. To some extent, these characteristics are broadly accepted by many as representative of the key qualities that can be used to assess '*agentness*'.

Wooldridge and Jennings also describe a *strong notion* of agency, prevalent in AI which, in addition to the *weak* notion, also uses mental components such as belief, desire, intention, knowledge and so on. Similarly, Etzioni and Weld [42] summarise desirable agent characteristics as including *autonomy*, *temporal continuity* by which agents are not simply 'one-shot' computations, believable *personality* in order to facilitate effective interaction, *communication ability* with other agents or people, *adaptability* to user-preferences and *mobility* which allows agents to be transported across different machines and architectures. They further characterise the first of these, autonomy, as requiring that agents are *goal-oriented* and accept high-level requests, *collaborative* in that they can modify these requests and clarify them, *flexible* in not having hard, scripted actions, and *self-starting* in that they can sense changes and decide when to take action. Other characteristics are often considered, both implicitly and explicitly, with regard to notions of agency including, for example, *veracity*, *benevolence* and *rationality*.

Krogh [73], for example, notes that there have been many attempts to find one central common denominator and, with a certain amount of pessimism, predicts that any such attempts will fail. However, he does comment that these definitions are technically useful even though they are usually flawed. As an example, he cites the definition of software agents by Genesereth and Ketchpel [52].

"An entity is a software agent if and only if it communicates correctly in an agent communication language such as ACL."

Krogh argues that this definition is inappropriate for the following reasons.

- If it does not communicate 'correctly' then it is not an agent.
- If it does not communicate at all then it is not appropriate to ascribe agenthood to an entity.

Instead, Krogh argues that there are many situations in which we would wish to ascribe agenthood to entities that cannot communicate correctly or cannot communicate at all. Without fully elaborating, Krogh further suggests that in some cases it is appropriate to consider entities that are not computer programs as agents.

Recognising that there is no commonly accepted definition of what constitutes an agent, Krogh chooses to *delineate* a class of agents that have certain *dimensions* as described above. In particular, these are independent, selfish, interacting, heterogeneous and persistent. However, the terms are not defining in themselves and can introduce even more ambiguity since, as stated earlier, the meanings attributed to these dimensions are not themselves uniform.

1.2.2 Problems with Definition

Wooldridge and Jennings recognise that many such qualities have been proposed by others as being necessary for agenthood but, in a joint paper with Sycara [68], suggest that the four characteristics enumerated in their *weak notion* above are the "essence" of agenthood. Despite some broad acceptance of this view, there are still many problems. For example, in a more recent paper, Müller [95] seeks to survey *autonomous* agent architectures by considering the three strands of *reactive* agents, *deliberative* (or pro-active) agents and *interacting* (or social) agents. The properties here correspond perfectly to three of these four key characteristics, but instead of being used to represent all agents, they are used to break down the classes of agents into three distinct streams of research.

The difficulty with this approach of *characterising* agents through identifying their properties is exemplified by considering *mobile agents* [15, 131], which are quite distinct and identifiable in the focus on movement of code between host machines. Here, the key characteristic is precisely this mobility, and indeed mobility has been regarded by some as an intrinsic agent property. A critical analysis of the area of mobile agents would, however, unearth a recognition that this mobility augments other, more central agent characteristics in mobile agents, so that mobility is valuable in identifying the kind of agent, rather than understanding all agents. Similarly, some of the more specific labels for agents describe other characteristics that do not impact on agents as a whole, but relate to a particular domain or capability.

This area is fraught with difficulty, yet there have been several efforts to address these issues. For example, in attempting to distinguish agents from programs, Franklin and Graesser constructed an agent taxonomy [47] aimed at identifying the key features of agent systems in relation to different branches of the field. Their aim, amply described by the title of the paper, "Is it an agent or just a program?", highlights what might be regarded as the problem of the *Emperor's clothes*, as to whether there is any value to the notion of agents. The definition provided, that an "autonomous agent is a system situated within and a part of an environment that senses that environment and acts on it, over time, in pursuit of its own agenda and so as to affect what it sense in the future," serves to distinguish some non-agent programs from agents through the introduction of *temporal continuity*, for example, but still suffers from simply providing a *characterisation*. Using this, Franklin and Graesser then move to classify existing notions of agents within a taxonomic hierarchy. While interesting and valuable, it still does not provide a solution to the problem of identifying agentness. As Petrie points out, for example, *autonomy* remains *unelaborated*, yet it is a key part of the definition [103].

In somewhat similar fashion, Müller [95] also provides a taxonomy of intelligent agents that reflects different application areas, and which can be used to identify classes of agent architectures that are suited to particular problems. While this is also a valuable aid to understanding the range of work done in this area, it does not help in clarifying the issues discussed above. Nwana [98], too, offers an interesting typology of agent systems in his review of the field, but importantly warns against the dangers associated with the "rampant" use of the agent buzzword, its overselling and the possibility of it becoming a "passing fad" as a result.

Thus, while agent properties illustrate the range and diversity both of the design and potential application of agents, such a discussion is inadequate for a more detailed and precise analysis of the basic underlying concepts. If we are to be able to make sense of this rapidly growing area, then we need to progress beyond a vague appreciation of the nature of agents. Indeed, as Wooldridge argues [135], to avoid the term 'agent' becoming meaningless and empty and attached to everything, only those systems that merit the agent label should have it.

To summarise, there is a distinct lack of precision and consensus in work dealing with agents and their dimensions. Consequently, there is no common currency for the notion of agenthood, or indeed for dimensions of agency. For example, the notions of reflexive and reactive agents are often confused. This is not an isolated case: terms are often used interchangeably without real regard for their significance and relevance. Another example, of this kind, is that agency is often taken to imply some degree of autonomy and the two terms are often used interchangeably [47].

This book adopts the stance that agency and autonomy relate to very specific and distinct, though related, qualities. It offers a precise understanding of these terms and the relationship between them, both of which are of fundamental importance in defining the nature of agent-based systems.

1.3 Multi-Agent Systems

Now, multi-agent systems are typically distributed systems in which several distinct components, each of which is an independent problem-solving agent come together to form some coherent whole. There is generally no pre-established architecture or configuration incorporating the agents, and the interactions between them are not pre-defined, as is usually the case with traditional processes in concurrent programs. More importantly, there is no global system goal, the agents being heterogeneous with their own goals and capabilities. In consequence, agents in a multi-agent system need to *coordinate* their activities and cooperate with each other, in order to avoid duplication of effort, to avoid unwittingly hindering other agents in achieving goals, and to exploit other agents' capabilities. These basic points motivate the consideration of several additional issues regarding agents that don't arise when considering individual agents in isolation. Each is outlined below.

Agent Modelling
As discussed, an agent may need a *model* of its world. If this world contains agents then it may be beneficial to model these other agents, too.

Multi-Agent Planning
In some cases agents will share plans in order to coordinate their behaviour or to achieve a goal using others.

Social Relationships
Agents may have *social relationships* with other agents. For example, if one agent has performed a service for another agent, the second agent may be under an *obligation* to reciprocate in some way. If two agents are working together to achieve a task, the agents are typically said to be *cooperating*.

Interaction
Agents may *interact*. In a multi-agent world in which interaction is not pre-defined, agents may need models of each other to decide how to interact, and to decide on

their success or failure. This may impact in different ways on the social relationships between the agents.

Communication

Agents may *communicate* to exploit interaction and ensure coordination. An agent may persuade others to adopt its goals and alter their plans [7].

The same problems regarding the undefined nature of agents discussed earlier arise in multi-agent systems. It is difficult to consider these issues in any structured or principled way without agreement on the basic components that are involved. In order to understand fully the issues introduced above, it is first necessary to understand the nature of individual agents themselves.

1.4 Desiderata for a Conceptual View of Agents

Agent systems that can act independently in complex environments are very appealing and, judging by the recent effort invested in their development and application, are here to stay. However, single-agent systems are fundamentally limited by their own particular dimensions. Individual agents in multi-agent systems, by contrast, can exploit the capabilities of other agents, allowing for a much greater range of collective functionality than an isolated agent. Multi-agent systems, however, are more complex in design and construction since this increased functionality arises through the interaction of the individual agents involved. Furthermore, in many cases, these agents are autonomous and the interaction emerges in a fashion that is essentially unplanned. An understanding of the way in which such systems operate can only be achieved through an analysis of the relationships that arise between agents, and any pre-existing architectural structure.

This book provides a detailed examination and analysis of the general social organisation of multi-agent systems and develops models of dimensions (or capabilities) of agents that need to function effectively and efficiently within them. A key aspect of this analysis is that it must be directed at the individual interacting agents themselves. More specifically, this book has the following salient concerns.

– To provide principled *definitions* for agency and autonomy, and to explicate the nature of the relationship between them. The distinction between agency and autonomy is critical to understanding the nature of the relationships in multi-agent systems.
– To provide a *unifying framework* that incorporates these definitions within which existing work and definitions can be situated. This is achieved by constructing high-level models of agents and autonomous agents and their operation in a way that is not architecture-specific. The framework should serve as a foundation both for the development of agent systems and for analysing agent relationships.
– To *analyse* and define key relationships that arise between agents. These relationships are universal and fundamental, arising as a natural consequence of the definitions of agency and autonomy.

- To build models of the *dimensions* of *deliberative* agents that are required for them to recognise and exploit social relationships in order that they may interact effectively in multi-agent systems.
- To demonstrate the practical applicability of the models constructed to existing theories and systems so that they may be readily analysed and evaluated.

In satisfying these aims, this book adheres to four main principles. First, it is concerned with the development of a theory that subsumes, as far as possible, existing work, so that it is useful and widely applicable. It is not our intention to produce yet another set of definitions that do not relate to any previous attempts. Second, a major criticism of many existing definitions and concepts is that they are vague and ambiguous. In order to avoid such problems, we must ensure that we are precise and unambiguous at all times. The book therefore uses formal methods to provide a rigorous and precise underpinning to the work in this book. Third, abstraction in analysis and design is an important tool because it enables an appropriate level of description to be chosen. Consequently, the book provides a means of moving between different levels of agent specification from the most abstract to the least abstract, from primitive definitional specifications through deliberative agent dimensions to instances of systems and theories. Finally, agent theories should serve as specifications [136]. This book aims to provide an explicit design and specification environment for the development of real systems; the formal models will relate directly to computational systems.

1.5 A Formal Framework for Agent Definition and Development

1.5.1 Formal Frameworks

To address the concerns identified above in relation to the agent field, it is sensible for a well-defined and precise vocabulary for the fundamental elements of agents and multi-agent systems to be developed. If such a vocabulary is also situated in a structured framework, it can provide the right kind of platform on which to base further research. Formal specification techniques are appropriate for this task.

It has been claimed elsewhere that formal specification can be used to construct *formal frameworks* within which common properties of a family of systems can be identified [37, 48, 49, 50]. As a result of such specifications, it becomes possible to consider different systems as instances of one design, and to show how new designs can be constructed from an existing design framework.

More precisely, a formal framework must satisfy three distinct requirements, as follows.

- It must provide meanings for common concepts and terms precisely and unambiguously, and do so in a readable and understandable manner. The availability of readable explicit notations allows a movement from a vague and conflicting understanding of a class of models towards a common conceptual framework. A

common conceptual framework exists if there is a generally held understanding of the salient features and issues involved in the relevant class of models.
- It must be sufficiently well-structured to provide a foundation for subsequent development of new and increasingly more refined concepts. In particular, it is important that a practitioner is in a position to choose the level of abstraction suitable for their current purpose.
- It must enable alternative designs of particular models and systems to be presented explicitly, compared and evaluated. It must provide a description of the common abstractions found within that class of models as well as a means of further refining these descriptions to detail particular models and systems.

Over the course of this book, a principled theory of agency is developed by describing just such a framework, called the SMART *agent framework*. Using the Z specification language, a sophisticated model of agents and their relationships is built up and illustrated with application to three distinct case-studies.

1.5.2 Notation

There is a large and growing number of formal techniques and languages available to specify properties of software systems [26]. These include state-based languages such as VDM [71], Z [121] and B [76], process-based languages such as CCS [90] and CSP [63], temporal logics [40], modal logics [14] and statecharts [128], with each technique having its advocates for use in modelling various aspects of computing.

This book adopts the language Z, deliberately selecting a technique which not only enables designs of systems to be developed formally, but allows for the systematic refinement of these specifications to implementations. The choice of Z is a direct response to (arguably) the most problematic aspect of many formal techniques for agent-based computing — that they do not directly relate to the construction of agent software.

Furthermore, Z is a specification language that is increasingly being used both in industry and academia, as a strong and elegant means of formal specification, and is supported by a large array of books (e.g. [3, 58]), articles (e.g. [4, 5]) industrial case studies (e.g. [17, 23, 130]), well-documented refinement methods (e.g. [132]), and available tools for animation (e.g. [60, 108, 120]).

Additionally, Z has other benefits.

- It is more *accessible* than many other formalisms since it is based on existing *elementary* components such as set theory and first order predicate calculus. (A summary of the notation is provided in Table 1.1, but a more detailed tutorial introduction is provided in the Appendix.)
- It is an extremely expressive language, allowing a consistent, unified and structured account of a computer system and its associated operations.
- It is gaining increasing acceptance as a tool within the artificial intelligence community (e.g. [22, 55, 91, 134]) and is therefore appropriate for the current work in terms of standards and dissemination capabilities.

Table 1.1. Summary of Z Notation

Definitions and declarations		Functions	
a, b	Identifiers	$A \nrightarrow B$	Partial function
p, q	Predicates	$A \rightarrow B$	Total function
s, t	Sequences	$A \twoheadrightarrow B$	Total Surjection
x, y	Expressions	$A \rightarrowtail B$	Partial Injection
A, B	Sets	$A \rightarrowtail B$	Bijection
$a == x$	Abbreviated definition	**Sequences**	
$[a]$	Introduction of given set	$\langle x, y, \ldots \rangle$	Sequence
$a ::= b \langle\!\langle B \rangle\!\rangle$		$\operatorname{seq} A$	Finite sequences
$\mid c \langle\!\langle C \rangle\!\rangle$	Free type declaration	$\operatorname{seq}_1 A$	Non-empty seqs
$\mu d \mid P$	Definite description	$\operatorname{iseq} A$	Injective seqs
Logic		$\operatorname{iseq}_1 A$	Non-empty inj seqs
$\neg p$	Logical negation	$s \frown t$	Concatenation
$p \wedge q$	Logical conjunction	$head\ s$	First element of seq
$p \vee q$	Logical disjunction	$last\ s$	Last element of seq
$p \Rightarrow q$	Logical implication	$s \operatorname{in} t$	Subsequence
$p \Leftrightarrow q$	Logical equivalence	**Schema notation**	
$\forall X \bullet q$	Universal quantification		
$\exists X \bullet q$	Existential quantification		
Sets			

Schema notation:

$$
\begin{array}{|l}
\hline\ S \underline{\quad} \\
\quad d \\
\hline
\quad p \\
\hline
\end{array} \quad \text{Vertical schema}
$$

$$
\begin{array}{|l}
\quad d \\
\hline
\quad p \\
\end{array} \quad \text{Axiomatic definition}
$$

$$
\begin{array}{|l}
\hline\ S \underline{\quad} \\
\quad T \\
\quad d \\
\hline
\quad p \\
\hline
\end{array} \quad \text{Schema inclusion}
$$

$$
\begin{array}{|l}
\hline\ \Delta S \underline{\quad} \\
\quad S \\
\quad S' \\
\end{array} \quad \text{Operation schema}
$$

Sets		Conventions	
$x \in y$	Set membership	$z.a$	Component inclusion
$x \notin y$	Non-membership	$a?$	Input to an operation
$\{\,\}$	Empty set	$a!$	Output from an op
$A \subseteq B$	Set inclusion	a	Variable before op
$A \subset B$	Strict set inclusion	a'	Variable after op
$\{x, y, \ldots\}$	Set of elements	S	Schema before op
$(x, y, \ldots)$	Ordered tuple	S'	Schema after op
$A \times B \times \ldots$	Cartesian product	ΔS	Change of state
$\mathbb{P} A$	Power set	ΞS	No change of state
$\mathbb{P}_1 A$	Non-empty power set		
$A \cap B$	Set intersection		
$A \cup B$	Set union		
$A \setminus B$	Set difference		
$\bigcup A$	Generalised union		
$\bigcap A$	Generalised intersection		
$\# A$	Size of finite set		
Relations			
$A \leftrightarrow B$	Relation		
$\operatorname{dom} R$	Domain of relation		
$\operatorname{ran} R$	Range of relation		
R^{-1}	Inverse of relation		
$R \rhd A$	Range restriction		
$A \lhd R$	Anti-domain restriction		
R^{-1}	Relational Inverse		
R^+	Transitive Closure		
$R(\!\mid A \mid\!)$	Relational Image		
$R_1 \oplus R_2$	Relational Overriding		

1.5.3 Specification Structure Diagrams

Over the course of this book, the formal description of the framework is presented in Z, but the structure of the specification is also presented graphically. In particular, diagrams are used to detail the way in which schemas are used to produce a *specification structure*, which provides a graphical overview of the way in which the formal models in this thesis are constructed. The key to these diagrams is presented in Figure 1.1 and is explained below.

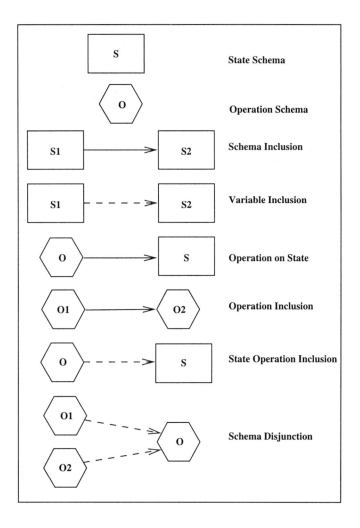

Fig. 1.1. Structuring Schemas

State Schema
State schemas are represented by a box enclosing the schema name.

Operation Schema
Operation schemas are represented by a hexagon enclosing the schema name.

Schema Inclusion
A solid arrow between boxes represents state schema inclusion. In the case shown in Figure 1.1, $S1$ is included in $S2$.

$S2$

$S1$

$\ldots$

Variable Inclusion
A dashed arrow between boxes represents a schema being included in the declarative part of the second schema as a type. In the case shown in Figure 1.1 a variable included in the state schema $S2$ is declared in terms of the type defined by state schema $S1$. For example, the schema below includes a variable that is defined as a set of elements of the schema type $S1$.

$S2$

$variable_1 : \mathbb{P}\, S1$

$\ldots$

Operation on State
A solid arrow between a hexagon, O, and a box, S, indicates that the operation schema, O, is defined in terms of a state change to the state schema, S.

O

ΔS

$\ldots$

Operation Inclusion
A solid arrow between two hexagons represents operation inclusion. In the case shown in Figure 1.1 the operation schema $O2$ includes the operation schema $O1$.

State Operation Inclusion
A dashed arrow between a hexagon and a box indicates that the state schema has been included in the definition of an operation schema. In the case shown in Figure 1.1 the state schema S is included but its state is unaffected.

Schema Disjunction
A set of converging dashed arrows between a set of hexagons $O1, O2$ and another hexagon O indicates that the operation schema O is defined as the disjunction of the

operation schemas $O1$ and $O2$. The pre-condition of O is the logical disjunction of the preconditions of $O1$ and $O2$.

In this book, the SMART agent framework is developed mathematically using Z, but it is also completely described in the accompanying text. The specification structure diagrams described above are also used throughout the book to illustrate how the formal description is organised. They serve as a reference point for all of the schemas that comprise the SMART framework. All of the concepts are introduced intuitively and informally before proceeding to a formal specification, so that the mathematically naive reader will also benefit from the book. Nevertheless, a tutorial introduction to Z is provided in the Appendix, and readers unfamiliar with the notation (which is summarised here in Table 1.1) may choose to consult it before proceeding. Alternatively, the texts mentioned above may also be valuable.

2. The SMART Agent Framework

2.1 Introduction

Though agents are becoming increasingly popular across a wide range of applications, the rapid growth of the field has led to much confusion regarding agents and their functionality. One part of this confusion is that it is now generally recognised that there is no agreement on what it is that makes something an agent. For example, Franklin and Graesser [47] provide evidence of the degree of current difficulties, citing *ten* different agent definitions of leading researchers. This lack of consensus sets up barriers to the development of an accepted foundation on which to build a rigorous scientific discipline. It can also be argued that this problem, which has resulted in a plethora of different terms and notions, hinders current research since integration and comparison of different approaches is made very difficult.

To address this confusion, it is sensible that a well-defined and precise vocabulary for the fundamental elements of agents and multi-agent systems be developed. If such a vocabulary is also situated in a structured framework, it can provide the right kind of platform on which to base further research.

This chapter lays the foundations for a principled theory of agency by describing just such a framework of Structured and Modular Agents and Relationship Types, which we refer to as the SMART framework. This framework is essentially a four-tiered hierarchy comprising entities, objects, agents and autonomous agents where agents are viewed as objects with *goals*, and autonomous agents are agents with *motivations*. The next sections address the issues of agency and autonomy, beginning with the base initial concepts, and continuing with descriptions of entities that provide a template to define objects, agents and autonomous agents in turn. Then the framework is applied to specify an example architecture for *tropistic agents*.

The basic strategy for introducing new aspects of the formal framework and later models in this book is as follows. First, an intuitive description is provided of what is required and why, and then, where appropriate, a textual definition is given. Finally, the specification that formalises the intuition and definition is provided.

2.2 Initial Concepts

According to Shoham [111], an *agent* is any entity to which mental state can be ascribed. Such mental state consists of components such as beliefs, capabilities and commitments, but there is no unique correct selection of them. This is sensible, and we too do not demand that all agents necessarily have the same set of mental components. Indeed, we recognise the limitations associated with assuming an environment comprising homogeneous agents and consequently deliberately direct this discussion at heterogeneous agents with varying capabilities. However, the SMART framework does specify what is minimally required of an entity for it to be considered an agent. This encompassing approach is intended to be inclusive in providing a way of relating different classes of agent, rather than attempting attempt to exclude through rigid definition.

Initially, the environment must be described and then, through increasingly detailed description, objects, agents and autonomous agents must be defined to provide an account of a general agent-oriented system. The definition of agency that follows is intended to subsume existing concepts as far as possible. In short, a four-tiered hierarchy comprising *entities*, *objects*, *agents* and *autonomous agents* is proposed. The basic idea underlying this hierarchy is that an environment consists of entities, some of which are objects. Of this set of objects, some are agents, and of these agents, some are autonomous agents.

These four classes are the fundamental components that comprise this view of the world. Though the choice of autonomy as a fundamental distinguishing quality in this framework may not be immediately obvious, its importance arises through the functionality of goals. As will be seen below, goals define agency, and the generation of goals defines autonomy. In this sense, autonomy is not simply one of many possible characterising properties or qualities, but is foundational in its significance, and serves as a platform on which other properties can be imposed, just as agency.

The specification is structured so that it reflects the view of the world as shown in the Venn diagram of Figure 2.1. It must be built up in such a way that, starting from a basic description of an entity, each succeeding definition can be a refinement of that previously described. In this way, an object is a refinement of an entity, an agent is a refinement of an object, and an autonomous agent is a refinement of an agent. Accordingly, the specification is thus structured into four parts.

- **Entity and Environment**
  The most abstract description provided is of an entity, which is simply a collection of attributes. An environment can then be defined as a collection of entities.
- **Object**
  Objects in the environment can also be considered as collections of attributes, but a more detailed description may also be given by, in addition, describing their capabilities. The capabilities of an object are defined by a set of action primitives which, theoretically, can be performed by the object in some environment and consequently change the environment's state.
- **Agent**
  If we consider objects more closely, some objects that are serving some purpose or, equally, can be attributed some set of goals, can be distinguished. This then becomes the definition of an agent, as an object with goals. With this increased

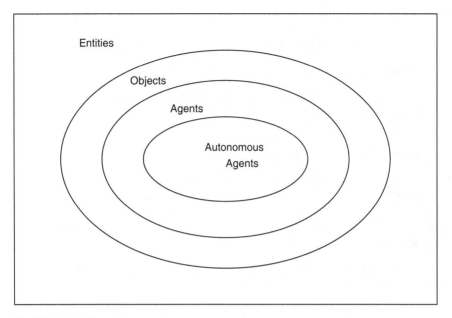

Fig. 2.1. Entity Hierarchy overview

level of detail in the description, the greater functionality of agents over objects can be modelled.

– **Autonomous Agent**
Refining this description further enables a subclass of agents that are autonomous to be distinguished. These autonomous agents are self-motivated agents in the sense that they create and pursue their own *agendas* as opposed to functioning under the control of another agent. An autonomous agent is thus defined as an agent with motivations and, in turn, it is shown how these agents behave in a more sophisticated manner than non-autonomous agents.

Before it is possible to construct agent models it is necessary to define the building blocks or *primitives* from which these models are created. We start by defining three primitives: *attributes*, *actions* and *motivations*, which are used as the basis for development of the SMART agent framework described in this chapter, and all subsequent models. Formally, these primitives are specified as given sets which means that we say nothing about how they might be represented for any particular system. In addition, two secondary concepts, *goals* and *environments*, are specified in terms of attributes.

Attributes are simply features of the world, and are the only characteristics that are manifest. They need not be perceived by any particular entity, but must be potentially perceivable in an omniscient sense. This notion of a feature allows anything to be included such as, for example, the fact that a tree is green, or is in a park, or is twenty feet tall.

Definition 2.2.1. *An* attribute *is a perceivable feature.*

The set of all such attributes is defined.

[*Attribute*]

An environment is then simply a set of attributes that describes *all* the features within that environment. Thus a new type, *Environment*, is defined to be a (non-empty) set of attributes.

$Environment == \mathbb{P}_1\, Attribute$

The second primitive that needs defining is an *action*. Actions can change environments by adding or removing attributes. For example, the action of a robot, responsible for attaching tyres to cars in a factory, moving from one wheel to the next, will delete the attribute that the robot is at the first wheel and add the attribute that the agent is at the second.

Definition 2.2.2. *An* action *is a discrete event that can change the state of the environment when performed.*

[*Action*]

A goal defines a state of affairs that is desirable in some way. For example, a robot may have the goal of attaching a tyre to a car.

Definition 2.2.3. *A* goal *is a state of affairs to be achieved in the environment.*

A goal can therefore be very simply defined as a non-empty set of attributes that describes a state of affairs in the world.

$Goal == \mathbb{P}_1\, Attribute$

Motivations can also be introduced, a detailed consideration of them is delayed until a time at which they are more relevant.

Definition 2.2.4. *A* motivation *is any desire or preference that can lead to the generation and adoption of goals and that affects the outcome of the reasoning or behavioural task intended to satisfy those goals.*

As with actions and attributes, motivations are defined using given sets.

[*Motivation*]

The formal specification that follows in this book is constructed solely from these three primitive types to provide models and definitions of entities, objects, agents and autonomous agents, which are related as shown in the Venn diagram of Figure 2.1. In this view, all autonomous agents are agents, all agents are objects and all objects are entities. Furthermore, there is a critical distinction between autonomous agents and non-autonomous agents that will provide the basis for the analysis described in subsequent chapters.

2.3 Entities

The *entity*, as defined in this section, serves as an *abstraction mechanism*; it provides a *template* from which objects, agents and autonomous agents can be defined. Since the specification should initially describe components in a multi-agent system at the highest possible level of abstraction, anything that is considered to be a single component is represented as an *entity*. For example, a tea-cup is an entity, as is a robot. These entities may have complex descriptions, but at the very highest level they are just collections of attributes. It is not important which attributes are grouped together to describe a given entity, nor how that is achieved. It is only important to be able to describe a collection of attributes as a single component. An entity is defined using the existing primitives.

Definition 2.3.1. *An* entity *is something that comprises a non-empty set of attributes, a set of actions, a set of goals and a set of motivations*.

The schema below formalises the definition of an entity. It has a declarative part containing four variables. Critically, the set of attributes of the entity, *attributes*, is non-empty. The remaining components of the schema are discussed subsequently.

$$
\begin{array}{|l|}
\hline
\_\,Entity _____ \\
attributes : \mathbb{P}\,Attribute \\
capabilities : \mathbb{P}\,Action \\
goals : \mathbb{P}\,Goal \\
motivations : \mathbb{P}\,Motivation \\
\hline
attributes \neq \{\,\} \\
\hline
\end{array}
$$

The *attributes* of an entity are limited to those features that are *permanent*. That is to say that attributes are features that can be ascribed to the entity itself rather than aspects of its particular state. Attributes relating to such transient things as the entity's orientation, configuration (which refers to elements such as the angle of a robot's arm), location, and so on, which are not solely dependent on the entity, but are also a factor of its environment, are not represented. By contrast, colour, age, mass, density and size, for example, which are fixed and which are a function only of the entity itself, are represented. Returning to the example of the tea-cup, the attributes of the cup may state that it is stable, blue, hard, and so on. They would not specify its temperature, position, whether it was standing on its base or whether it was full. A robot's attributes may specify that it is red, large, heavy, and has three arms, but would not include the current position of those arms.

Unless an entity refers to everything, such as the universe, it must be situated in an environment. Conversely, an environment must include all the entities within it. The *Env* schema formalises an environment whose state is represented by the *environment* variable of type *Environment*, which must consist of a non-empty set of attributes. The *entities* variable refers to the set of entities in the environment, and the last predicate formalises the requirement that the sum of the attributes of the entities in an environment is a subset of all the attributes of that environment.

$$
\begin{array}{|l|}
\hline \textit{Env} \\
\hline
\textit{environment} : \textit{Environment} \\
\textit{entities} : \mathbb{P}\,\textit{Entity} \\
\hline
\textit{environment} \neq \{\,\} \\
\bigcup\{e : \textit{entities} \bullet e.\textit{attributes}\} \subseteq \textit{environment} \\
\hline
\end{array}
$$

2.3.1 Entity State

Once an entity is placed in an environment, aspects such as its orientation and location, which are part of its *state*, can be specified.

Those features of an entity that are not fixed (as represented by *attributes*), but include aspects of its current *state*, are collectively referred to as the entity's *situation*. For example, the situation of a cup might now include that it is upright and situated on a table, while the situation of a robot may specify that it is located in the first floor of a car factory, holding a tyre. The attributes and situation are both part of the environment, but an attribute cannot be part of both the entity's attributes and its situation.

The next schema formalises the state of an entity in an environment and includes the schema representing the entity itself, *Entity*, and the schema representing the current environment, *Env*. This is equivalent to incorporating all of the declarations and predicates from both schemas. In addition, an extra variable, *situation*, is used to denote the entity's current situation. The union of attributes and situation is a *proper* subset of the environment, since equality would entail that the entity is isolated, and the environment is effectively nonexistent.

$$
\begin{array}{|l|}
\hline \textit{EntityState} \\
\hline
\textit{Entity} \\
\textit{Env} \\
\textit{situation} : \mathbb{P}\,\textit{Attribute} \\
\hline
\textit{situation} \neq \{\,\} \\
\textit{attributes} \cap \textit{situation} = \{\,\} \\
\textit{attributes} \cup \textit{situation} \subset \textit{environment} \\
\hline
\end{array}
$$

2.3.2 Entity Operations

The constraints on the way in which an entity changes its state in an environment can now be specified. Changes to the state of entities do not affect their attributes, only their situation. For example, a cricket ball may change its orientation and location during the course of a cricket match since these are aspects of its situation. However, if the ball is hit hard, it may lose its shape, which is one of the ball's attributes, so that it can no longer be used for cricket. In general, if the attributes of an entity change, then a new entity is instantiated.

To describe this, an *operation schema* that describes the relationship between two states must be introduced; the state before the operation, and the state afterwards. The *ΔEntityState* schema specifies that a change to the *EntityState* schema will leave the *Entity* schema unchanged, indicated by '*ΞEntity*'. In addition, the resulting situation of an entity will always be contained in the new environment as shown by the only schema predicate.

```
┌── ΔEntityState ──────────────────────────────────────────
│ Object
│ objectactions : Environment → ℙ Action
├──────────────────────────────────────────────────────────
│ ∀ environment : Environment •
│         (objectactions environment) ⊆ capabilities
└──────────────────────────────────────────────────────────
```

2.3.3 Object State

As with an entity, an object must be situated in an environment and will have a *situation* as specified previously. The environment, which includes the object's situation, can be used to determine those actions that it is to perform next.

The state of an object in its environment in the *ObjectState* schema is defined by refining the schema, *EntityState*, which contains the attributes and situation of the object, and the environment in which the object is situated, and also includes the *ObjectAction* schema. The variable, *willdo*, specifies the next actions that the object will perform. Its value is found by applying the *objectactions* function from the *ObjectAction* schema to the current *environment*, and amounts to a subset of the capabilities of the object.

```
┌── ObjectState ───────────────────────────────────────────
│ EntityState
│ ObjectAction
│ willdo : ℙ Action
├──────────────────────────────────────────────────────────
│ willdo = objectactions environment
│ willdo ⊆ capabilities
└──────────────────────────────────────────────────────────
```

For example, the tyre-attaching robot, in a situation which includes holding a tyre, may now have *willdo* as a set of actions to attach the tyre to the car.

2.3.4 Object Operations

So far, objects and the way in which their actions are selected have been defined. Next, we specify the way in which the performance of these actions affects the environments in which the objects are situated. Those variables that relate to the state of the object (its situation and next actions) can change, while the other variables that are not concerned with state but with the *nature* of the object itself (namely, its attributes, capabilities and action-selection function) remain unchanged. If these later variables ever did change, then a *new* object would be instantiated. In this view a robot without a power supply is a different object from a robot with a power supply.

The *ΔObjectState* schema shows how these constraints are formalised. It refines the *ΔEntity* schema, which asserts that *situation* rather than *attributes* change, and further states that none of the variables in *ObjectAction* (which includes *Object*) are affected by a change of state.

$$
\begin{array}{|l}
\underline{\quad \varDelta ObjectState \underline{\hspace{5cm}}} \\
ObjectState \\
ObjectState' \\
\varDelta EntityState \\
\varXi ObjectAction \\
\hline
\end{array}
$$

Now, when actions are performed in an environment, we say that an *interaction* takes place. An interaction changes the state of the environment by adding and removing attributes. In this model, all actions result in the same change to an environment whether taken by an object, agent or autonomous agent. The function that formalises how the environment is affected by actions performed within it can therefore be defined *axiomatically*; it maps the current environment and the performed actions to the resulting environment.

$$
effectinteraction : Environment \rightarrow \mathbb{P}\,Action \nrightarrow Environment
$$

This allows an object interacting with its environment to be modelled. Both the state of the object and the environment change as specified by the schema *ObjectInteracts*. The resulting environment is determined by applying the function, *effectinteraction*, to the current state of the environment and the current set of actions. In turn, this environment then determines the next set of actions to be performed by the object through applying *objectactions* again.

$$
\begin{array}{|l}
\underline{\quad ObjectInteracts \underline{\hspace{5cm}}} \\
\varDelta ObjectState \\
\hline
environment' = effectinteraction\ environment\ willdo \\
willdo' = objectactions\ environment' \\
\hline
\end{array}
$$

2.4 Agents

2.4.1 Introduction

There are many dictionary definitions for an agent. Wooldridge and Jennings [136] quote the definition of an agent as "one who, or that which, exerts power or produces an effect."[1] However, they omit the second sense of agent, which is given as "one who acts for another ...". This is important, for it is not the acting alone that defines agency, but the acting for *someone or something* that is defining. Indeed, Wooldridge and Jennings acknowledge the difficulties in a purely action-based analysis of agency.

In the SMART view agents are just objects with certain dispositions. Specifically, an object is regarded as an agent if it is serving some purpose. They may always be agents, or they may revert to being objects in certain circumstances. This is explored further in the next chapter. For the moment, we concentrate on the nature of the disposition that characterises an agent. An object is an agent if it serves a useful purpose either to a different agent, or to itself, in which latter case the agent is *autonomous*. Specifically, an agent is something that satisfies a goal or set of goals (often of another). Thus if I want to use some object for my purpose, then that object becomes my agent. It has been *ascribed* or, if we anthropomorphise, has *adopted*, my goal. An agent is thus defined in relation to its goals.

2.4.2 Agent Specification

As stated previously, a goal is defined as a state of affairs to be achieved in the environment. An agent is defined in terms of an object as follows.

Definition 2.4.1. *An* agent *is an object with a goals.*

The formal description of an agent is specified by the *Agent* schema. This refines the object schema and constrains the set of goals to be non-empty.

Agent
───────────────────────────────
  Object
  ─────────
  goals $\neq \{\ \}$

Thus an agent has, or is *ascribed*, a set of goals that it retains over any instantiation (or lifetime). One object may give rise to different instantiations of agents, and an agent is instantiated from an object in response to another agent. Thus agency is *transient*, and an object that becomes an agent at some time may subsequently revert to being an object.

Note that this definition means that in the limiting case, very simple non-computational entities without perception can be agents. For example, a cup is an object. It can be regarded as an agent and ascribe to it mental state, but it serves no useful purpose to do so without considering the circumstances. A cup is an agent *if* it is containing liquid and it is doing so to some end. In other words, if I fill a cup with tea, then the cup is my agent; it serves my purpose. Alternatively, the cup would also be an agent if it were placed upside down on a stack of papers and used

---

[1] *The Concise Oxford Dictionary of Current English (7th edition)*, Oxford University Press, 1988.

as a paperweight. It would *not* be an agent if it were just sitting on a table without serving any purpose to any one. In this case it would be an object. As this example shows, an entity is not required to be intelligent for it to be an agent. Clearly, the example of the cup is counter-intuitive and it is much more intuitive to talk about robots, but it is important to realise that any object, computational or otherwise, can be an agent once it is serving a purpose.

Consider the robot example, and suppose now that the robot has a power supply. If the robot has no goal, then it cannot use its actuators in any sensible way but only, perhaps, in a random way, and must be considered an object. Alternatively, if the robot has some goal or set of goals that allow it to employ its actuators in some directed way, such as picking up a cup, or fixing a tyre onto a car, then it is an agent. The goal need not be explicitly represented, but can instead be implicit in the hardware or software design of the robot. It is merely necessary for there to be a goal of some kind.

Returning to the example of the cup as my agent, it is clear that not everyone will know about this *agentness*. If, for example, I am in a cafe and there is a half-full cup of tea on my table, there are several views that can be taken. It can be regarded by the waiter as an agent for me, storing my tea, or it can be regarded as an object serving no purpose if the waiter thinks it is not mine or that I have finished. The view of the cup as an object or agent is relevant to whether the waiter will remove the cup or leave it at the table. Note that we are not suggesting that the cup actually possesses a goal, just that there is a goal that it is satisfying.

These examples highlight the range of behaviour that is available from agents. The tea-cup is passive and has goals *imposed* upon and *ascribed* to it, while the robot is capable of actively manipulating the environment by performing actions designed to satisfy its goals.

2.4.3 Agent Perception

Perception can now be introduced. An agent in an environment may have a set of percepts available, which are the possible attributes that an agent could perceive, subject to its capabilities and current state. We refer to these as the *possible percepts* of an agent. However, due to limited resources, an agent will not normally be able to perceive all those attributes possible, and will base its actions on a subset, which we call the *actual percepts* of an agent. Indeed, some agents will not be able to perceive at all. In the case of a cup, for example, the set of possible percepts will be empty and consequently the set of actual percepts will also be empty. The robot, however, may have several sensors that allow it to perceive. Thus it is not a requirement of an agent that it is able to perceive.

To distinguish between representations of mental models and representations of the *actual* environment, a type, *View*, is defined to be the perception of an environment by an agent. This has an equivalent type to that of *Environment*, but now physical and mental components of the same type can be distinguished.

$$View == \mathbb{P}_1\, Attribute$$

It is also important to note that it is only meaningful to consider perceptual abilities in the context of goals. Thus when considering objects without goals, perceptual abilities are not relevant. Objects respond directly to their environments and make no use of percepts even if they are available. We say that perceptual capabilities are *inert* in the context of objects.

An agent has a (possibly empty) set of actions that enable it to perceive its world, which we call its *perceiving actions*. The set of percepts that an agent is potentially capable of perceiving is a function of the current environment, which includes the agent's situation and its perceiving actions. Since the agent is resource-bounded, it may not be able to perceive the entire set of attributes and selects a subset based on its current goals. For example, the distributed Multi-Agent Reasoning System (dMARS) [29], may have a set of events to process, where events correspond to environmental change. Each of these percepts is available to the agent but because of its limited resources it may only be able to process one event, and must make a selection based on its goals.

The perception capabilities of an agent are defined in the *AgentPerception* schema, which includes the *Agent* schema and refines it by introducing three variables. First, the set of perceiving actions is denoted by *perceivingactions*, a subset of the capabilities of an agent. The *canperceive* function determines the attributes that are potentially available to an agent through its perception capabilities. Notice that this function is applied to a physical environment (in which it is situated) and returns a mental environment. The second argument of this schema is constrained to be equal to *perceivingactions*. Finally, the function, *willperceive*, describes those attributes actually perceived by an agent. This function is always applied to the goals of the agent and in contrast to the previous function, takes a mental environment and returns another mental environment.

__*AgentPerception*_____

Agent
perceivingactions : $\mathbb{P}\,Action$
canperceive : *Environment* $\rightarrow$ $\mathbb{P}\,Action$ $\nrightarrow$ *View*
willperceive : $\mathbb{P}\,Goal$ $\rightarrow$ *View* $\rightarrow$ *View*

─────────────────────────

perceivingactions $\subseteq$ *capabilities*
$\forall\,env$: *Environment*; as : $\mathbb{P}\,Action$ •
      $as \in$ dom(*canperceive env*) $\Rightarrow$ as = *perceivingactions*
dom *willperceive* = {*goals*}

_____

2.4.4 Agent Action

Any agent is still an object and can be viewed as such, so that the selection of actions is dependent solely on the environment. However, at the agent level of abstraction, goals and perceptions as well as the environment can be viewed as directing behaviour. This is specified by the *agentactions* function in the *AgentAction* schema below, which is dependent on the goals of the agent, the actual perceptions of the agent and the current environment. Since the *objectactions* function is still applicable for modelling the agent solely at the object level, the *ObjectAction* schema is included. The first predicate requires that *agentactions* returns a set of actions within the agent's capabilities, while the last predicate constrains its application to the agent's goals. If there are no perceptions, then the action-selection function is dependent only on the environment, as it is with *objectactions*.

```
___ AgentAction _____
  Agent
  ObjectAction
  agentactions : ℙ Goal → View → Environment → ℙ Action
_____
  ∀ gs : ℙ Goal; v : View; env : Environment •
            (agentactions gs v env) ⊆ capabilities
  dom agentactions = {goals}
_____
```

2.4.5 Agent State

To describe an agent with capabilities and behaviours for perception and action situated in an environment, the two schemas previously defined for action and perception are included as well as the schema defining the agent as a situated object. The *AgentState* schema, which formalises an agent situated in an environment, therefore includes the schemas *AgentAction*, *AgentPerception* and *ObjectState*.

In addition, since the attributes of the environment are now accessible, it is possible to specify the *possible percepts* and *actual percepts* of the agent. These are denoted by the variables, *possiblepercepts* and *actualpercepts*, which are calculated using the *canperceive* and *willperceive* functions respectively.

```
___ AgentState _____
  AgentPerception
  AgentAction
  ObjectState
  posspercepts, actualpercepts : View
_____
  actualpercepts ⊆ posspercepts
  posspercepts = canperceive environment perceivingactions
  actualpercepts = willperceive goals posspercepts
  perceivingactions = { } ⇒ posspercepts = { }
  willdo = agentactions goals actualpercepts environment
_____
```

Consider again the robot agent and the cup agent, which are attaching tyres and storing tea respectively. Now, suppose that the robot also has perceptual capabilities that allow it to perceive attributes in its environment. Potentially, as a consequence of its current environment, the robot may be able to perceive a multitude of attributes including that the car is red, a tyre is flat, the car door is open, and so on. Again, however, due to limited perceptual and processing abilities, and to the goal of attaching tyres, the actual percepts of the robot may only include that the tyre is flat and not the relatively insignificant attribute of the car being red. The cup agent, on the other hand, has no perceiving capabilities and consequently no possible or actual percepts.

Since goals are fixed for any agent, it is changes to the actual percepts of an agent that affect its selection of actions. An agent without perceptions does not therefore have any increased functionality as a result of its goals, but the behaviour of an such as agent can still be viewed and modelled in terms of goals affecting its action selection. In addition, as will be shown in the next chapter, it is necessary to model such entities as agents in order to analyse key inter-agent relationships.

2.4.6 Agent Operations

Operations characterising agent behaviour are constrained to affect only certain aspects. The attributes, capabilities, goals, perceptual capabilities, and action and perception selection functions are unchanged by any operation. If any of these variables change, a new agent is instantiated. The only variables that may change are necessarily associated with the state of the agent such as its situation and percepts. These constraints are formalised in the $\Delta Agent$ schema, which defines a change in agent state. It includes $\Delta ObjectState$ to ensure that only the state properties of objects change and, in addition, that variables included in the *AgentAction*, and *AgentPerception* schemas are unaltered.

```
┌─ ΔAgentState ─────────────────────────────────────────
│ AgentState
│ AgentState′
│ ΔObjectState
│ ΞAgentAction
│ ΞAgentPerception
└───────────────────────────────────────────────────────
```

When an agent acts in an environment, the environment changes according to the specific actions performed. This is not dependent on whether the entity is an object or an agent. Thus the schema describing object interaction is still directly applicable. Formally, the *AgentInteracts* schema includes *ObjectInteracts* and affects the state of an agent as specified by $\Delta AgentState$. The three predicates of this schema show explicitly how the schema variables are updated.

```
┌─ AgentInteracts ──────────────────────────────────────
│ ΔAgentState
│ ObjectInteracts
├───────────────────────────────────────────────────────
│ posspercepts′ = canperceive environment′ perceivingactions
│ actualpercepts′ = willperceive goals posspercepts′
│ willdo′ = agentactions goals actualpercepts′ environment′
└───────────────────────────────────────────────────────
```

2.5 Autonomy

2.5.1 Introduction

The definition of agents developed so far relies upon the existence of other agents to provide the goals that are adopted when an agent is instantiated. In order to ground this chain of goal adoption, to escape what could be an infinite regress, and also to bring out the notion of *autonomy*, *motivation* in introduced.

Grounding the hierarchies of goal adoption demands that some agents can generate their own goals. These agents are *autonomous* since they are not dependent on the goals of others, and possess goals that are *generated* from within rather than *adopted* from other agents. Such goals are generated from *motivations* , higher-level non-derivative components characterising the nature of the agent, but which are related to goals. Motivations are, however, qualitatively different from goals in that they are not describable states of affairs in the environment. For example, consider the motivation *greed*. This does not specify a state of affairs to be achieved, nor is it describable in terms of the environment, but it may (if other motivations permit) give rise to the generation of a goal to rob a bank. The distinction between the motivation of greed and the goal of robbing a bank is clear, with the former providing a reason to do the latter, and the latter specifying what must be done. The definition of motivation can now be re-stated.

Definition 2.5.1. A motivation *is any desire or preference that can lead to the generation and adoption of goals and that affects the outcome of the reasoning or behavioural task intended to satisfy those goals.*

A *motivated agent* is thus an agent that pursues its own agenda for reasoning and behaviour in accordance with its internal motivation. Since motivations ground the goal-generation regress, motivation is critical in achieving autonomy. An *autonomous agent* must be a *motivated* agent.

Although it draws on Kunda's work on motivation in psychology [74], the definition used for motivation above expresses its role but does not tie us to any particular implementation. Indeed, there are several views as to exactly how the role of motivation as defined here can be fulfilled. Simon, for example, takes motivation to be "that which controls attention at any given time," and explores the relation of motivation to information-processing behaviour, but from a cognitive perspective [113]. More recently, Sloman has elaborated on Simon's work, showing how motivations are relevant to emotions and the development of a computational theory of mind [114, 115]. Some have used motivation and related notions such as *motives* [97], and *concerns* [92], in developing computational architectures for autonomous agents while others have argued for an approach based on rationality that relies on utility theory [107].

In SMART, a neutral stance on such detail is taken by specifying motivation as a *given set*, omitting any further information. This allows use of the concept of distinct and possibly conflicting motivations influencing the behaviour of the agent, but also defers the choice of the actual mechanism to a subsequent point of refinement or implementation. Moreover, while others have been concerned with modelling motivation [92, 97], this chapter is concerned with its use in defining autonomy.

2.5.2 Autonomous Agent Specification

An autonomous agent may now be defined.

Definition 2.5.2. *An* autonomous agent *is an agent with motivations.*

It is specified simply as an agent with a non-empty set of motivations.

$$
\begin{array}{|l}
\hline
\_\_AutonomousAgent_____ \\
\;\; Agent \\
\hline
\;\; motivations \neq \{\,\} \\
\hline
\end{array}
$$

In illustration of these ideas, note that the cup cannot be considered autonomous because, while it can have goals ascribed to it, it cannot *generate* its own goals. In this respect it relies on other entities for purposeful existence. The robot, however, is potentially autonomous in the sense that it may have a mechanism for internal goal generation. Suppose the robot has motivations of achievement, hunger and self-preservation, where achievement is related to attaching tyres onto a car on a production line, hunger is related to maintaining power levels, and self-preservation is related to avoiding system breakdowns. In normal operation, the robot will generate goals to attach tyres to cars through a series of subgoals. If its power levels are low, however, it may replace the goal of attaching tyres with a newly-generated goal of recharging its batteries. A third possibility is that in satisfying its achievement motivation, it works for too long and is in danger of overheating. In this case, the robot can generate a goal of pausing for an appropriate period in order to avoid any damage to its components. Such a robot is autonomous because its goals are not imposed, but are generated in response to its environment. The views of the cup and robot in terms of the agent hierarchy are shown in Table 2.1, which provides example instantiations of the different requirements for each level.

Table 2.1. Example: Descriptions of a Robot and Cup in the Agent Framework

Schema	Variable	Cup	Robot
Entity	*attributes*	$\{stable, hard, \ldots\}$	$\{red, large, heavy, \ldots\}$
Object	*capabilities*	$\{support, store, \ldots\}$	$\{lift, carry, hold, \ldots\}$
Agent	*goals*	$\{store\_tea\}$	$\{fix\_tyres\}$
AutonomousAgent	*motivations*	$\{\,\}$	$\{achievement, hunger, \ldots\}$

2.5.3 Autonomous Agent Perception

With autonomous agents, therefore, it is both goals and motivations that are relevant to determining what is perceived in an environment. The schema below thus specifies a modified version of the non-autonomous agent's *willperceive* function as *autowillperceive*. That which an autonomous agent is potentially *capable* of perceiving at any time is independent of its motivations . Indeed, it will always be independent of goals and motivations, and there is consequently no equivalent increase in functionality to *canperceive*.

$$
\begin{array}{|l}
\hline
\_\_AutonomousAgentPerception_____ \\
AutonomousAgent \\
AgentPerception \\
autowillperceive : \mathbb{P}\,Motivation \rightarrow \mathbb{P}\,Goal \rightarrow Environment \rightarrow View \\
\hline
\mathrm{dom}\,autowillperceive = \{motivations\} \\
\hline
\end{array}
$$

2.5.4 Autonomous Agent Action

An autonomous agent will have some potential means of evaluating behaviour in terms of the environment and its motivations. In other words, the behaviour of the agent is determined by both external and internal factors. This is qualitatively different from an agent that merely has goals because motivations are non-derivative and governed by internal inaccessible rules, while goals are derivative but relate to motivations. Specifically, the action-selection function for an autonomous agent is produced at every instance by the motivations of the agent. The next schema defines the action-selection function, *autoactions*, and includes the *AgentAction* and *AutonomousAgent* schemas. The domain of the *autoactions* function is equal to the motivations of the agent.

$$
\begin{array}{|l}
\hline
\_\_AutonomousAgentAction_____ \\
AutonomousAgent \\
AgentAction \\
autoactions : \\
\quad \mathbb{P}\,Motivation \rightarrow \mathbb{P}\,Goal \rightarrow View \rightarrow Environment \rightarrow \mathbb{P}\,Action \\
\hline
\mathrm{dom}\,autoactions = \{motivations\} \\
\hline
\end{array}
$$

2.5.5 Autonomous Agent State

In exactly the same way that the state of an agent is defined by refining the definition of the state of an object, the state of an autonomous agent is defined using the state of an agent. The actions performed by an autonomous agent are a function of its motivations, goals, percepts and environment.

___AutonomousAgentState_____
| AgentState
| AutonomousAgentPerception
| AutonomousAgentAction
|_____
| willdo = autoactions motivations goals actualpercepts environment
|_____

2.5.6 Autonomous Agent Operations

In considering the definition of a change in state for an autonomous agent, there are some subtle but important differences with previous schemas. Whereas previously goals were fixed for agents as capabilities were for objects, it is not explicitly stated whether motivations change when actions are performed. If they do change, then the agent functions, *willperceive* and *agentactions*, will also change. If they do not change, motivations may generate new and different goals for the agent to pursue. In any of these cases, the characterising features of an agent are in flux so that an autonomous agent can be regarded as a continually re-instantiated non-autonomous agent. In this sense, autonomous agents are permanently agents as opposed to transient non-autonomous agents, which may revert to being objects.

___ΔAutonomousAgentState_____
| AutonomousAgentState
| AutonomousAgentState$'$
|_____
| ΔAgentState
| autowillperceive$'$ = autowillperceive
| autoactions$'$ = autoactions
|_____

Finally, the operation of an autonomous agent performing its next set of actions, is specified as a refinement of the *AgentInteracts* schema.

___AutonomousAgentInteracts_____
| ΔAutonomousAgentState
| AgentInteracts
|_____
| posspercepts$'$ = canperceive environment$'$ perceivingactions
| actualpercepts$'$ = autowillperceive motivations$'$ goals$'$ posspercepts$'$
| willdo$'$ = autoactions motivations$'$ goals$'$ actualpercepts$'$ environment$'$
|_____

2.6 Applying SMART: Tropistic Agents

2.6.1 Tropistic Agents

SMART specifies a set of generic architectures. The types, functions and schemas it contains can be applied to other systems and concepts. In order to illustrate its use in this way, *tropistic agents* [51] are reformulated as an example of an agent architecture. It is one of a set of core agent architectures used by Genesereth and Nilsson to demonstrate some key issues of intelligent agent design. The activity of tropistic agents, as with reflexive agents, is determined entirely by the state of the environment in which they are situated. First, the original description of tropistic agents is summarised and then reformulated using elements of SMART.

According to Genesereth and Nilsson, the set of environmental states is denoted by S. Since agent perceptions are limited in general, it cannot be assumed that an arbitrary state is distinguishable from every other state. Perceptions thus partition S in such a way that environments from different partitions can be distinguished whilst environments from the same partition cannot. The partitions are defined by the sensory function, *see*, which maps environments contained in S to environments contained in T, the set of all observed environments. The effectory function, *do*, which determines how environments change when an agent performs an action, taken from the set of the agent actions, A, maps the agent's action and the current environment to a new environment. Finally, action-selection for a tropistic agent, *action*, is determined by perceptions and maps elements of T to elements of A. Tropistic agents are thus defined by the following tuple.

$$(S, T, A, see : S \rightarrow T, do : A \times S \rightarrow S, action : T \rightarrow A)$$

2.6.2 Reformulating Perception

The SMART framework can be applied to reformulate tropistic agents by first defining types: equating the set S to the SMART type, *Environment*; the set T (as it refers to agent perceptions), to the type *View*; and the set, A, to the type *Action*. The following type definitions can then be written.

$$S == Environment \land T == View \land A == Action$$

According to SMART, tropistic agents are not autonomous. Thus the agent-level of conceptualisation is the most suitable level, and these are the models chosen. The functions defining architecture at this level are *canperceive*, *willperceive* and *agentactions*, defining the possible percepts, actual percepts and performed actions, respectively. The effect of actions on environments is independent of the level chosen in the agent hierarchy and defined by *effectinteraction*. Recall that these functions have the following type signatures.

$$canperceive : Environment \rightarrow \mathbb{P}\,Action \nrightarrow View$$
$$willperceive : \mathbb{P}\,Goal \rightarrow View \rightarrow View$$
$$agentactions : \mathbb{P}\,Goal \rightarrow View \rightarrow Environment \rightarrow \mathbb{P}\,Action$$
$$effectinteraction : Environment \rightarrow \mathbb{P}\,Action \rightarrow Environment$$

These functions include explicit reference to agent goals, which are not represented in the model of tropistic agents since they are implicitly fixed in the hard-coded functions. In what follows, the value of these goals is taken to be *gs* and accordingly set all goal parameters of SMART functions to this value.

The goals of a tropistic agent do not constrain the selection of its perceptions from those that are available, and *willperceive* is defined as the identity function on observed environments. In SMART, the perceiving actions are used at every perceiving step so that the second argument of *canperceive* is always applied to the perceiving actions (*perceivingactions*) of the agents as specified in the *AgentPerception* schema. Accordingly, tropistic perception is reformulated in the second predicate below. There is an implicit assumption that tropistic agents are capable perceivers; perceptions are always a subset of the actual environment. This assumption is formalised in the last of the three predicates below that together define tropistic perception.

$$willperceieve\ gs = \{v : View \bullet (v, v)\}$$
$$\forall e : S \bullet see\ e = willperceive\ gs\ (canperceive\ e\ perceivingactions)$$
$$\forall e, v : S \bullet willperceive\ gs\ (canperceive\ e\ perceivingactions) \subseteq e$$

The set of partitions in S can be calculated using set comprehension.

$$partitions == \{e, v : Environment \mid v = see\ e \bullet see \rhd \{v\}\}$$

2.6.3 Reformulating Action

The difference between the SMART framework and tropistic agent effectory functions is simply that the former allows for a set of actions to be performed rather than a single action.

$$\forall e : Environment;\ a : Action \bullet do\ (a, e) = effectinteraction\ e\ \{a\}$$

The action *selected* by a tropistic agent is dependent solely on its perceptions. In SMART, the actions *performed* are additionally dependent on goals and the environment. The environment can affect the performance of selected actions if, for example, an agent has incorrect or incomplete perceptions of it. By contrast it is assumed that a tropistic agent correctly perceives its static environment and performs actions that are equivalent to those selected. These assumptions mean that the environment does not affect the performance of actions once they have been selected. In order to specify this in SMART, the *Environment* parameter of *agentactions* is fixed to the empty set, and *action* is defined using *agentactions* as follows.

$$\forall v : T \bullet action\ v = agentactions\ gs\ v\ \{\}$$

2.6.4 Discussion

Reformulating tropistic agents using SMART highlights several issues of note. First, SMART provides a more intuitive conceptualisation of an agent as an object with a purpose. Goals are hard-coded into tropistic agent actions and perception functions; they are neither *ascribed* to the agents nor are there any explicit mechanisms by which agent goals direct behaviour. Second, explicitly incorporating agent goals in SMART provides a more sophisticated design environment. It incorporates the premise that agent goals change over time and that the selection of actions and perceptions must be adapted accordingly. Clearly, it is inefficient to have to re-write the functions defining action and perception selection every time new goals are adopted. Third, features of SMART are more generally applicable than those described for tropistic agents, and it can therefore be used to explicitly formalise any assumptions (implicit or otherwise) regarding the tropistic agent, its environment, and the interaction between them.

2.7 Specification Structure of SMART

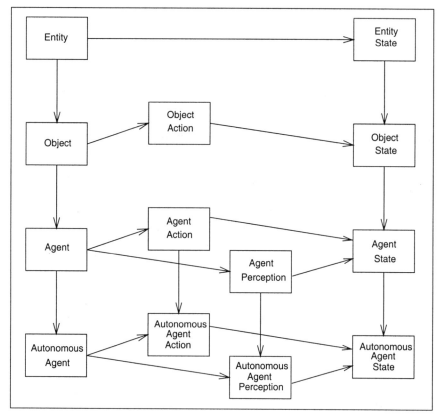

Fig. 2.2. Schema Structure for SMART

This chapter has described a formal model of a four-tiered framework that defines, at decreasing levels of abstraction, entities, objects, agents and autonomous agents.

It has been constructed in such a way that the set of entities in an environment includes the set of objects, the set of objects includes the set of agents, and the set of agents includes the set of autonomous agents. As well as definitions, SMART provides functional and operational models of the architecture and operation of entities at each level in the hierarchy.

Entities offer the most abstract description of components and are collections of attributes that are grouped together in some way. Entities with capabilities are objects, which can affect their environments by interacting with them. Agents are objects whose capabilities affect the environment in a way that is *purposeful*, and can therefore be ascribed goals. Autonomous agents are agents that generate their own goals through non-derivative internal motivations and are consequently capable of *independent* purposeful behaviour.

The specification structure used to formalise this four-stage hierarchy is shown in Figure 2.2. Components are specified at the highest level of abstraction in the *Entity* schema and then, through schema inclusion, this is refined to define objects, agents and autonomous agents in the *Object*, *Agent* and *AutonomousAgent* schemas respectively. For objects, agents and autonomous agents, behaviour is described by the *ObjectAction*, *AgentAction* and *AutonomousAgentAction* schemas. For agents and autonomous agents, their perception in an environment is detailed in *AgentPerception* and *AutonomousAgentPerception*. Similarly, for entities, objects, agents and autonomous agents, their state when situated in an environment is defined in *EntityState*, *ObjectState*, *AgentState* and *AutonomousAgentState*. Since the relationships between the different levels are well-defined, easy movement between them is facilitated. This enables the appropriate level of abstraction to be chosen to describe a given system component. It is then possible, for example, to describe a robot at either the object level or the agent level as appropriate.

Finally, in order to describe interaction, operations that affect the state of components situated in an environment, rather than the components themselves, are defined as changes of state to *EntityState*, *ObjectState*, and so on, as shown in Figure 2.3.

2.8 Related Work

There exists a small body of work that provides a similar view to that presented here. For example, Covrigaru and Lindsay describe a set of properties that *characterise* autonomous systems, relating to such factors as type and number of goals, complexity, interaction, robustness, and so on [20]. In contrast, SMART *defines* what is necessary for a system to be autonomous in very precise terms, and distinguishes clearly between objectness, agency and autonomy. One particular consequence of the difference in views is that SMART allows a rock, for example, to be considered an agent *if* it is being used for some purpose, such as a hammer for tent-pegs. Covrigaru and Lindsay deny the rock the quality of autonomy because it is not goal-directed, but ignore the possibility of agency, skipping over an important part of SMART.

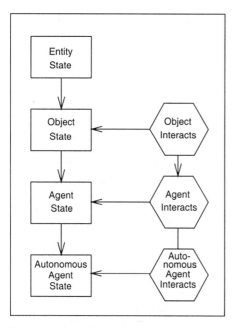

Fig. 2.3. Schema Structure for SMART Operation

Castelfranchi shares some of the views expressed in this chapter in arguing that autonomy is characterised in terms of agents having their own goals, making decisions about these goals and adopting the goals of others only when they choose to [8]. However, whilst Castelfranchi's notions are extremely important they are often vague and rely on an existing analysis of the possible social relationships and dependencies between agents. He also considers which aspects of an agent architecture determine whether it is autonomous, and characterises types of autonomy such as social, executive and motivational autonomy [10]. Though Castelfranchi recognises that motivations are significant in descriptions of autonomy, he does not consider them to be *sufficient* qualities. In addition, these notions of autonomy are *relative* to his proposed social theory in contrast to SMART, by which we take autonomy to be an absolute concept that is constant regardless of the context in which it occurs. Furthermore it is not dependent on specific agent architectures. In SMART, autonomy either exists or it does not, depending solely on whether an agent has motivations.

Demazeau and Müller [25] discuss the *minimal features* of a generic agent and also make explicit a conceivable distinction between agents and autonomous agents. In their view, a minimal agent possesses knowledge, goals, a set of possible plans or solutions to achieve these goals, reasoning capabilities to produce these plans and, lastly, decision capabilities to choose which plan to pursue. The goals of an agent can either be implicitly encoded in the algorithms of that agent or explicitly acquired. An autonomous agent is taken to mean an agent whose "existence is not justified by the existence of others." Some of these ideas are subsumed by the agent framework but also conflict as discussed below.

First, the definition of a minimal agent appears to be far too strong. For example, whilst in many cases agents may be able to plan, it is surely not a necessary characteristic. In addition, no model of how these different aspects of agency are related is provided and, further, the definitions exclude non-computational entities being agents. The SMART definition of agency on the other hand is more clearly defined and can be more generally applied. For example, it does not rule out non-computational entities as agents. This is important since there are examples of existing agent systems in which non-computational entities are modelled as agents [101]. In fact, SMART does not distinguish between computational and non-computational agents at all. Programs, robots and cups can all be agents depending on whether they serve a purpose.

Demazeau and Müller's view of a goal is, however, accommodated within the framework, since according to SMART, goals can be either explicitly represented and acquired by an agent or implicitly ascribed. Similarly, their definition of autonomy is subsumed by that within the framework, since a motivated agent creates its own goals and does not rely on others for purposeful existence. In addition, SMART defines the precise relationship between agency and autonomy, a question not investigated by Demazeau and Müller, since it can only be settled by definition as has been done in this chapter.

Research by Maruichi et al. [88], with a bias towards agent-oriented programming, takes what at first appears to be a similar view to the one in this chapter, defining agents in terms of objects and then distinguishing those agents that are autonomous. They model agents as concurrent objects and argue that since these objects automatically execute methods in response to messages without evaluating their meaning or considering their own internal state, they are not autonomous. Autonomy, it is argued, is achieved when an object or agent can control method execution after evaluation of both the meaning of the message and the internal state. However, in that work the authors do not distinguish between objects and agents. Subsequent work by Tokoro offers a related view in which he distinguishes objects, concurrent objects, autonomous agents and volitional agents [125], again similar in spirit to the view taken in this chapter, though not so precisely defined or so widely applicable.

More recently. Franklin and Graesser [47] have attempted to distinguish *agents* from *programs*. In their view, any software agent is a program but a program may not be a software agent. They argue that there is an important distinction between a program and an agent and provide the following definition.

"An autonomous agent is a system situated within and part of an environment that senses that environment and acts on it, over time, in pursuit of its own agenda and so as to affect what it senses in the future."

This definition does not appear to be at odds with SMART but the last remark concerning acting so as to affect what it senses is vague and open to several interpretations and may simply be a consequence of any goal-directed behaviour. Crucially however, the authors have not fulfilled their promise of a definition of *agency* but have instead moved straight to a definition of an *autonomous agent* without first considering what it is to be an agent. This is a key aspect of SMART.

2.9 Summary

As a result of this chapter, there are formal definitions for agents and autonomous agents that are clear, precise and unambiguous. The work is not biased towards any existing classifications or notions because there is little consensus. Recent papers define agents in wildly different ways, if at all, and this makes it extremely difficult to be explicit about their nature and functionality. The SMART framework explicates those factors that are necessary for agency and autonomy, and is sufficiently abstract to cover the gamut of agents, both hardware and software, intelligent and unintelligent,

The definitions have been constructed so that they relate to existing work but in such a way as not to specify a prescribed internal architecture. This makes good sense, since it allows a variety of different architectural and design views to be accommodated within a single unifying structure. All that is required by the specification is a minimal adherence to features of, and relationships between, the entities described therein. Thus a cup can be viewed as an object or an agent depending on the manner in which it functions. Similarly, a robot can be viewed as an object, an agent or an autonomous agent depending on the nature of its control structures. Just how those control structures should function is not specified here, but instead how the control is directed.

SMART provides an important basis for reference. Both human and artificial agents can be classified equally well. As an example, consider the relationship of a programmer to a program. Programs are always designed to satisfy goals, but these goals are rarely explicit or able to be modified independently of the programmer. The programs lack goal-generating motivations, but can be ascribed goals. In this respect, they are agents and not autonomous agents. Programmers typically develop programs according to several motivations which determine how the program is constructed. Time and effort must be balanced against cost, ease of use, simplicity, functionality and other factors. Programmers consider these factors in determining the design of programs and in the goal or goals of programs. Programmers can change the goals of programs by modifying code if desired, and can modify their own goals to suit circumstances. In this respect, programmers are autonomous agents.

The difference between these kinds of programs as agents and much recent use of the term is that the relationship between the user (or programmer) and the program has become explicit. Software agents assist users. They adopt the goals of the users in the tasks that they perform. Whether or not they are autonomous depends on the ability of the agents to function independently of those users, and to modify their goals in relation to circumstances.

3. Agent Relationships

3.1 Introduction

It is the interaction between individual agents by which goals are typically achieved in multi-agent systems [124]. The form of such interaction can range over interleaved actions, combined actions, message-passing or high-level linguistic utterances such as speech acts, depending on the nature of the agents themselves. This suggests that an account of interaction is only possible through an understanding of the agents involved.

The previous chapter defined agency and autonomy in terms of goals. Agents *satisfy* goals, while autonomous agents may, additionally, generate them. Goals may be adopted by either autonomous agents, non-autonomous agents or objects without goals However, since non-autonomous agents must satisfy goals for others, they *rely* on other agents for purposeful existence, which indicates that goal adoption creates critical inter-agent relationships. The combined total of these agent relationships defines a social organisation that is not artificially or externally imposed but arises as a natural and elegant consequence of the definitions of agency and autonomy. Moreover, the SMART framework allows an explicit and precise analysis of multi-agent systems with no more conceptual primitives than were introduced in the previous chapter for individual agents.

As before, the discussion of multi-agent systems in this chapter is not limited to computational entities, since it is the relationships in which they participate that are significant. For example, if I use a cup to store tea, or a robot to attach a tyre to my car, then the relationships I have with each are important, and I would not wish either of these relationships to be broken or constrained. However, while the components of a multi-agent system need not be computational, it is only computational entities that can recognise and exploit the relationships therein. There are thus two parts to this work. The first is to understand the key inter-agent relationships that arise in multi-agent systems, and the second is to consider how these relationships can be recognised and exploited by computational components. This chapter considers the former, while the latter is considered later.

3.2 Multi-Agent Systems

3.2.1 Multi-Agent System Definition

A multi-agent system is one that contains a collection of two or more agents. Now, since goals cannot exist without having been generated by autonomous agents, it is impossible for agents to exist without autonomy somewhere in the system. In addition therefore, a multi-agent system must contain at least *one* autonomous agent. It may contain multiple autonomous agents but this is not a necessary condition. One further requirement for a set of agents to make up a multi-agent system is that there must be some *interaction* between the agents, since otherwise each would be acting independently of the others and it would make little sense to consider such a collection of components as one system. Moreover, this interaction must specifically result from one agent satisfying the goals of another.

Definition 3.2.1. *A* multi-agent system *is any system that contains*

1. *two or more agents;*
2. *at least one autonomous agent; and*
3. *at least one relationship between two agents where one satisfies the goal of the other.*

3.2.2 Server-Agents and Neutral-Objects

In what follows, it is useful to identify further sub-categories of entity. Before proceeding, therefore, those objects that are not agents, and those agents that are not autonomous, are distinguished and referred to as *neutral-objects* and *server-agents* respectively. They are defined in the following schemas.

```
┌─ NeutralObject ──────────────────────────────
│  Object
│ ─────────────
│  goals = { }
│  motivations = { }
└──────────────────────────────────────────────
```

```
┌─ ServerAgent ────────────────────────────────
│  Agent
│ ─────────────
│  motivations = { }
└──────────────────────────────────────────────
```

A multi-agent system is one that contains a collection of entities of which some are objects; of these objects some are neutral-objects and some are agents; and of these agents some are server-agents and some are autonomous agents. This is shown in a modified Venn diagram in Figure 3.1. A term written across a boundary signifies the set of elements contained within it.

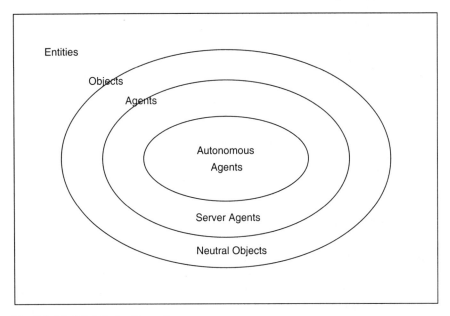

Fig. 3.1. Modified Entity Hierarchy

3.2.3 Multi-Agent System Specification

The specification of a multi-agent system is given in the schema below, which that contains all four hierarchical categories from the SMART framework as well as the new categories of neutral-object and server-agent. It captures the way in which different classes of entity are related. The first predicate of the schema states that *autonomousagents* is a subset of *agents*, that *agents* is a subset of *objects*, and that *objects* is a subset of *entities*. The following two predicates then state that the set of all agents is the union of all autonomous agents and all server-agents, and that the set of all objects is the union of all agents and all neutral-objects. Finally, the remainder of the schema requires there to be at least two agents of which one is autonomous, and that at least two of the agents in the system share a minimum of one goal. These predicates provide a formal realisation of the multi-agent system definition above.

```
┌─ MultiAgentSystem ──────────────────────────────────────────
│ entities : ℙ Entity
│ objects : ℙ Object
│ agents : ℙ Agent
│ autonomousagents : ℙ AutonomousAgent
│ neutralobjects : ℙ NeutralObject
│ serveragents : ℙ ServerAgent
├─────────────────────────────────────────────────────────────
│ autonomousagents ⊆ agents ⊆ objects ⊆ entities
│ agents = autonomousagents ∪ serveragents
│ objects = agents ∪ neutralobjects
│ #agents ≥ 2
│ #autonomousagents ≥ 1
│ ∃ aa1, aa2 : agents • aa1.goals ∩ aa2.goals ≠ { }
└─────────────────────────────────────────────────────────────
```

In order to construct a multi-agent system, one agent must adopt the goal of another. Before this can happen, however, the goal must first be created. In the next section, the way in which goals are generated by autonomous agents from their motivations is discussed.

3.3 Goal Generation

3.3.1 Discussion

An account of how autonomous agents generate goals from their motivations is an important topic of investigation in the design of autonomous agents, and many people have looked at specific computational architectures for achieving this aim [92, 97]. Though the issues in the development of particular architectures or mechanisms involved in the generation of goals are not addressed, a high-level functional description that can be refined to describe particular architectures is considered. The model that follows is therefore not architecture-specific but simply illustrates how the control of goal generation is directed. It is important to understand the original generation of goals since it is their creation and subsequent propagation that defines the set of inter-agent relationships considered in this chapter.

For an agent to assess the relative benefit of *generating* one goal over others, it must have a repository of known goals that is referred to as a *goal library*. This goal library may be fixed permanently, but is more generally updated over time through learning, while the goals themselves capture knowledge of limited and well-defined aspects of the world by describing particular *sub-states* of environments. An autonomous agent thus tries to find a way to mitigate motivations, either by selecting an action to achieve an existing goal, or by retrieving a goal from the goal library and including it in its current goals. The first of these alternatives was addressed by the *autoactions* function in the *AutonomousAgentAction* schema seen earlier, while the second is considered here.

In order to retrieve goals to mitigate motivations, an autonomous agent must have some way of assessing the effects of competing or alternative goals. Clearly, the goals that make the greatest positive contribution to the motivations of the agent should be selected, unless a greater motivational effect can be achieved by *destroying* some subset of its current goals. The motivational effect of generating or destroying goals is not only dependent on the current motivations but also on the current goals of the agent and its current perceptions. For example, it is sensible to require that an autonomous agent should not generate a goal that is incompatible with the achievement or satisfaction of its existing goals, and neither should it generate a goal that is already satisfied in the current environment.

Once generated, it is possible that goals may be changed or modified if it seems appropriate to do so in the light of any changes to the environment or unexpected problems in the goal-achievement process. Goals can thus be *dynamically* re-evaluated as a result of considering the implications of the original and alternative goals in terms of the actions required to achieve them.

3.3.2 Goal Generation Specification

Formally, the ability of autonomous agents to generate their own goals is specified in the schema, *AssessGoals*, which describes how autonomous agents monitor their motivations for goal generation. First, the *AutonomousAgentState* schema is included, and the new variable, *goallibrary*, is declared to represent the repository of available known goals. Then, there are two functions to evaluate the benefit of generating and destroying current goals. The *motiveffectgenerate* function returns a numeric value representing the motivational effect of satisfying a new set of additional goals with a set of motivations, current goals and current perceptions. Similarly, the *motiveffectdestroy* function returns a numeric value representing the motivational effect of removing some subset of existing goals with the same set of motivations, goals and perceptions. The predicate part specifies that the current goals must be in the goal library. For ease of expression, a function is defined that is related to *motiveffectgenerate*, called *satisfygenerate*, which returns the motivational effect of an autonomous agent satisfying an additional set of goals. The function *satisfydestroy*, is analogously related to *motiveffectdestroy*.

```
┌─ AssessGoals ──────────────────────────────────────────────────
│ AutonomousAgentState
│ goallibrary : P₁ Goal
│ motiveffectgenerate : P Motivation → P Goal → View → P Goal → Z
│ motiveffectdestroy : P Motivation → P Goal → View → P Goal → Z
│ satisfygenerate, satisfydestroy : P Goal → Z
├────────────────────────────────────────────────────────────────
│ goals ⊆ goallibrary
│ ∀ gs : P goallibrary •
│     satisfygenerate gs =
│         motiveffectgenerate motivations goals actualpercepts gs ∧
│     satisfydestroy gs =
│         motiveffectdestroy motivations goals actualpercepts gs
└────────────────────────────────────────────────────────────────
```

The *GenerateGoals* operation schema formally describes the generation of a new set of goals, which changes the state of the agent. The remaining part of the schema states that there is a set of goals in the goal library that has a greater motivational effect than any other set of goals, and the current goals of the agent are updated to include the new goals.

```
┌─ GenerateGoals ────────────────────────────────────────────────
│ ΔAutonomousAgentState
│ AssessGoals
├────────────────────────────────────────────────────────────────
│ ∃ gs : P Goal | gs ⊆ goallibrary •
│     (∀ os : P Goal |
│         os ∈ (P goallibrary) •
│         (satisfygenerate gs ≥ satisfygenerate os) ∧
│             goals' = goals ∪ gs)
└────────────────────────────────────────────────────────────────
```

Once generated by an autonomous agent, goals persist in the relevant multi-agent system until, for whatever reason, they are explicitly destroyed by that autonomous agent. The destruction of goals is defined analogously to the generation of goals in the *DestroyGoals* schema, which states that an agent destroys the subset of its goals that provide the greatest motivational advantage for doing so.

```
┌─ DestroyGoals ─────────────────────────────────────────────────
│ ΔAutonomousAgentState
│ AssessGoals
├────────────────────────────────────────────────────────────────
│ ∃ gs : P Goal | gs ⊆ goallibrary •
│     (∀ os : P Goal |
│         os ∈ (P goallibrary) •
│         (satisfydestroy gs ≥ satisfydestroy os) ∧ goals' = goals \ gs)
└────────────────────────────────────────────────────────────────
```

This section has provided a high-level description of how goals are generated from motivations. In particular, it has considered how the current perceptions, goals and motivations of an autonomous agent affects the generation of new goals, or the destruction of existing ones. Since goals can only be generated by autonomous agents a multi-agent system must contain at least one autonomous agent. However, in attempting to achieve their goals, autonomous agents may attempt to involve others, which is considered next.

3.4 Goal Adoption

Agents can make use of the capabilities of others if these others *adopt* their goals. Let us consider an example of two autonomous agents who are librarians, Anne and Bill, sharing an office. Now, if Anne needs to move a table which cannot be lifted alone, she must get someone else to adopt her goal before it can be moved. Similarly, if she wants tea, then she must make use of a kettle to boil water, a teapot to make the tea and subsequently a cup from which to drink it. Each of these objects can be ascribed, or viewed, as adopting Anne's goals in order that her thirst can be relieved.

In general, entities may serve the purposes of others by adopting their goals. Since they must have capabilities they must be objects. The discussion that follows, therefore, considers only objects. However, the ways in which objects adopt the goals of others depends on the *kind* of object. An object is either a neutral-object, a server-agent or an autonomous agent, and each category requires a separate analysis by the agent with a goal to be adopted, which is referred to as the *viewing* agent.

- A neutral-object serves no purpose and can be instantiated as an agent by the viewing agent without regard to others. Here, agents are created from objects with the addition of relevant associated goals.
- A server-agent is not isolated since it must already be serving a purpose for one or more other agents. An additional goal may affect the achievement of existing goals so for goal adoption to take place, the viewing agent must analyse both the server-agent and the agents that are engaging it in order to avoid conflict.
- An autonomous agent generates its own goals, adopting the goals of a viewing agent either by recognising that goal or by negotiation with the viewing agent or some intermediary agent. The viewing agent must therefore consider the motivations of the autonomous agent to determine whether it will adopt the goal of the viewing agent.

These three scenarios are illustrated in Figure 3.2. A *target* agent or object is one that is intended to adopt goals, an *engaging* agent is one whose goals are currently (already) adopted by the target agent, and (as stated above) a *viewing* agent is an agent that seeks to *engage* a target agent or object by having it adopt goals. (The engagement relationship between agents is examined in more detail in the next section.) It is a viewing agent because the way in which goal adoption is attempted is determined by its view of the situation. In (a), the viewing agent must analyse the target neutral-object in order for the neutral-object to adopt the goal of the viewing agent. Second, in (b) the viewing agent must analyse the target server-agent and any agents which are engaging the target agent. Third, in (c) the viewing agent analyses the target autonomous agent only. Each of these is considered below.

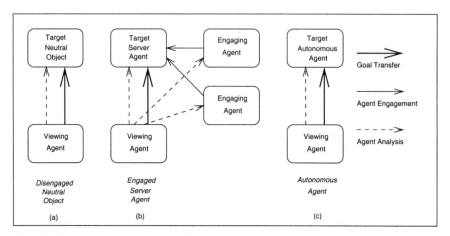

Fig. 3.2. Goal Adoption in Neutral-Objects, Server-Agents and Autonomous Agents

3.4.1 Goal Adoption by Neutral-Objects

The simplest case involves instantiating an agent from a neutral-object with the goals to be adopted. Here, the simple act of goal transfer causes an agent to be created from a neutral-object. Thus, for example, a cup in Anne and Bill's office, which is just a neutral-object, becomes an agent when it is used for storing Anne's tea. In this case it *adopts* or *is ascribed* her goal of storing the liquid. It is possible to create the agent from the object because the cup is not being used by anyone else; it is not *engaged* by another agent. Neutral-objects are not engaged but *disengaged*.

Below, a function is specified that creates a new entity by ascribing a set of goals to an existing entity. It takes an entity and a set of goals, *gs*, and creates a new entity with the same set of attributes, actions and motivations but with the additional goals, *gs*. The function is *total* and is thus valid for any entity and any set of goals.

$$EntityAdoptGoals : (Entity \times \mathbb{P}\,Goal) \to Entity$$

$\forall\, gs : \mathbb{P}\,Goal;\ old, new : Entity \bullet EntityAdoptGoals(old, gs) = new \Leftrightarrow$
$\quad new.goals = old.goals \cup gs \land$
$\quad new.capabilities = old.capabilities \land$
$\quad new.attributes = old.attributes$

When a neutral-object adopts a set of goals it becomes a server-agent, as specified below. Thus, a neutral-object and a set of goals are inputs, and the sets of objects and agents are updated accordingly by removing the object and including the newly instantiated server-agent.

NeutralObjectAdoptGoals
$no?$: *NeutralObject*
$gs?$: $\mathbb{P}\,Goal$
$\Delta MultiAgentSystem$

$no? \in neutralobjects$
$neutralobjects' = neutralobjects \setminus \{no?\}$
$serveragents' = serveragents \cup \{EntityAdoptGoals\,(no?, gs?)\}$
$autonomousagents' = autonomousagents$

For completeness, the related operation is specified by which an entity is released from all of its agency obligations and a server-agent reverts to a neutral-object. It is possible that a cup can be engaged for two separate goals. It may be engaged as a vase for flowers and as a paper-weight for loose papers if there is a breeze coming from a nearby open window. If the window is closed and the flowers are removed, the cup is released from all its agency obligations and reverts to being a neutral-object.

Formally, this operation is defined by the *RevertToNeutralObject* schema. It uses the axiomatic function, *EntityRemoveGoals*, defined similarly to *EntityAdoptGoals*, which removes a set of goals from an entity.

$EntityRemoveGoals : (Entity \times \mathbb{P}\,Goal) \to Entity$

$\forall gs : \mathbb{P}\,Goal;\; old, new : Entity \bullet$
$\quad EntityRemoveGoals(old, gs) = new \Leftrightarrow$
$\qquad new.goals = old.goals \setminus gs \wedge$
$\qquad new.capabilities = old.capabilities \wedge$
$\qquad new.attributes = old.attributes$

The predicates in the following schema check that the input goals are the same as the set of current goals of the server-agent. This ensures that the server-agent is released from *all* of its agency obligations. The variables, *neutralobjects*, *serveragents* and *autonomousagents*, are updated accordingly.

RevertToNeutralObject
$sa?$: *ServerAgent*
$gs?$: $\mathbb{P}\,Goal$
$\Delta MultiAgentSystem$

$sa? \in serveragents$
$gs? = sa?.goals$
$neutralobjects' =$
$\quad neutralobjects \cup \{EntityRemoveGoals\,(sa?, sa?.goals)\}$
$serveragents' = serveragents \setminus \{sa?\}$
$autonomousagents' = autonomousagents$

3.4.2 Goal Adoption by Server-Agents

If the target object is *engaged* by other agents then it is itself an agent, so the protocol for goal adoption changes. In this case, there are alternative ways to *engage* the target object.

The first involves supplying the target object with more goals that do not affect the existing agency obligations. In this case the agent is *shared* between the viewing agent and the existing engaging agents. The second involves trying to persuade any engaging agents to *release* the engaged object so that it becomes a *neutral*-object and can therefore subsequently be engaged by the viewing agent as required. (This may relate to the issue of goal adoption for autonomous agents, which is considered later). The third possibility involves *displacing* the engaging agent so that the engaged object becomes a neutral-object and can then subsequently be ascribed other goals. This possibility is dangerous since it may cause conflict with the previous engaging agents.

As an example, suppose that a cup is currently in use as a paper-weight for Anne, so that the cup is *Anne's* agent with her goal of securing loose papers. Suppose also, that Bill wishes to use the cup to have some tea. The first way for Bill to engage the cup is for him to attempt to use the cup without destroying the existing agent relationship between Anne and the cup. Since this would involve an awkward attempt at making tea in, and subsequently drinking from, a stationary cup, he may decide instead to try other alternatives. The second alternative is to negotiate with Anne to release the cup so that it can be used for storing tea while the third alternative is for Bill to displace the goal ascribed to the cup by removing the cup from the desk and pouring tea into it. The cup is no longer an agent for Anne and is now ascribed the goal of storing tea for Bill. It has switched from being engaged by Anne to being engaged by Bill, and this is equivalent to the agent reverting to an object and then being re-instantiated as a new agent. This method may not be an appropriate strategy, however, because in destroying the agency obligation of the cup as a paper-weight, there is a risk of conflict between Anne and Bill.

The adoption of goals by server-agents is formalised in the next schema, in which a server-agent is ascribed an additional set of goals. This describes the alternative where the cup is serving as a paper weight and is then subsequently given the goal of storing flowers. The initial target agent is removed from the set of server-agents, which is further updated to include the newly-instantiated target agent. The preconditions ensure that the target agent currently exists, and that the new goals are distinct from the existing goals.

```
┌─ ServerAgentAdoptGoals ────────────────────────────────
│ sa? : ServerAgent
│ gs? : ℙ Goal
│ ΔMultiAgentSystem
├────────────────────────────────────────────────────────
│ sa? ∈ serveragents
│ gs? ∩ sa?.goals = { }
│ neutralobjects' = neutralobjects
│ serveragents' = serveragents \ {sa?} ∪ {EntityAdoptGoals (sa?, gs?)}
│ autonomousagents' = autonomousagents
└────────────────────────────────────────────────────────
```

In some situations, a server-agent is released from some but not all of its agency obligations. Suppose, for example, that a window is open in the librarians' office and that a cup is being used as a paperweight by Anne and a vase by Bill. If the window is subsequently closed, then the cup may be released from its agency obligations as a paperweight while still remaining an agent because it is holding flowers. Formally, the operation schema representing this change of agency obligation is specified in the next schema. Notice that the goals that are removed from an agent in this operation must be a *proper* subset of its goals. The server-agent, *sa?*, is removed from the set of server-agents and replaced with the agent that results from removing the goals, *gs?*, from *a?*.

```
┌─ ServerAgentReleaseGoals ──────────────────────────────
│ sa? : ServerAgent
│ gs? : ℙ Goal
│ ΔMultiAgentSystem
├────────────────────────────────────────────────────────
│ sa? ∈ serveragents
│ gs? ⊂ sa?.goals
│ neutralobjects' = neutralobjects
│ serveragents' =
│     (serveragents \ {sa?}) ∪ {EntityRemoveGoals (sa?, gs?)}
│ autonomousagents' = autonomousagents
└────────────────────────────────────────────────────────
```

3.4.3 Autonomous Goal Adoption

In the example above, the second possibility for goal adoption by server-agents involves Bill persuading Anne to first release the cup from its existing agency. The cup would then become a neutral-object and could be instantiated as required by Bill. In general, such persuasion or negotiation may be more difficult than the direct physical action required for goal adoption in non-autonomous entities. Autonomous agents are motivated and, as such, only participate in an activity and assist others if it is to their motivational advantage to do so. They create their own agendas and for them, goal adoption is a *voluntary* process as opposed to an *obligatory* one for non-autonomous agents. In a similar example, Anne might ask Bill to assist in moving a table, but Bill may refuse.

Formally, the operation of an autonomous agent adopting the goals of another is specified in the following schema where the set of autonomous agents is updated to include the newly instantiated target autonomous agent. Note that this does not detail the persuasion involved, but simply the state change resulting from the goal adoption.

$$
\begin{array}{l}
\underline{\quad AutonomousAgentAdoptGoals \quad} \\
aa? : AutonomousAgent \\
gs? : \mathbb{P}\, Goal \\
\Delta MultiAgentSystem \\
\hline
aa? \in autonomousagents \\
autonomousagents' = (autonomousagents \setminus \{aa?\}) \cup \\
\qquad\qquad\qquad\qquad\qquad \{EntityAdoptGoals\,(aa?, gs?)\} \\
agents' = agents \;\wedge\; objects' = objects
\end{array}
$$

In general, goals must be adopted through explicit autonomous agent initiative, as opposed to an ascription of goals for non-autonomous agents. However, in some contexts the ascription of goals to autonomous agents may be meaningful. Suppose, as a dramatic yet unlikely example, that Anne incapacitates Bill in some way and places him by the door to function as a draft excluder. In this situation, the autonomous agent, Bill, could be *ascribed* the goal of keeping out the draft even though he has not explicitly adopted this goal. Such cases can be described by considering the autonomous agent as an agent in an obligatory relationship. This book, however, restricts *autonomous goal adoption* to the explicit and voluntary generation of goals that have been recognised in others.

Several points arise as a consequence of autonomous agents having to adopt goals.

- An autonomous agent can only explicitly adopt the goals of another if these can be represented in its goal library. For example, consider an agent whose goal base consists entirely of formulae in predicate calculus. If the goal base can represent predicates of the form $On(x, y)$ but not of the form $NextTo(x, y)$ then it can adopt the goal $On(block_A, block_B)$ but not the goal $NextTo(block_A, block_B)$.
- In order for an autonomous agent to adopt a goal, it must *generate* this goal through its motivations so that autonomous goal adoption is, in fact, a special case of goal generation. The generated goal is first recognised and then considered in terms of its motivational effect.
- Autonomous agents only adopt the goals of another if, at that time, this adoption provides the greatest motivational effect compared with the generation of any other possible set of goals.

3.4.4 Autonomous Goal Destruction

For a number of reasons an autonomous agent may destroy adopted goals. For example, suppose Anne wishes to move a table and has persuaded Bill to help. If Anne subsequently destroys some important agent relationship of Bill's, it is possible that Bill may then destroy the goal he has adopted from Anne of moving the table. As with goal adoption, for an autonomous agent to destroy goals, this must be considered the most motivationally beneficial course of action. This scenario is formalised below and is similar to the previous schema.

$$
\begin{array}{|l}
\underline{\textit{AutonomousAgentDestroysGoals}} \\
\textit{aa?} : \textit{AutonomousAgent} \\
\textit{gs?} : \mathbb{P}\,\textit{Goal} \\
\Delta\textit{MultiAgentSystem} \\
\textit{AssessGoals} \\
\hline
\textit{aa?} \in \textit{autonomousagents} \\
\textit{gs?} \subseteq \textit{aa?}.\textit{goals} \\
\textit{autonomousagents}' = (\textit{autonomousagents} \setminus \{\textit{aa?}\}) \cup \\
 \{\textit{EntityRemoveGoals}\,(\textit{aa?}, \textit{gs?})\} \\
\textit{agents}' = \textit{agents} \wedge \textit{objects}' = \textit{objects}
\end{array}
$$

Figure 3.3 gives an overview of the schemas used to define a multi-agent system as a collection of different categories of entity. The *MultiAgentSystem* schema is defined using the four entity schema types of SMART as well as introducing neutral-objects and server-agents. There are then six operation schemas describing goal adoption that change the state of this schema.

3.5 Engagement

Now, whenever an agent uses another non-autonomous entity, there is a relationship between the agent and the entity. In keeping with existing work concerning the nature of interdependencies between agents agent relationships are considered as specific kinds of *social* relationship [8], which must be recognised by computational components. For example, if Bill is collecting dirty cups for washing, it is important how he views the relationship of Anne to each cup. If she is using a cup, then there is a relationship and the cup should remain, otherwise it can be removed.

3.5.1 Direct Engagement

The social relationship between a non-autonomous entity that has adopted the goals of another agent and that agent is termed an *engagement*, and the agent is said to be *engaging* the entity. If Anne is using the cup to drink tea then she is said to be *engaging* the cup. In addition, Anne is engaging the cup through *direct* intervention. Such a relationship is referred to as a *direct engagement*. This distinguishes direct engagements from other engagements in which there are intermediary agents.

A direct engagement takes place whenever a neutral-object or a server-agent adopts the goals of another. Thus, an agent with some goals, called the *client*, uses another agent, called the *server*, to assist them in the achievement of those goals. Note that according to the previous definition, a server-agent is non-autonomous, and either exists already as a result of some other engagement, or is instantiated from a neutral-object for the current engagement. There is no restriction placed on a client-agent, and it may be autonomous or non-autonomous.

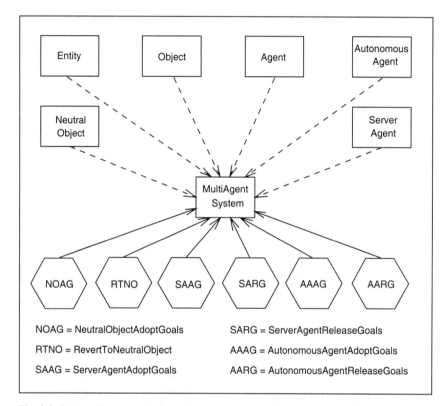

Fig. 3.3. Schema Structure for Specifying Multi-Agent Systems and Goal Adoption

Definition 3.5.1. *A direct engagement between an agent and a server-agent exists when, through the direct intervention of the first agent, the server-agent has adopted a goal of the agent.*

The following schema provides a formal definition of a direct engagement, in which there is a client agent, *client*, a server-agent, *server*, and the goal that *server* satisfies for *client*. An agent cannot engage itself, and both agents must have the goal of the engagement.

$\underline{\quad DirectEngagement\ \rule{6cm}{0.4pt}}$
client : Agent
server : ServerAgent
goal : Goal

client $\neq$ server
goal $\in$ (client.goals $\cap$ server.goals)

3.5.2 Direct Engagements in a Multi-Agent System

A multi-agent system may contain many engagements between individual agents. Formally, the set of *all* direct engagements in a multi-agent system is represented by the *directengagements* variable in the *SystemEngagements* schema. The first predicate states that for any direct engagement in *directengagements*, there can be no intermediate *direct* engagements of the same goal. In addition, the set of all server-agents, *serveragents*, in any multi-agent system is equal to the set comprising all server-agents involved anywhere in *directengagements*. In other words, a non-autonomous entity is only an agent if it is engaged by another. The set of all client agents is also defined, and the union of client and server agents defined to be a subset of the set of all agents.

$\underline{\quad SystemEngagements\ \rule{5.5cm}{0.4pt}}$
MultiAgentSystem
directengagements : $\mathbb{P}\,DirectEngagement$
clientagents : $\mathbb{P}\,Agent$

$\forall\,eng : directengagements \bullet$
$\quad \neg\,(\exists\,A : Agent;\ e_1, e_2 : directengagements\ |$
$\qquad e_1.goal = e_2.goal = eng.goal \bullet e_1.server = eng.server \wedge$
$\qquad\quad e_2.client = eng.client \wedge e_1.client = e_2.server = A)$
serveragents $= \{d : directengagements \bullet d.server\}$
clientagents $= \{d : directengagements \bullet d.client\}$
(clientagents $\cup$ serveragents) $\subseteq$ agents

3.5.3 Engagement Chains

Once autonomous agents have generated goals and engaged other server-agents, these server-agents may, in turn, engage other non-autonomous entities with the purpose of achieving or pursuing the original goal. This process can then, in principle, continue indefinitely. For example, the librarian Anne (A) may generate the goal of finding the location of a library book, and if A engages a workstation (W) to run a program (P) to search a database (D) for this information, there is a direct engagement between Anne and the workstation, between the workstation and the program, and between the program and the database, all with the goal of locating the book as illustrated in Figure 3.4. These chains of engagement provide more information with which to analyse multi-agent systems than using engagements alone, since the flow of goal adoption is explicitly represented. An *engagement chain* thus represents the goal and all the agents involved in the sequence of direct engagements. Since goals are grounded by motivations, the agent at the head of the chain must be autonomous.

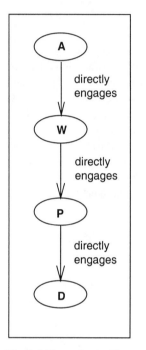

Fig. 3.4. Example: An Engagement Chain

Definition 3.5.2. *An* engagement chain *consists of a goal, the autonomous agent that generated that goal, and a non-empty sequence of server-agents such that*

1. *the autonomous agent engages the agent at the head of the chain with respect to the goal and,*
2. *each agent in the sequence directly engages the next with respect to the goal.*

Formally, an engagement chain comprises a goal, *goal*, the autonomous client-agent that generated the goal, *autoagent*, and a sequence of server-agents, where each agent in the sequence is directly engaging the next called *agentchain*. For any engagement chain, there must be at least one server-agent and the same agent cannot be involved more than once, so that *agentchain* is represented as a non-empty injective sequence. The predicate states that all the agents involved must share the goal of the chain. Note that this does not preclude the possibility that an autonomous agent may have generated the goal by adopting it from another autonomous agent.

─── *EngagementChain* ───────────────────────────────
goal : *Goal*
autoagent : *AutonomousAgent*
agentchain :iseq$_1$ *ServerAgent*
───
goal ∈ *autoagent.goals*
goal ∈ ⋂{*s* : *ServerAgent* | *s* ∈ ran *agentchain* • *s.goals*}
───

3.5.4 Engagement Chains in a Multi-Agent System

In general, a multi-agent system contains many engagement chains. For any two consecutive agents in an engagement chain there must be a corresponding direct engagement between those two agents with the goals of the chain.

Formally, the set of all such engagement chains is represented by the *engchains* variable in the *SystemEngagementChains* schema. This set can be related to the set of direct engagements, *directengagements*, as follows. For every engagement chain, *ec*, there must be a direct engagement between the autonomous agent, *ec.autoagent*, and the first client, *head ec.agentchain*, of *ec* with respect to the goal of *ec*. There must also be a direct engagement between any two agents that are adjacent to each other in *ec.agentchain* with respect to *ec.goal*. Given two sequences, *s* and *t*, of the same type, the relation, *s* in *t*, holds when *s* is a subsequence of *t*. The definition of the subsequence relation can be found in Appendix A.2.4. In addition, *autonomousagents* can be related to the *engchains* set, since the autonomous agents involved in an engagement chain are a subset of the set of all autonomous agents of the system.

─── *SystemEngagementChains* ───────────────────────────
SystemEngagements
engchains : ℙ *EngagementChain*
───
∀ *ec* : *engchains*; *s*$_1$, *s*$_2$: *Agent* •
        (∃ *d* : *directengagements* •
                d.goal = *ec.goal* ∧
                d.client = *ec.autoagent* ∧
                d.server = *head* (*ec.agentchain*)) ∧
        ⟨*s*$_1$, *s*$_2$⟩ in *ec.agentchain* ⇒
                (∃ *d* : *directengagements* •
                        d.client = *s*$_1$ ∧
                        d.server = *s*$_2$ ∧
                        d.goal = *ec.goal*)
        {*ec* : *engchains* • *ec.autoagent*} ⊆ *autonomousagents*
───

Engagement chains provide a means of categorising the relationships between agents. An understanding of engagements alone rather than engagement chains would not, in general, be sufficient to understand why the relationship exists. Engagement chains capture the flow of control from agent to agent and the understanding that every direct engagement must eventually be traced back to an autonomous agent. Understanding a program engaged by a workstation with the goal of locating a book is important, but may not be sufficient. What is crucial is the sequence of direct engagements that led to the creation of this direct engagement, the autonomous agent that generated the original goal, and the motivations that led to the goal's original generation.

3.6 Cooperation

The server-agents in the engagement relationships of the previous section have no means of resisting these relationships, so that they are *obligatory*. Autonomous agents, by contrast, generate their own goals and decide when to adopt the goals of others. Any relationship entered into by an autonomous agent is therefore *voluntary*, and referred to as a *cooperation*. An autonomous agent is said to be *cooperating* with another autonomous agent, if that agent has adopted the goal or goals of the other. The notion of autonomous goal acquisition applies both to the origination of goals by an autonomous agent for its own purposes, and the *adoption* of goals from others. For autonomous agents, the goal of another can only be adopted if it has a positive motivational effect, and this is also exactly why and how *cooperations* originate. Thus, as stated previously, goal adoption is just a special case of goal generation, where goals are generated in response to recognising them in others.

Thus the term, *cooperation*, is reserved for use only when the parties involved are autonomous and potentially capable of resisting. The difference between engagement and cooperation is in the autonomy or non-autonomy of the entities involved. It is senseless, for example, to consider a workstation cooperating with its user, but meaningful to consider the user engaging the workstation. Similarly, while it is not inconceivable for a user to engage a secretary, it makes better sense to say that the secretary is cooperating with the user, since the secretary can withdraw assistance at any point.

For example, if Anne and Bill both independently discover a broken library shelf and in response, both independently generate the goal of getting it repaired, then they are *not* cooperating. Certainly, both agents have the same goal but neither has adopted the goal of the other and neither agent can be said to be cooperating with the other. Cooperation cannot occur unwittingly if, by chance, two autonomous agents both generate the same goal. An agent can only cooperate with another if it has first recognised a goal in that other and — partly as a result of that recognition — has generated that goal for itself.

Definition 3.6.1. *An agent, A, is said to* cooperate *with another agent, B, if they are both autonomous, and A has autonomously adopted the goal of B.*

Note that this definition entails that cooperation is not symmetric. That is, if A is cooperating with B then it does not follow that B is cooperating with A.[1]

Definition 3.6.2. *A cooperation comprises a goal, the autonomous agent that generated the goal, and the non-empty set of autonomous agents that autonomously adopted the goal from the original autonomous agent.*

The schema below defines a cooperation to be a goal, *goal*, the autonomous agent that generated the goal, *generatingagent*, and the non-empty set of autonomous agents that adopted the goal, *cooperatingagents*. The predicates assert that all involved agents have the cooperation goal and that agents cannot cooperate with themselves.

┌─ *Cooperation* ─────────────────────────────────
│ *goal* : *Goal*
│ *generatingagent* : *AutonomousAgent*
│ *cooperatingagents* : $\mathbb{P}_1$ *AutonomousAgent*
├───
│ *goal* $\in$ *generatingagent.goals*
│ $\forall$ *aa* : *cooperatingagents* • *goal* $\in$ *aa.goals*
│ *generatingagent* $\notin$ *cooperatingagents*
└───

Cooperation therefore arises through autonomous agents acting in their self-interest. Some authors have proposed explicit mechanisms for this including, for example, Ito and Yano [65], who show how cooperation can arise from collections of agents trying to maximise benefit to themselves. We do not consider it further in this book however.

3.6.1 Cooperations in a Multi-Agent System

The set of cooperations in a multi-agent system is defined by the *cooperations* variable in the *SystemCooperations* schema. The predicate part of the schema states that for any cooperation, the union of the cooperating agents and the generating agent of that cooperation are a *subset* of all autonomous agents that have that goal. The subset relation is used rather than the equality relation because two agents sharing a goal are not necessarily cooperating. In addition, the set of all agents involved as co-operating agents in a cooperation is a subset of (rather than is equal to) the set of all autonomous agents of the system, since not all autonomous agents are necessarily involved in cooperations.

---

[1] This definition of cooperation is quite different from the standard, symmetrical one, which typically includes references to "working together". However, in this book, we make the point more forcibly that while the concept of "cooperation" can be a symmetrical process it is not necessary. For example, suppose that Anne is expecting a visitor later in the day and starts to tidy the office in preparation. If Bill recognises Anne's goal to tidy the office he may decide to adopt her goal and help. In some cases, Anne may not even be aware that Bill has adopted her goal and in this case, whilst Bill is cooperating with Anne, Anne cannot be said to be cooperating with Bill.

__ *SystemCooperations* _____

MultiAgentSystem

cooperations : $\mathbb{P}$ *Cooperation*
_____

$\forall c : cooperations \bullet$
    $(c.cooperatingagents \cup \{c.generatingagent\}) \subseteq$
        $\{a : autonomousagents \mid c.goal \in a.goals \bullet a\}$
$\bigcup\{c : cooperations \bullet$
    $(c.cooperatingagents \cup$
        $\{c.generatingagent\})\} \subseteq autonomousagents$

3.6.2 Discussion and Example

Suppose that Bill informs Anne that he needs to borrow a car, and further suppose that Anne wishes to help Bill achieve his goal but is not in a position to lend her car because it is in a garage awaiting repair. If she adopts the goal to provide a car that Bill can borrow, she may ask another friend, Charlie, to borrow his car. Now, if Anne does not tell Charlie that the car is intended for Bill, then Anne is cooperating with Bill, and Charlie is cooperating with Anne, but Charlie *is not* cooperating with Bill. This can be represented by two cooperations, *coop*1 and *coop*2, as follows.

$coop1.generatingagent = Bill$
$coop1.cooperatingagents = \{Anne\}$
$coop1.goal = Bill\_use\_car$

$coop2.generatingagent = Anne$
$coop2.cooperatingagents = \{Charlie\}$
$oop2.goal = Anne\_use\_car$

Alternatively, if Anne informs Charlie that the car is intended for Bill, then Charlie can be seen to be cooperating with Bill. This is represented as follows using the cooperation, *coop*.

$coop.generatingagent = Bill$
$coop.cooperatingagents = \{Anne, Charlie\}$
$coop.goal = Bill\_use\_car$

The definitions provided here state *necessary* conditions for cooperation. An agent must be autonomous and adopt the goal of another for cooperation to ensue. Further categories of goal adoption can be seen as refinements to this basic notion. For example, according to Conte et al. [19], cooperation includes a notion of goal adoption but also stipulates that agents should *depend* on each other for the shared goal. They also define three types of cooperation known as accidental, unilaterally intended and mutual cooperation. However, their definition requires a notion of dependence on each other for the goal to be achieved. In the SMART view, Anne can cooperate with Bill even if Bill could achieve his goal independently of Anne.

This definition of cooperation also provides necessary conditions for a group of entities becoming what Castelfranchi et al. call a *collective entity* [9, 11]. In addition to sharing a common goal, each agent in such a collective is required 'to do its share' to achieve the common goal of the group. In this way, a collective entity can be viewed as a refinement of a set of cooperative autonomous agents as described above. Similarly, Hirayama and Toyada [62] consider *coalitions* amongst agents that work together to benefit members of the coalition only.

The distinction between autonomous and non-autonomous agents enables us to detail precisely the nature of the relationships between agents. Autonomy implies independence and freedom to make decisions according to an agent's own priorities and also to decide with whom to cooperate. By contrast, non-autonomous agents are naturally disposed to adopt the goals of others whenever possible, and typically have no choice in the matter. They are therefore *benevolent* agents.

The distinction between engagement and cooperation is similar to the

distinction made between *vertical* cooperation and *horizontal* cooperation proposed by Fischer et al. [44, 45], which are two particular *cooperation settings* arising from different possible configurations of agents. They use a transportation domain as an example, where the former setting is a standard protocol for task allocation between a shipping company and its trucks, whilst the latter is a protocol for negotiation between companies that takes into account the fact that other companies are autonomous and therefore self-interested entities. Clearly, the trucks of a shipping company can be considered as server-agents for that company and are thus naturally disposed to adopt the goals of the company so that they can simply be engaged. In the latter case, negotiation must take place since autonomous companies need to *cooperate* with each other. The model proposed in this chapter provides a means of analysing these relationships so that the form of the interaction or negotiation can be reasoned about in advance.

3.7 The Agent Society

Engagements, engagement chains and cooperations are collectively referred to as the SMART *agent relationship types*, and use the term *agent society* to refer to the set of all entities and agent relationships in a multi-agent system. Formally, using the definitions of engagement, engagement chains and cooperations, the existing multi-agent system definition, *MultiAgentSystem*, can be refined to define the agent society. This schema defined a multi-agent system as a collection of entities, objects, agents and autonomous agents with the condition that at least one entity was an autonomous agent and there were at least two agents in the system. To this can be added the set of *engagements*, *engagement chains* and *cooperations* between entities, which define the entire set of agent relationships that arise from the definitions in the SMART framework.

As previously stated, a multi-agent system must contain at least one relationship in which one agent satisfies the goal of another. For there to be at least one such relationship between agents, it is necessary that at least two agents satisfy the same goal. It is now possible to state *sufficient* conditions in terms of the SMART agent relationships, that there must be at least one engagement or one cooperation.

Formally, the the set of agent relationships that arise in multi-agent systems is defined in the *AgentSociety* schema. The way this schema has been defined using the schemas defining cooperations, engagements and engagement chains is shown in Figure 3.5. These schemas, in turn, require the set of entities, objects, agents and autonomous agents defined in the *MultiAgentSchema* schema, as well as schemas defining the individual relationships. The predicate in the schema states that there is at least one agent relationship.

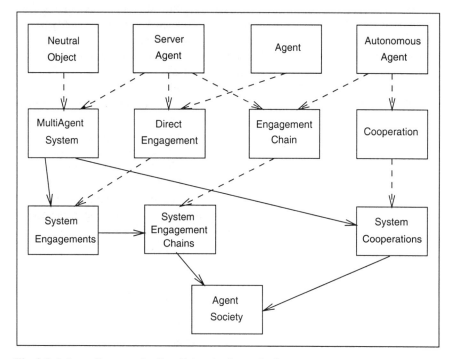

Fig. 3.5. Schema Structure for Specifying the Agent Society

AgentSociety
MultiAgentSystem
SystemEngagementChains
SystemCooperations

$\#cooperations + \#directengagements \geq 1$

3.8 Agent Relationships Taxonomy

By considering the entire set of engagements, engagement chains and cooperations, a map of the relationships between individual agents can be constructed for a better understanding of their current social interdependence. Different situations each suggest different possibilities for interaction. For example, if Anne alone is engaging an entity, then she can interact with it without regard to others.

This section provides a taxonomy of the relationships (or dependencies) between two agents that result from the agent relations that underly multi-agent systems, and are therefore *derived* from them. In what follows, eight types of agent relation are defined: *dengages, engages, indengages, owns, downs, uowns, sowns* and *cooperates* which may hold between two agents. For each, an initial description is provided, followed by a definition and formal specification. The definitions of these relationships are interdependent, with some relying on others, imposing an ordering on them.

3.8.1 Direct Engagement Relation

The first relation defined specifies agents directly engaging others. One agent is related to another by the direct engagement relation if and only if there is a direct engagement for which the first agent is the client and the second agent is the server. For example, users directly engage their workstations and tea-shop customers directly engage their cups.

Definition 3.8.1. *An agent, c, directly engages another server-agent, s, if, and only if, there is a direct engagement between c and s.*

$$
\begin{array}{|l}
\_Dengages_____ \\
AgentSociety \\
dengages : Agent \leftrightarrow ServerAgent \\
\hline
dengages = \{e : directengagements \bullet (e.client, e.server)\}
\end{array}
$$

3.8.2 Generic Engagement Relation

The notion of direct engagement implies a tight coupling between the behaviours of the agents involved. Certainly, there can be no intermediate entity in a direct engagement. Suppose, however, that a user is engaging a workstation to access a printer. The user is not *directly* engaging the printer but is *indirectly* engaging the printer since the printer is still serving as an agent for the user. The entities an agent engages are those that, either directly or indirectly, serve some purpose for that agent. In general, any agent involved in an engagement chain engages all those agents that appear subsequently in the chain.

Definition 3.8.2. *An agent* engages *another (server) agent if there is some engagement chain that includes the server such that either the engaging agent precedes the server-agent or the engaging agent is the autonomous agent of the engagement chain.*

In order to formally specify the engages relation, it is necessary to define the generic *before* relation that holds between a pair of elements and a sequence of elements if the first element of the pair precedes the second element in the sequence.

$$
\begin{array}{l}
\boxed{}[X]\boxed{} \\[4pt]
before : (X \times X) \leftrightarrow \operatorname{seq} X \\[6pt]
\hline \\[-6pt]
\forall a, b : X;\; s : \operatorname{seq} X \bullet ((a, b), s) \in before \Leftrightarrow \\
\qquad (\exists t, u, v : \operatorname{seq} X \bullet s = t \,^\frown \langle a \rangle \,^\frown u \,^\frown \langle b \rangle \,^\frown v)
\end{array}
$$

The engages relation comprises a set of pairs (c, s), where there is an engagement chain, ec, such that s is in $ec.agentchain$ and either c is *before* s in the chain or c is the autonomous agent of ec.

$$
\begin{array}{l}
\underline{\quad Engages \quad\quad\quad\quad\quad\quad\quad\quad\quad\quad\quad\quad\quad} \\[4pt]
AgentSociety \\
engages : Agent \leftrightarrow ServerAgent \\[6pt]
\hline \\[-6pt]
engages = \\
\quad \{ec : engchains;\; c : Agent;\; s : ServerAgent \mid \\
\qquad s \in (\operatorname{ran} ec.agentchain) \wedge \\
\qquad ((c = ec.autoagent) \vee \\
\qquad\quad ((c, s), ec.agentchain) \in before) \bullet (c, s)\}
\end{array}
$$

3.8.3 Indirect Engagement Relation

To distinguish those engagements involving an intermediate agent the indirect engagement relation *indengages* is introduced.

Definition 3.8.3. *An agent* indirectly engages *another if it engages it, but does not directly* engage *it.*

The relation is formalised below in the *Indengages* schema, which includes the definition of generic engagements and direct engagement. Two agents are related by *indengages* if and only if they are related by *engages* but not by *dengages*.

$$
\begin{array}{l}
\underline{\quad Indengages \quad\quad\quad\quad\quad\quad\quad\quad\quad\quad\quad\quad} \\[4pt]
Engages \\
Dengages \\
indengages : Agent \leftrightarrow ServerAgent \\[6pt]
\hline \\[-6pt]
indengages = engages \setminus dengages
\end{array}
$$

3.8.4 Generic Ownership Relation

If many agents directly engage the same entity, then no single agent has complete control over it. Any actions that an agent takes affecting the entity may destroy or hinder the engagements of the other engaging agents. This in turn, may have a deleterious effect on the engaging agents themselves. It is therefore important to understand *when* the behaviour of an engaged entity can be modified without any deleterious effect. This can certainly occur between an agent and an entity when there is no other agent using the entity for a *different* purpose. In this case the agent *owns* the entity.

For example, suppose Anne is running several applications on a workstation with each satisfying a different goal. If the machine is not being used by any others, then all the goals that can be ascribed to the workstation belong solely to Anne. In this way, Anne *owns* the workstation, and can decide whether, for example, it is currently appropriate to re-boot the machine. In scenarios where the workstation is being used by other agents to run applications remotely, no agent *owns* the workstation and more care is required by all users when taking action, since this may affect other agent relationships. For example, if the workstation is being used to run remote applications and Anne re-boots the machine, it may have a deleterious effect on Anne's relationship with the agents running remote applications.

Definition 3.8.4. *An agent, c, owns another agent, s, if, for every sequence of server-agents in an engagement chain in which s appears, c precedes it, or c is the autonomous client-agent that initiated the chain.*

The pair (c, s) is in the relation *owns*, if and only if, for every engagement chain, *ec*, in which *s* appears, *c* is the autonomous agent of *ec* or *c* appears before *s* in the chain.

__*Owns*__ _____

AgentSociety
owns : *Agent* $\leftrightarrow$ *ServerAgent*

$\forall c : Agent;\ s : ServerAgent \bullet (c, s) \in owns \Leftrightarrow$
$\qquad (\forall ec : engchains \mid s \in \text{ran } ec.agentchain \bullet$
$\qquad\qquad ec.autoagent = c \ \lor$
$\qquad\qquad ((c, s), ec.agentchain) \in before)$

3.8.5 Direct Ownership Relation

If an agent owns another agent and directly engages it then the first agent *directly owns* the second.

Definition 3.8.5. *An agent, c, directly owns another agent, s, if it owns it, and directly engages it.*

Formally, this relation is the intersection of the direct engagement relation, *downs*, and the generic ownership relation, *owns*.

```
┌─ Downs ──────────────────────────────────────────────
│  Dengages
│  Owns
│  downs : Agent ↔ ServerAgent
│ ─────────────────────────────────────────────────────
│  downs = owns ∩ dengages
└──────────────────────────────────────────────────────
```

3.8.6 Unique Ownership Relation

A further distinction of direct ownership can be made. Either no other agent directly owns the entity, or there is another agent that is also directly engaging that entity for the same purpose. The first case occurs normally but the second situation can occur if the entity is engaged by two agents each for the same purpose as generated by a single autonomous agent. This situation arises, for example, when two different software agents are both searching a database for the same entry. To distinguish these situations we define the relation, *uniquely owns*, which holds when an agent *directly* and *solely* owns another.

Definition 3.8.6. *An agent c* uniquely owns *another agent s, if it directly owns it, and no other agent is engaging it.*

Formally, the agent pair (c, s) is in this relation if c directly owns s, and there is no other distinct agent, a, that engages c.

```
┌─ Uowns ──────────────────────────────────────────────
│  Engages
│  Downs
│  uowns : Agent ↔ ServerAgent
│ ─────────────────────────────────────────────────────
│  ∀ c : Agent; s : ServerAgent • (c, s) ∈ uowns ⇔
│        (c, s) ∈ downs ∧ ¬ (∃ a : Agent | a ≠ c • (a, s) ∈ engages)
└──────────────────────────────────────────────────────
```

3.8.7 Specific Ownership Relation

There is also one further category of generic ownership, since an agent may own another with respect to either multiple distinct goals or a single goal. Since multiple goals may conflict, this is an important distinction. For example, if Anne owns a workstation to find the location of *two* books for two different users then it is likely that achieving one goal may affect the achievement of the other. An agent *specifically owns* a server-agent if the server-agent has only a single goal.

Definition 3.8.7. *An agent, c,* specifically owns *another agent, s, if it owns it, and c has only one goal.*

The formal definition states that the agent pair (c, s) is an element of *sown* if c owns s and the number of goals of S is equal to 1.

```
┌─ Sowns ──────────────────────────────────────────────
│ Owns
│ sowns : Agent ↔ ServerAgent
├──────────────────────────────────────────────────────
│ ∀c : Agent; s : ServerAgent •
│         (c, s) ∈ sowns ⇔ (c, s) ∈ owns ∧ #(s.goals) = 1
└──────────────────────────────────────────────────────
```

3.8.8 Generic Cooperation Relation

The last relation to be defined holds between two agents when one is cooperating with another. If Anne generates the goal to move a table and persuades Bill to help then he has autonomously adopted her goal. In this situation, Bill *cooperates* with Anne.

Definition 3.8.8. *An agent, A_2, cooperates with agent, A_1, if and only if both agents are autonomous, and there is some cooperation in which A_1 is the generating agent, and A_2 is in the set of cooperating agents.*

```
┌─ Cooperates ─────────────────────────────────────────
│ AgentSociety
│ cooperates : AutonomousAgent ↔ AutonomousAgent
├──────────────────────────────────────────────────────
│ cooperates =
│     ⋃{A₁, A₂ : AutonomousAgent |
│         (∃c : cooperations • A₁ = c.generatingagent ∧
│         A₂ ∈ c.cooperatingagents) •
│             {(A₁, A₂)}}
└──────────────────────────────────────────────────────
```

Notice that the relationship is not symmetric: if agent $aa1$ is cooperating with $aa2$, this does not entail that $aa2$ is cooperating with $aa1$. Formally, this can be stated as follows.

$$\neg \, (\forall \, system : Cooperates; \; aa1, aa2 : AutonomousAgent \; | $$
$$\{aa1, aa2\} \subseteq system.autonomousagents \wedge \; aa1 \neq aa2 \; \bullet$$
$$(aa1, aa2) \in system.cooperates \Rightarrow (aa2, aa1) \in system.cooperates)$$

The set of all these relationships are defined in the schema below. Figure 3.6 shows how schema inclusion is used to define the agent relationships taxonomy.

```
┌─ AgentRelationshipsTaxonomy ─────────────────────────
│ Sowns
│ Uowns
│ Indengages
│ Cooperates
└──────────────────────────────────────────────────────
```

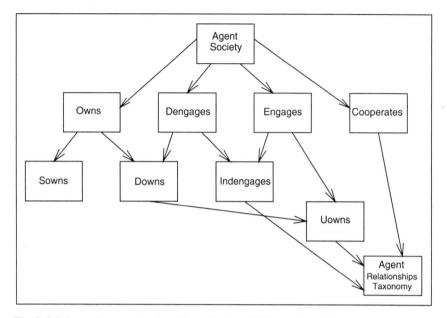

Fig. 3.6. Schema Structure for Specifying the Agent Relationships Taxonomy

3.9 Summary

Agents are limited entities and, as such, may need the help of *other agents* to achieve
their goals. Any system in which agents help others to achieve goals is classified as
a multi-agent system.

The SMART agent framework relies on the existence of autonomous agents that
can generate their goals from their *motivations*, and the adoption of goals by, and in
order to create, other agents so that a multi-agent system must contain at least one
autonomous agent. Components in SMART may be either neutral-objects, server-
agents or autonomous agents, and these three specific and distinct categories give
rise to three distinct cases of goal adoption. Neutral-objects can adopt goals without
regard to any existing agent relationships. Since autonomous agents make their own
decisions about the adoption of goals they must be persuaded to do so. Goal adoption by existing server-agents is the most complex situation, since it may affect the
pursuit or maintenance of existing goals.

The generation and subsequent transfer of goals between entities through interaction produces *relationships* between agents, and the distinction between agency
and autonomy enables us to distinguish between *voluntary* and *compulsory* relationships. The distinction arises naturally and elegantly from the SMART framework.
Server-agents do not have motivations and therefore rely on the existence of others
to become agents and are naturally disposed to adopt the goals of others. These compulsory relationships are called *engagements*. Autonomous agents, however, only

enter into relationships if it is to their advantage, and must therefore volunteer their help. These voluntary relationships are called *cooperations*.

The distinction between engagement and cooperation is important since much existing work has defined cooperation only in terms of helpful agents that are predisposed to adopt the goals of others (e.g. [16, 118]). This assumes that agents are already designed with common or non-conflicting goals that facilitate the possibility of helping each other satisfy additional goals. The collection of engagements, engagement chains and cooperations are called the agent relationships, which together with the set of system entities describe the agent society. This definition can subsequently be used as the platform from which to analyse the possible relationships or dependencies between two agents.

The inter-agent relationships identified in the chapter are not imposed on multi-agent systems, but arise naturally from agents interacting. They therefore underlie all multi-agent systems. Furthermore, the precise interdependence of agents in terms of the goals agents are achieving for others can then be analysed once the agent society is defined.

Not only are the agent relationships important in allowing users to analyse multi-agent systems, they are a crucial feature that need to be considered by computational entities designed to act within them. Any agent not recognising these relationships may (inadvertently) destroy or hinder these relationships in its interactions with others. Engaging agents without regard to their current social context may bring about short-term gains, but may be detrimental to the agent's achievement of its goals in the longer term. After a while, other autonomous agents may neither cooperate with this agent nor allow other non-autonomous entities to be engaged by it.

Agents not only need access to the information that identifies existing relationships so as not to destroy them, they may also need, or wish, to take advantage of the current set of agent relationships. If a software agent is engaged by an autonomous agent to find users that are engaging a particular application on a network, and another autonomous agent also wishes to establish this information, then it may either engage the software agent directly by requesting the results, or persuade the original autonomous agent to cooperate and pass on relevant information.

The analysis of the relationships between *agents* provides computational entities with a means of determining how they should approach interactions with those agents. For example, if I own an entity, I can do as I please, and other agents would be ill-advised to attempt to use this entity for another purpose. If I only engage it, then I may be more constrained in my interaction with it and may anticipate other agents engaging it.

Whenever an agent uses objects or resources, exploits others, communicates or interacts in any way, the relationships described here are present and have to be recognised. This chapter has shown how the notions of agency and autonomy can be used to provide an analysis of universal relationships that facilitates a better understanding of multi-agent systems, so that agent interaction can be effective and efficient.

4. An Operational Analysis of Agent Relationships

4.1 Introduction

As elaborated in the previous chapter, fundamental to the operation of multi-agent systems is the concept of cooperation and engagement between individual agents. If single-agent systems can both cooperate and engage others, they can exploit the capabilities and functionality of others to achieve their own individual goals. Once this is achieved, then such systems can potentially move beyond the advantages of robustness in traditional distributed systems in the face of individual component failure since components can be replaced and cooperation configurations realigned. In principle then, the multi-agent system paradigm allows the specific expertise and competence of different agents to complement each other so that in addition to general resilience, the overall system exhibits significantly greater functionality than individual components.

Since the set of agent relationships is critical to defining and understanding multi-agent systems, it is important to be able to model and analyse them in detail in the context of a well-founded framework. Moreover, the ways in which cooperative relationships come about are also important for a complete understanding of the nature of cooperation. This is especially true if such an analysis is to be relevant to real systems for which the invocation and destruction of such relationships is critical.

Previous chapters have provided an analysis of key agent relationships that can be found in multi-agent systems. This chapter provides an *operational* analysis of how these relationships are created and destroyed, and how this affects the agent society.

The four principal operations that arise from the investigation of goal adoption in Section 3.4 and which are considered in this chapter are as follows.

- A server-agent adopting the goals of an agent gives rise to a new engagement. The formal operational description is called *SystemEngage*.
- A server-agent being released from some or all of its agency obligations by an engaging agent destroys a direct engagement, called *SystemDisengage*.
- An autonomous agent adopting the goal of another to generate a new cooperation or extend an existing one. This is called *SystemCooperate*.
- An autonomous agent destroying the goals of an existing cooperation either destroys a cooperation or reduces it. This operation schema is correspondingly labelled *SystemLeaveCooperation*.

Not only is it important to understand multi-agent systems by analysing the agent relationships they contain, it is also important to understand the ways in which these relationships arise. This is particularly true if such an analysis is to be relevant to, and useful for, the construction of real systems for which the invocation and destruction of such relationships is critical. This chapter provides an operational analysis of the invocation and destruction of engagement and cooperation. After a description of some initial concepts, the subsequent four sections describe each of the four operations summarised above. In particular, the chapter includes a worked example that shows how multi-agent systems can be modelled in SMART.

Note, however, that no fundamentally new concepts are added in this chapter since the focus is on providing an operational specification of agent relationships developed previously.

4.2 Initial Concepts

To provide an operational account of these relationships, we must specify how they are affected when new cooperations and engagements are invoked and destroyed. Before considering the operations in detail some general functions are specified to create schema types from individual components. Thus, *MakeEng*, *MakeEngChain* and *MakeCoop* below simply construct the corresponding relationship schema types. All three functions are injective since in general the same schema element cannot be created from two different sets of component elements. They are also surjective since every element of the schema type can be formed by choosing the appropriate components. In addition, the functions, *MakeEng* and *MakeCoop*, are partial; *MakeEng* is not defined if the two agents involved in the engagement are the same, and *MakeCoop* is not defined if the single autonomous agent initiating the cooperation is in the set of other cooperating autonomous agents.

The functions make use of the unique identifier expression [121]. For example, consider the mu-expression $\mu\, a : A \mid p$. In this case, the function μ assigns to the variable a the unique value of the type A that satisfies the predicate p. (For example, the expression $\mu\, n : \mathbb{N} \mid (n * n) \bmod 2 = 0 \wedge (n * n) \leq 10$ binds the variable n to the value 2.)

$MakeEng : (Goal \times Agent \times ServerAgent) \rightarrowtail DirectEngagement$
$MakeChain : (Goal \times AutonomousAgent \times \text{iseq}_1\ ServerAgent)$
$$\rightarrowtail EngagementChain$$
$MakeCoop : (Goal \times AutonomousAgent \times \mathbb{P}_1\ AutonomousAgent)$
$$\rightarrowtail Cooperation$$

$\forall g : Goal;\ a : Agent;\ aa : AutonomousAgent;\ s : ServerAgent;$
$\quad ch :\text{iseq}_1\ ServerAgent;\ aas : \mathbb{P}_1\ AutonomousAgent\ |$
$\quad a \neq s \wedge aa \notin aas \bullet$
$\quad MakeEng(g, a, s) = (\mu d : DirectEngagement\ |$
$\qquad\qquad\qquad\qquad\qquad d.goal = g \wedge d.client = a \wedge$
$\qquad\qquad\qquad\qquad\qquad d.server = s) \wedge$
$\quad MakeChain(g, a, ch) = (\mu ec : EngagementChain\ |$
$\qquad\qquad\qquad\qquad\qquad\quad ec.goal = g \wedge ec.autoagent = a \wedge$
$\qquad\qquad\qquad\qquad\qquad\quad ec.agentchain = ch) \wedge$
$\quad MakeCoop(g, aa, aas) = (\mu c : Cooperation\ |$
$\qquad\qquad\qquad\qquad\qquad\quad c.goal = g \wedge c.generatingagent = aa \wedge$
$\qquad\qquad\qquad\qquad\qquad\quad c.cooperatingagents = aas)$

Defined next is the generic function, *cut*, which takes an injective sequence (where no element appears more than once) and an element, and removes all the elements of the sequence that appear after this element. If the element does not exist in the sequence, the sequence is left unaltered.

$=[X]=$

$cut : (\text{iseq}\ X \times X) \rightarrowtail \text{iseq}\ X$

$\forall x : X;\ s, t :\text{iseq}\ X \bullet$
$\quad x \notin \text{ran}\ s \Rightarrow (cut(s, x) = s) \wedge$
$\quad x \in \text{ran}\ s \Rightarrow (cut(s, x) = t \Leftrightarrow$
$\qquad last\ t = x \wedge (\exists u : \text{seq}\ X \bullet s = t ^\frown u))$

Lastly, two further functions, *extendchain* and *cutchain*, are defined. The first function takes an engagement chain and an object, and extends the engagement chain to include the object. The second function cuts an engagement chain after the occurrence of an object.

$extendchain : EngagementChain \times Object \rightarrow EngagementChain$
$cutchain : EngagementChain \times Agent \nrightarrow EngagementChain$

$\forall c : EngagementChain;\ e : Object \bullet$
$\quad extendchain(c, e) = (\mu\, new : EngagementChain\ |$
$\qquad new.goal = c.goal \wedge new.autoagent = c.autoagent \wedge$
$\qquad new.agentchain = c.agentchain^\frown$
$\qquad\qquad \langle EntityAdoptGoals(e, \{c.goal\}) \rangle) \wedge$
$\quad cutchain(c, e) = (\mu\, new : EngagementChain\ |$
$\qquad new.goal = c.goal \wedge new.autoagent = c.autoagent \wedge$
$\qquad new.agentchain = cut(c.agentchain, e)))$

Finally, some generic definitions are introduced that enable the assertion that an element is *optional*. The following definitions provide for a new type, *optional T*, for any existing type, *T*, along with the predicates *defined* and *undefined*, which test whether an element of *optional T* is defined or not. The function, *the*, extracts the element from a defined member of *optional T*.

$$optional\, [X] == \{xs : \mathbb{P}\, X \mid \#\, xs \leq 1\}$$

$=[X]$ ===============

$defined\ \_,\ undefined\ \_ : \mathbb{P}(\ optional\, [X])$
$the: optional\, [X] \nrightarrow X$

$\forall xs : optional\, [X] \bullet$
$\quad defined\ xs \Leftrightarrow \#\, xs\ =\ 1 \wedge$
$\quad undefined\ xs \Leftrightarrow \#\, xs\ =\ 0$
$\forall xs : optional\, [X] \mid defined\ xs \bullet$
$\quad the\ xs = (\mu\, x : X \mid x \in xs)$

4.3 Making Engagements

When a new direct engagement is formed between an agent and a server-agent, the associated engagement chain may be altered in several ways. The different possibilities depend on whether the engaging agent is at the tail, the head, or in the middle of the chain. Consider an engagement chain where *A* is the autonomous agent at the head of the chain who is directly engaging the server-agent, *S1*, which is directly engaging server-agent, *S2*, which is, in turn, directly engaging *S3* as shown in Figure 4.1(a).

– If the autonomous agent, *A*, directly engages *O*, a new engagement chain is created solely comprising *A* and *O*, as in Figure 4.1(b).
– If the last agent in the chain, *S3*, engages an object, *O*, the chain is extended to include the engagement between *S3* and *O*, as in Figure 4.1(c).

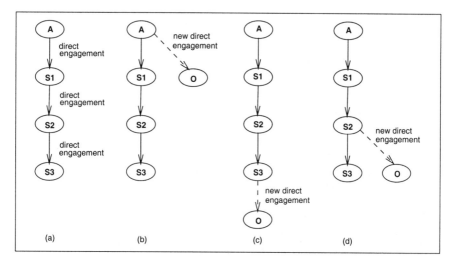

Fig. 4.1. Alternative New Engagements

– If any *server*-agent, other than that at the tail of the engagement chain, engages
O, then a new engagement chain is formed comprising the original chain up to
the server-agent but extended to include O. Thus if $S2$ engages O, the existing
chain is unchanged, but a new chain is formed from the engagements up to and
including $S2$ in the original chain, with the addition of the new engagement of O
by $S2$, as in Figure 4.1(d).

The aspects of forming a new engagement common to all three scenarios are
described in the next schema. Here, the engaging agent, *agent?*, the engaged object,
e?, the goal of the engagement, *goal?*, and an optional engagement chain, *chain?*,
are inputs to the operation, and the set of relationships in the multi-agent system
changes. The predicate part states that the object is a system object (but not an
autonomous agent), and the agent is a known agent with the goal, *goal?*. If no engagement chain already exists, so that *chain?* is not defined, then *agent?* must be
autonomous as in Figure 4.1(b). If *chain?* is defined, *agent?* must be a server-agent,
the goal of *chain?* must be *goal?*, and *agent?* must be part of *chain?*. There is no
change to the set of cooperations, but the set of direct engagements is updated to
include the new engagement between the agent and the object.

GeneralEngage ─────────────────────────────────
agent? : *Agent*
e? : *Object*
goal? : *Goal*
chain? : *optional* [*EngagementChain*]
Δ*AgentSociety*

---
e? $\in$ *objects* \ *autonomousagents*
agent? $\in$ *agents*
goal? $\in$ *agent?.goals*
undefined chain? $\Leftrightarrow$ *agent?* $\in$ *autonomousagents*
defined chain? $\Leftrightarrow$ (*agent?* $\in$ *serveragents* $\wedge$
(*the chain?*).*goal* = *goal?* $\wedge$
agent? $\in$ ran(*the chain?*).*agentchain*)
cooperations' = *cooperations*
directengagements' = *directengagements* $\cup$
    {*MakeEng*(*goal?*, *agent?*, (*EntityAdoptGoals* (*e?*, {*goal?*})))}

The distinct aspects of the ways in which the set of engagement chains are affected in each scenario are detailed below.

First, the engaging agent is autonomous, and a new engagement chain is formed from *goal?*, *agent?*, and the sequence consisting solely of the newly instantiated agent.

NewChain ─────────────────────────────────
GeneralEngage

---
undefined chain? $\Rightarrow$
  engchains' = *engchains* $\cup$
    {*MakeChain*(*goal?*, *agent?*, $\langle$*EntityAdoptGoals* (*e?*, {*goal?*})$\rangle$)}

Second, the engaging agent is the server-agent at the end of the chain so that the chain is extended to include this new direct engagement.

ExtendChain ─────────────────────────────────
GeneralEngage

(*defined chain?* $\wedge$
(*e?* = *last* (*the chain?*).*agentchain*)) $\Rightarrow$
    engchains' =
        (*engchains* \ *chain?*) $\cup$ {*extendchain*((*the chain?*), *e?*)}

Third, if *agent?* is in the chain of server-agents but not at its head then the original chain is unchanged, and a new chain is formed from the direct engagements in the original chain up to the agent, plus the new direct engagement between *agent?* and the newly instantiated object.

```
┌─ AddChain ──────────────────────────────────────────────────
│ GeneralEngage
├─────────────────────────────────────────────────────────────
│ defined chain? ∧ e? ≠ last ( the chain?).agentchain ∧
│     engchains' = engchains ∪
│         {extendchain((cutchain(( the chain?), agent?)), e?)}
└─────────────────────────────────────────────────────────────
```

The operation of making an engagement can then be defined using schema disjunction. Thus, when the *Engage* operation is applied, either of the three operation schemas *NewChain*, *ExtendChain* or *AddChain* occur.

$$Engage == ExtendChain \lor NewChain \lor AddChain$$

Considering the analysis of goal adoption of the previous chapter, either a new direct engagement creates a server-agent from a neutral-object, or a new server-agent from an existing server-agent. The schemas defining these cases of goal adoption can be directly reused in order to specify the overall change to the agent society. The two cases are then specified in the following schemas.

```
┌─ SystemEngageObject ────────────────────────────────────────
│ Engage
│ NeutralObjectAdoptGoals
├─────────────────────────────────────────────────────────────
│ gs? = {goal?}
└─────────────────────────────────────────────────────────────
```

```
┌─ SystemEngageAgent ─────────────────────────────────────────
│ Engage
│ ServerAgentAdoptGoals
├─────────────────────────────────────────────────────────────
│ gs? = {goal?}
└─────────────────────────────────────────────────────────────
```

The operation specifying the change to both the agent components and relationships and is defined by the disjunction of these two schemas.

$$SystemEngage == SystemEngageObject \lor SystemEngageAgent$$

The structure of the specification used to describe this operation is illustrated in Figure 4.2, which shows that the operation alters the agent society. The schema, *GeneralEngage*, defines those aspects of a new engagement that are common to all three scenarios above. The three schemas, *ExtendChain*, *NewChain* and *CutAndAddChain*, are then all refinements of *GeneralEngage*, each detailing the particular aspects of the three different scenarios, and the *Engage* schema is defined by their logical disjunction. To specify the change of state of multi-agent system entities, as well as the change to the agent relationships, the schemas that define individual goal adoption by entities must be included. There are two possibilities as discussed previously: An existing server-agent is instantiated as a new server-agent or a neutral-object is instantiated as a server-agent.

The change to the entire system described by the first case is defined by *SystemEngageAgent* and includes the *Engage* and *ServerAgentAdoptGoals* schemas. The *SystemEngageObject* schema defines the second case and includes *Engage* and *NeutralObjectAdoptGoals*. The operation is finally specified by *SystemEngage*, which is simply defined as the logical disjunction of *SystemEngageAgent* and *SystemEngageObject*.

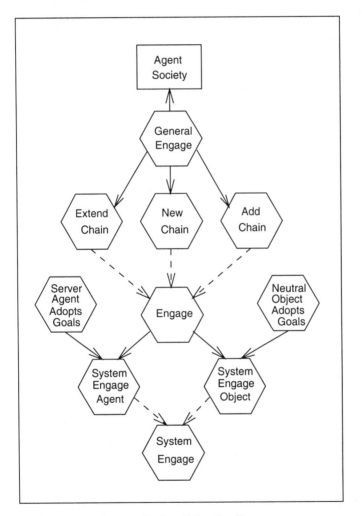

Fig. 4.2. Schema Structure for Specifying New Engagements

4.4 Breaking Engagements

If an autonomous agent or a server-agent in an engagement chain *disengages* a
server-agent it is directly engaging, either through destroying the goal itself or because the agent is no longer required to achieve it, all subsequent engagements in
the chain are destroyed. This is because the subsequent agents no longer satisfy a
goal that can be attributed to an autonomous agent. Figure 4.3 shows how broken
direct engagements propagate down through an engagement chain in this way. Initially, the engagement chain consists of the autonomous agent, *A*, and a chain of
agents *S*1, *S*2 and *S*3. If *A* disengages *S*1, then *S*1 necessarily disengages *S*2 and *S*2
disengages *S*3.

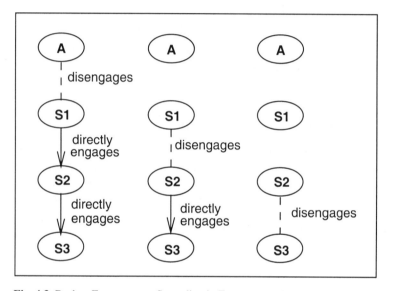

Fig. 4.3. Broken Engagements Spreading in Engagement Chains

The situation above is addressed by the *Disengage* schema, which formally defines the breaking of a direct engagement between engaging and engaged agents,
engaging? and *engaged*?, respectively, and specifies the propagation of broken direct engagements for the goal, *goal*?, down through the associated engagement
chain, *chain*?. All of these components are inputs. The predicates ensure that there
is a direct engagement between *engaging*? and *engaged*? with respect to *goal*?, that
chain? is an engagement chain, and that the goal of the chain is equal to the input *goal*?. The set of cooperations remains unchanged, but the engagement chain,
chain?, is removed from the system and replaced with the chain resulting from cut-
ting the original chain at the engaging agent. Finally, the direct engagements are
updated accordingly.

─── *Disengage* ──

engaging? : *Agent*
engaged? : *ServerAgent*
goal? : *Goal*
chain? : *EngagementChain*
$\Delta AgentSociety$

───

$MakeEng(goal?, engaging?, engaged?) \in directengagements$
$chain? \in engchains$
$chain?.goal = goal?$
$cooperations' = cooperations$
$engchains' = engchains \setminus \{chain?\} \cup \{cutchain(chain?, engaging?)\}$
$directengagements' = (directengagements \setminus$
$\quad \{d : DirectEngagement \mid$
$\quad\quad (\langle d.client, d.server \rangle \text{ in } chain?.agentchain) \wedge$
$\quad\quad\quad\quad\quad\quad\quad\quad d.goal = chain?.goal \bullet d\}) \cup$
$\quad \{d : DirectEngagement \mid$
$\quad\quad (\langle d.client, d.server \rangle \text{ in }$
$\quad\quad\quad\quad (cutchain(chain?, engaging?)).agentchain \wedge$
$\quad\quad\quad\quad\quad\quad d.goal = chain?.goal) \bullet d\}$

───

The act of disengaging an entity either creates a neutral-object from a server-agent, or it creates a new server-agent from an existing server-agent. Analogous to *SystemEngage*, the *RevertToNeutralObject* and *ServerAgentReleaseGoals* schemas can be directly reused, as defined in Section 3.4, to formalise these two scenarios.

─── *SystemDisengageToObject* ──────────────────────────

Disengage
RevertToNeutralObject

───

$\{goal?\} = engaged?.goals$

───

─── *SystemDisengageToAgent* ───────────────────────────

Disengage
ServerAgentReleaseGoals

───

$\{goal?\} \subset engaged?.goals$

───

The *SystemDisengage* schema, which defines the entire system change, is the logical disjunction of *SystemDisengageToObject* and *SystemDisengageToAgent*.

$$SystemDisengage == SystemDisengageToObject \vee SystemDisengageToAgent$$

The structure of the specification used to describe this operation is illustrated in Figure 4.4. This shows that the schemas *Disengage* and *RevertToNeutralObject* are used to define the schema, *SystemDisengageToObject*, and the schemas *Disengage* and *ServerAgentReleaseGoals* to define *SystemDisengageToAgent*. The logical disjunction of these schemas is called *SystemDisengage* and defines the overall state change when an agent disengages another.

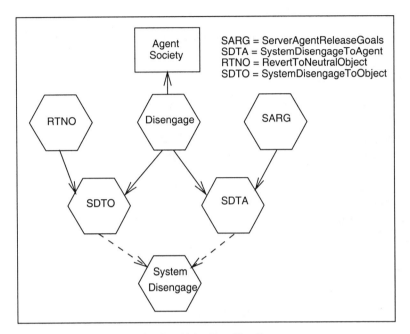

Fig. 4.4. Schema Structure for Specifying Breaking Engagements

4.5 Joining Cooperations

A cooperation occurs when an autonomous agent generates a goal by recognising that goal in another autonomous agent. There are two scenarios when one autonomous agent, *B*, adopts the goal, *g*, of another, *A*. If no cooperation exists between any other autonomous agents and *A* with respect to *g*, then a new cooperation structure is created. Alternatively, if a cooperation already exists between another agent and *A* with respect to *g*, then *B* joins this cooperation.

Formally, the *GeneralCooperate* schema describes the general system change when a cooperating agent, *coopagent?*, adopts the goal, *goal?*, of the generating agent, *genagent?*. The predicate part of the schema states that *genagent?* has *goal?*, that *coopagent?* does not, and that both agents are autonomous. The sets of direct engagements and engagement chains remain unchanged.

GeneralCooperate _____

goal? : Goal
genagent?, coopagent? : AutonomousAgent
ΔAgentSociety

---
goal? ∈ genagent?.goals
goal? ∉ coopagent?.goals
{genagent?, coopagent?} ⊆ autonomousagents
directengagements' = directengagements
engchains' = engchains

The two scenarios are illustrated in Figure 4.5. Either *B* adopts the goal of *A* and a new cooperation is created, or *B* adopts the goal of *A* that others (in this case *B*1 and *C*1) have also adopted, in which case *B* joins an existing cooperation. Formally, the two scenarios are defined by the schemas, *NewCooperation* and *JoinCooperation*, where *coopagent?* adopts the goal, *goal?* of the autonomous agent *genagent?*. In the first case, a new cooperation is formed since there is no existing cooperation with the agent, *genagent?*, as the generating agent and *goal?* as the goal. In this case a new cooperation is formed between *coopagent?*, which now has the goal, *goal?*, and *genagent?*.

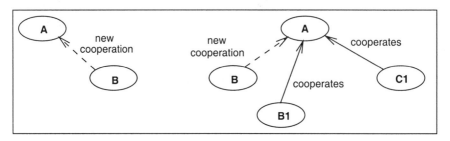

Fig. 4.5. New Cooperations

NewCooperation _____
GeneralCooperate

¬ (∃c : cooperations • c.goal = goal? ∧
              c.generatingagent = genagent?) ∧
cooperations' =
      cooperations ∪ {MakeCoop(goal?, genagent?, {coopagent?})}

However, if such a cooperation does exist, then *coopagent?* adopts *goal?*, and joins.

```
 ┌─ JoinCooperation ─────────────────────────────────────
 │ GeneralCooperate
 ├──────────────────────────────────────────────────────
 │ ∃ c : cooperations •
 │      c.goal = goal? ∧ c.generatingagent = genagent? ∧
 │          cooperations' = cooperations \ {c} ∪
 │              {MakeCoop(goal?, genagent?, c.cooperatingagents ∪
 │                  {EntityAdoptGoals(coopagent?, {goal?})})}
 └──────────────────────────────────────────────────────
```

The *Cooperate* schema is defined using schema disjunction.

Cooperate == *NewCooperation* ∨ *JoinCooperation*

The change to the agent society that occurs when autonomous agents adopt the goals of others is described below and includes the schemas, *Cooperate* and *AutonomousAgentAdoptGoals*. The goals of the goal adoption, *gs?*, must be equal to the set containing the one goal of the new cooperation, *goal?*.

```
 ┌─ SystemCooperate ─────────────────────────────────────
 │ AutonomousAgentAdoptGoals
 │ Cooperate
 ├──────────────────────────────────────────────────────
 │ gs? = {goal?}
 └──────────────────────────────────────────────────────
```

The specification structure of this the operation is in Figure 4.6, which should by now be self-evident to the reader because of previous similar diagrams.

4.6 Leaving Cooperations

There are three cases for autonomous agents destroying the goal of a cooperation in which they are involved, illustrated in Figure 4.7. First, the generating agent, *A*, destroys the goal of a cooperation with the result that the cooperation is itself destroyed. This does not imply that *B2* and *B1* have destroyed the goal since, for example, they may not recognise that *A* no longer has the goal. Second, the cooperation is also destroyed when the only cooperating agent destroys the cooperation goal. Finally, when there are many cooperating agents, one of which destroys the cooperation goal, the cooperation is not destroyed but modified so that only one agent *leaves* the cooperation.

In all three cases the set of cooperations changes but the set of engagements is unaltered which is formalised in the *CommonLeaveCooperation* schema. A goal, *goal?*, a cooperation, *coop?*, and, optionally, two autonomous agents, *genagent?*, and *coopagent?* are inputs. The preconditions state that only one of *genagent?* or *coopagent?* is input, but not both. In addition, the schema checks that *genagent?* is the generating agent and that *Coopagent* is a cooperating agent of *coop?*. The sets of direct engagements and engagement chains are unaffected.

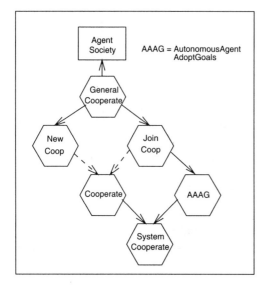

Fig. 4.6. Schema Structure for Specifying New Cooperations

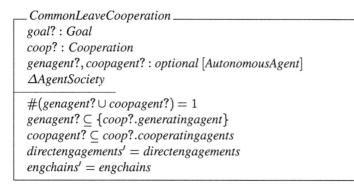

Fig. 4.7. Leaving Cooperations

Each of the three different scenarios can now be specified formally as refinements to this general operation schema. First, the generating agent of the cooperation destroys the goal of the cooperation. The cooperation, *coop?*, is destroyed and removed from *cooperations*.

___ *GeneratingAgentDestroysCooperation* _____
CommonLeaveCooperation

defined genagent? $\Rightarrow$ *cooperations'* = *cooperations* \ {*coop?*}

Second, the only cooperating agent destroys the goal of the cooperation. In this case, the cooperation is similarly destroyed and removed from *cooperations*.

___ *CooperatingAgentDestroysCooperation* _____
CommonLeaveCooperation

(*defined coopagent?* $\wedge$
  coopagent? = *coop?*.*cooperatingagents*) $\Rightarrow$
    cooperations' = *cooperations* \ {*coop?*}

Finally, a cooperating agent that is not the only cooperating agent destroys the goal of the cooperation. It is removed from the cooperation and the resulting cooperation is added to *cooperations*.

___ *CooperatingAgentLeavesCooperation* _____
CommonLeaveCooperation

(*defined coopagent?* $\wedge$
  coopagent? $\subset$ *coop?*.*cooperatingagents*) $\Rightarrow$
    cooperations' = (*cooperations* \ {*coop?*}) $\cup$
        {*MakeCoop*(*goal?*, *coop?*.*generatingagent*,
            (*coop?*.*cooperatingagents* \ *coopagent?*))}

Schema disjunction is then used to define *LeaveCooperation*.

LeaveCooperation ==
        GeneratingAgentDestroysCooperation $\vee$
        CooperatingAgentDestroysCooperation $\vee$
        CooperatingAgentLeavesCooperation

The overall change to the system state is then specified below by the schema, *SystemLeaveCooperation*. The specification structure used to define this operation is illustrated in Figure 4.8.

___ *SystemLeaveCooperation* _____
LeaveCooperation
AutonomousAgentDestroysGoals

{*goal?*} = *gs?*

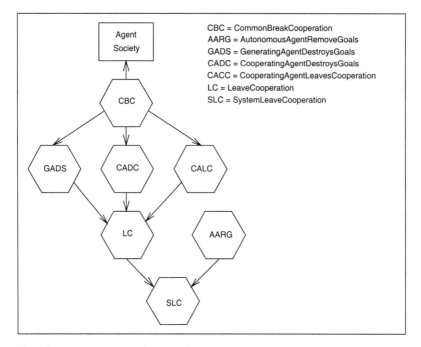

Fig. 4.8. Schema Structure for Specifying Leaving Cooperations

4.7 An Illustrative Example

This chapter has provided operational details of how the adoption and destruction of goals, engagements and cooperations affects the configuration of agent relationships as well as the entities themselves. In order to explicate the SMART model of agent relationships and how they are altered through the interaction of agents, a worked example follows.

Suppose a library member, Charlie (C), cannot find a copy of a particular book in his office and visits the library to try to locate a copy. The library contains books ($b1,b2,\ldots$) and workstations ($W1,W2,\ldots$) that can be used to find information about the books. If one of the librarians, Anne (A), is currently present in the library then the system can be represented in the model as follows.

$autonomousagents = \{C, A, \ldots\}$
$neutralobjects = \{W1, W2, \ldots, b1, b2, \ldots\}$

Now, suppose that Charlie has generated the goal to locate $b1$ and decides to try to gain Anne's assistance. Since Anne is *autonomous*, Charlie cannot *engage* her, but instead must persuade Anne to *cooperate* with him to achieve his goal. Let us suppose that Anne recognises Charlie's goal and generates it for herself. The operation defined by *SystemCooperate* then changes the current state of the library system, generating a new cooperation, *coop*, as follows.

$coop.goal = find\_b1$
$coop.generatingagent = C$
$coop.cooperatingagents = \{A\}$

Notice that since there are now two autonomous agents with a social relationship between them, according to the definition of Section 3.2 the system is now a *multi-agent system*.

In attempting to locate $b1$ Anne uses the workstation, $W1$, to invoke a computer program, $P1$, which, in turn, accesses the library database D, and performs the relevant query. The goal of locating the book can then be ascribed to Anne, the workstation, the program and the database. Anne directly engages the workstation, the workstation directly engaging the program, and the program directly engaging the database. In SMART model, three direct engagements, $deng1$, $deng2$, $deng3$ and one engagement chain, $engch1$, are created, through repeated application of the *SystemEngage* operation with the following values.

$deng1.goal = find\_b1$	$deng2.goal = find\_b1$	$deng3.goal = find\_b1$
$deng1.server = A$	$deng2.server = W1$	$deng3.server = P1$
$deng1.client = W1$	$deng2.client = P1$	$deng3.client = D$

$engch1.goal = find\_b1$
$engch1.autoagent = A$
$engch1.agentchain = \langle W1, P1, D \rangle$

This engagement chain is constructed through the engagement of agents by other agents in order to satisfy the goal of locating the book, and is shown in Figure 4.9. Note that in order to avoid complicating the diagrams in this section, not all of the relations between the entities are shown, though they can be inferred. For example, in Figure 4.9 Anne engages $W1$, $P1$ and D, $W1$ engages $P1$ and D, Anne indirectly engages $P1$ and so on.

Since the workstation can only ever be used by a single-agent (for the moment the assumption is that no remote logins are possible), Anne currently *owns* the workstation. In addition, Anne is *directly engaging* the workstation since there are no intermediate agents between Anne and the workstation, and therefore *directly owns* the workstation. Moreover, since no other agent is engaging the workstation with the same goal Anne *uniquely owns* the workstation. Lastly, if the workstation is only being used to find the location of the one book, $b1$, then Anne *specifically owns* the workstation since she has *only one goal*.

If only the workstation, $W1$, is able to run the program then a similar argument can be made about the relationship between $W1$ and $P1$, so that the workstation uniquely and specifically owns the program. In addition, Anne *specifically owns P1* since it is not necessary that she *directly* owns it for this relationship to exist. If the database is currently being searched by other programs, the program does not own the data base, since the database is being used by other agents for different purposes.

The agent relationships in the library multi-agent system therefore include the following.

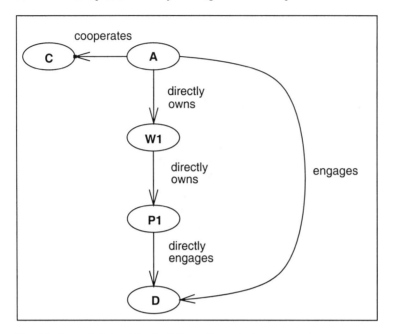

Fig. 4.9. Agent Relationships for Library Scenario I

$\{(C, A)\} \subseteq cooperates$
$\{(A, W1), (W1, P1), (P1, D)\} \subseteq dengages$
$\{(A, P1), (A, D), (W1, D)\} \subseteq indengages$
$\{(A, W1), (W1, P1), (P1, D), (A, P1), (A, D), (W1, D)\} \subseteq engages$
$\{(A, W1), (W1, P1), (A, P1)\} \subseteq owns$
$\{(A, W1), (W1, P1)\} \subseteq downs$
$\{(A, W1), (W1, P1), (A, P1)\} \subseteq sowns$
$\{(A, W1), (W1, P1)\} \subseteq uowns$

Suppose then that Charlie leaves Anne searching for the book, but inadvertently discovers $b1$ for himself. His goal is now satisfied and he destroys it since there is no motivational advantage in pursuing a satisfied goal. However, there still exists an autonomous agent who has generated this goal (albeit through recognising it first in another) and as such, the agent relationships are illustrated in Figure 4.10.

Charlie might inform Anne of the discovery of the book, since if she invests unnecessary effort in trying to achieve a goal that is already satisfied, it may affect any future cooperation between Anne and Charlie. In general, if the generating agent of a cooperation destroys the goal of that cooperation, whether it becomes satisfied or not, and does not inform other cooperating agents, the possibility of future cooperation may be deleteriously affected. If Charlie does inform Anne then she will, in general, destroy the goal of locating the book, kill the program, and log off from the workstation. In this case, the workstation and program, assuming that they do not figure in some other goal engagement graph, revert to natural objects and the

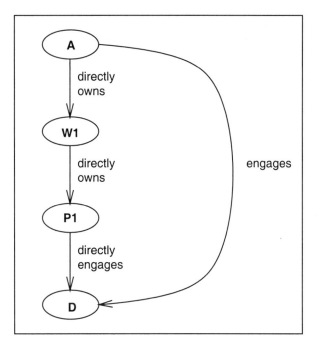

Fig. 4.10. Agent Relationships for Library Scenario II

engagement chain is destroyed. The database, if it is still being searched by other programs, remains an agent but with reduced agency obligations.

If, on the other hand, Anne, after destroying the goal to find the book, inadvertently leaves herself logged on to the workstation with the program still searching through the database, it might appear that the goal of locating the book can still be attributed to the workstation, program and database. However, in the SMART model, the goal of finding the book no longer exists since no autonomous agent has this goal. Certainly, the behaviour of the workstation and program might best be understood as server-agents rather than as neutral-objects, and many agents in the library might mistakenly infer that the workstation and program are being engaged.

Suppose again that Charlie does not find the book so that the situation is still as described in Figure 4.9. Also, suppose that Charlie's friend, Emily (*E*), generates the goal to locate another book, *b*2. Since the workstation, *W*1, is *owned* by Anne, and cannot be used by multiple agents, Emily cannot share it. In this situation Emily may give the current goal of Charlie priority over her own, and either wait or find an alternative workstation to run another program. Note that this last possibility is not constrained by the database being engaged by Anne, since it is not owned by Anne.

Another option is for Emily to take the workstation forcibly. However, this may drastically affect future cooperations with Anne, Charlie and other autonomous agents in general. Emily could also attempt to persuade Anne to release the workstation. If Anne cannot be persuaded, she may ask another librarian, Bill (*B*), to take part in separate cooperation negotiations to persuade Anne to release the worksta-tion. Emily may choose this option if she considers that Bill has a better chance than she does of persuading Anne to adopt her goal.

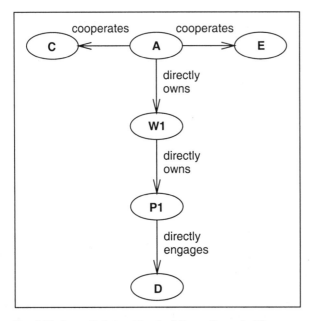

Fig. 4.11. Agent Relationships for Library Scenario III

One other option available to Emily is to persuade Anne to cooperate with her so that Anne now has *two* goals of finding *two* different books. In this, there are six di-rect engagements, *deng*1, *deng*2, *deng*3, *deng*4, *deng*5 and *deng*6, two engagement chains, *engch*1 and *engch*2, and, since Anne is cooperating with both Charlie and Emily, two cooperations *coop*1 and *coop*2, as follows.

$deng1.goal = find\_b1$	$deng2.goal = find\_b1$	$deng3.goal = find\_b1$
$deng1.server = A$	$deng2.server = W1$	$deng3.server = P1$
$deng1.client = W1$	$deng2.client = D$	$deng3.client = D$
$deng4.goal = find\_b2$	$deng5.goal = find\_b2$	$deng6.goal = find\_b2$
$deng4.server = A$	$deng5.server = W1$	$deng6.server = P1$
$deng4.client = W1$	$deng5.client = D$	$deng6.client = D$

$$engch1.goal = find\_b1 \qquad engch2.goal = find\_b2$$
$$engch1.autoagent = A \qquad engch2.autoagent = A$$
$$engch1.agentchain = \langle W1, P1, D \rangle \qquad engch1.agentchain = \langle W1, P1, D \rangle$$

$coop1.goal = find\_b1$ $coop2.goal = find\_b2$
$coop1.generatingagent = C$ $coop2.generatingagent = E$
$coop1.cooperatingagents = \{A\}$ $coop2.cooperatingagents = \{A\}$

The state of this model in terms of the *AgentSociety* schema defined in Section 3.7 is then as follows.

$autonomousagents = \{A, C, E\}$
$serveragents = \{W1, P1, D\}$
$neutralobjects = \{b1, b2, \ldots\}$
$directengagements = \{deng1, deng2, deng3, deng4, deng5, deng6\}$
$engagementchains = \{engch1, engch2\}$
$cooperations = \{coop1, coop2\}$

From the information contained in this state, it is now possible to derive the precise relation between any two agents as defined by the agent relations taxonomy in Section 3.8. For example, consider the relationship between Anne and the workstation. Since the workstation is not being used by *another* agent for a different purpose Anne still *owns* the workstation and the program. Since there are no intermediary agents between Anne and the workstation Anne *directly owns* the workstation and as she is the only agent engaging the workstation she also *uniquely owns* it. However, Anne is using the workstation for two separate goals and as such, does *not specifically own* the workstation. This may be an important consideration for Anne since it may be that the that the achievement of one goal may adversely affect the achievement of the other. Specifically, the following agent relationships can be derived.

$\{(A, C), (A, E)\} \subseteq cooperates$
$\{(A, W1), (W1, P1), (P1, D)\} \subseteq dengages$
$\{(A, P1), (A, D), (W1, D)\} \subseteq indengages$
$\{(A, W1), (W1, P1), (P1, D), (A, P1), (A, D), (W1, D)\} \subseteq engages$
$\{(A, W1), (W1, P1), (A, P1)\} \subseteq owns$
$\{(A, W1), (W1, P1)\} \subseteq downs$
$\{\,\} \subseteq sowns$
$\{(A, W1), (W1, P1)\} \subseteq uowns$

Finally, Figure 4.12 shows another situation that arises when Bill, after being asked by Emily. uses a different workstation, $W2$, to access a different program, $P2$, to locate $b2$.

4.8 Summary

Identifying the relationships between agents in multi-agent systems provides a way of understanding the nature of the system, its purpose and functionality. However, in

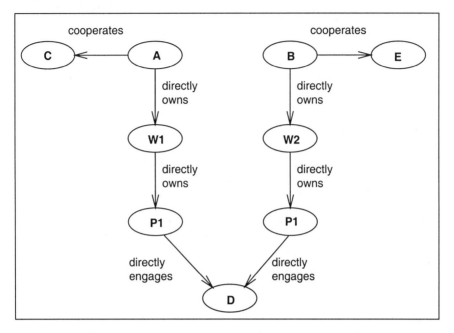

Fig. 4.12. Agent Relationships for Library Scenario IV

order to build systems that need to recognise and exploit these relationships, so that prior relationships are not destroyed when new ones are created, such analyses must be extended into *operational* areas. This chapter has provided just such an analysis, showing how different configurations of agents and relationships can evolve by invoking and destroying them. This analysis has considered a range of scenarios and the effects of changing relationships upon them.

Operational analysis is particularly important for system developers aiming to build programs that are capable of exploiting a dynamic multi-agent environment. It provides a vital link from the structural account to methods for accessing and manipulating these structures. If such analyses are avoided, then the merit of research that aims to lay a foundation for the practical aspects of multi-agent systems is limited.

Now that fundamental agent relationships have been analysed, and an operational account of their creation and destruction in multi-agent systems has been provided, the design of agents required to function in such systems can be considered. The next chapter, therefore, analyses the requisite dimensions of agents that have the ability to act effectively in multi-agent systems.

5. Sociological Agents

5.1 Introduction

Now that the inter-agent relationships that arise from the application of the SMART framework have been have identified and analysed, the requisite deliberative qualities of such agents for effective and efficient action in order to gain this benefit can be addressed. An individual agent can achieve this, first through the appropriate use of its own capabilities, and second through the successful exploitation of the capabilities of others.

In both these cases, however, an agent must be able to recognise existing relationships between entities in order that it can successfully perform the relevant task within the social constraints of the current situation. Not only can it then exploit them, but it can also reason about altering these relationships without inadvertently and deleteriously affecting its own relationships with others.

This chapter is concerned with the dimensions required by agents to achieve such behaviour; it identifies several key areas of interest. In particular, such an agent may:

- have an internal store which can be used to access percepts;
- model the entities in its environment;
- model the agent relationships in its environment;
- represent *plans* and be able to reason about them to take advantage of the capabilities of other entities; and
- be able to quantify how the current agent relationships affect the selection of plans for execution.

Thus, this chapter extends the previously developed models of agents to provide models of *deliberative* agents with prescribed dimensions of modelling others and representing and reasoning about plans. These models are presented as refinements at the SMART framework level of *agents* as opposed to *autonomous agents* for two reasons. First, an agent does not have to be autonomous in order to have the dimensions discussed in this chapter. Non-autonomous agents may be able to model others and reason about plans, and descriptions at the agent level are the most general. Second, when moving to issues of autonomy, the role of motivation in directing behaviour can be explicitly evaluated. This enables a clear analysis of the increased functionality that arises through the motivations of autonomous agents as opposed to their non-autonomous counterparts.

Agents able to represent plans, or model others, need an internal store to record the model or plan. Therefore, first *internal store* or *memory* agents that have this capacity are considered. Then agents that can *model* their environment, the entities within it, and the relationships between entities can be developed, and the models can then be applied by autonomous agents when making decisions that affect the current social state. Finally, the requisite data structures required for effective social planning are considered. A high-level account is provided of the basic functionality required for representing and reasoning about plans without detailing the nature of the agent's environment within which it is situated. This high-level description is then refined to the level of social environments containing other agents. In this way, initial high-level definitions of agents are provided that can apply equally well to single-agent systems, and those aspects of agent design that enable them to act effectively in multi-agent systems can be isolated.

5.2 Agent Store

The model of agent operation defined in the SMART framework relies solely on the environment, and the agent's perceptions, goals and motivations (if available) to determine action. However, if agents need to model their environment, or evaluate competing plans, they need more than just actions, goals and motivations; they will require an *internal store*. In general, agents without internal stores are extremely limited since their experience cannot direct behaviour, and actions can only be selected *reflexively* [6, 87]. As well as being able to capture historical information agents with a store can cache local information in order to avoid repeating complex computational tasks.

Modelling agents at a lower level facilitates distinguishing the *external* environment of an agent from some other, *internal*, repository that can be used to access percepts. The distinction between perceiving a tree in a physical environment and *recalling* a tree that was perceived previously, for example, is that the latter does not feature as a component of the possible percepts available in the current external environment and must be derived from an internal store. This *internal store* or em memory exists as part of an agent's state in an environment but it must also have existed *prior* to that current state. *Store agents* are defined as those with such memories. Store-agents therefore have the ability to access a shared or individual internal store, which can generate percepts.

In this section, these agents are outlined, providing the full specification, but omitting excessive technical explanation. Formally, the definition of a store-agent is a refinement of the agent schema defined in Section 2.4, and includes the variable *store*, represented as a non-empty set of attributes. Notice that the type of a store is *Environment* which, when accessed, produces perceptions of type *View*.

```
StoreAgent
Agent
store : Environment
```

Now, since there is both an external environment and a memory, it is necessary to distinguish between internal and external perceiving actions, where internal actions can access the store, and external perceiving actions can access the external environment. The internal perceiving actions must be non-empty since otherwise the store cannot be accessed. In defining perception, *StoreAgentPerception* includes both *AgentPerception* and *StoreAgent*, with *internalperceivingactions* and *externalperceivingactions* referring to the external and internal perceiving actions, respectively. The set of perceptions that can currently be generated from the agent's internal store is determined by the *storecanperceive* function, while *extcanperceive* determines those percepts possible from the external environment. The internal perceiving actions must be non-empty, while the internal and external perceiving actions are disjoint and together comprise the set of all perceiving actions. Note that the percepts the agent actually selects make up a subset of the available attributes and depend on the goals of the agent as defined previously. Thus the *willperceive* function from the *AgentPerception* schema is still applicable, since the store is carried through possible percepts and actual percepts to the action-selection function, *agentactions*.

StoreAgentPerception

StoreAgent
AgentPerception
$internalperceivingactions, externalperceivingactions : \mathbb{P} Action$
$storecanperceive, extcanperceive : Environment \rightarrow \mathbb{P} Action \nrightarrow View$

$internalperceivingactions \neq \{\,\}$
$internalperceivingactions \cup$
$\qquad externalperceivingactions = perceivingactions$
$internalperceivingactions \cap externalperceivingactions = \{\,\}$
$\mathrm{dom}\, storecanperceive = \{store\}$
$\forall\, env : Environment;\ as : \mathbb{P} Action \mid$
$\qquad env \in \mathrm{dom}\, storecanperceive \bullet$
$\qquad\qquad as \in \mathrm{dom}(storecanperceive\ env) \Rightarrow$
$\qquad\qquad\qquad as = internalperceivingactions$
$\forall\, env : Environment;\ as : \mathbb{P} Action \mid$
$\qquad env \in \mathrm{dom}\, extcanperceive \bullet$
$\qquad\qquad as \in \mathrm{dom}(extcanperceive\ env) \Rightarrow$
$\qquad\qquad\qquad as = externalperceivingactions$

StoreAgentAction

StoreAgent
AgentAction

The state of such an agent is specified by *StoreAgentState*. Once a store-agent is placed in an external environment, the values of the potential and actual sets of percepts, and the next set of actions can be determined. The latter two of these are specified in the original *AgentState* schema. However, the possible internal percepts, *possinternalpercepts*, are derived from applying the internal perceiving actions to the internal store, and the possible external percepts, *possexternalpercepts*, are derived by applying the external perceiving actions to the current external environment. The possible percepts then available to a store-agent are equal to the union of these two sets.

$$
\begin{array}{|l}
\_\_StoreAgentState_____ \\
StoreAgentPerception \\
StoreAgentAction \\
AgentState \\
possinternalpercepts, possexternalpercepts : View \\
extenv : Environment \\
\hline
possinternalpercepts = \\
\quad storecanperceive\ store\ internalperceivingactions \\
possexternalpercepts = \\
\quad extcanperceive\ environment\ externalperceivingactions \\
posspercepts = possinternalpercepts \cup possexternalpercepts \\
extenv \cup store = environment \\
\end{array}
$$

The consequences of an action on the external environment are represented by the same type as the base *effectinteraction* function. However, the way in which the internal store is updated is different and depends on the design of the agent as shown in *UpdateStore*. Such an update depends on the current percepts, internal store, current goals, and the actions the agent has most recently performed. Goals are relevant here because they may constrain what is recorded in the internal store, and what is not.

$$
externaleffectinteraction : Environment \nrightarrow \mathbb{P}\,Action \nrightarrow Environment
$$

$$
\begin{array}{|l}
\_\_UpdateStore_____ \\
StoreAgent \\
updatestore : \\
\quad View \rightarrow Environment \rightarrow \mathbb{P}\,Goal \rightarrow \mathbb{P}\,Action \rightarrow Environment \\
\end{array}
$$

Now, when an agent interacts with its environment, both the external environment changes, and the store changes, specified in *StoreAgentInteracts*, which is a refinement of *AgentInteracts*. When a store-agent acts, it does not necessarily record just those attributes that are currently available in the external environment, but may also store some other attributes regarding more general learned or acquired information. Certain agent designs may not allow for their store to be updated, in which case there is no learning facility, as specified by *FixedStoreAgentInteracts*.

—— *StoreAgentInteracts* ——————————————————————
Δ*StoreAgentState*
UpdateStore
AgentInteracts
——————————————————————
extenv' = *externaleffectinteraction extenv willdo*
store' = *updatestore actualpercepts' store goals willdo*
——————————————————————

—— *FixedStoreAgentInteracts* ——————————————————
StoreAgentInteracts
——————————————————————
store' = *store*
——————————————————————

The schema structure for specifying store agents is illustrated in Figure 5.1. By now it should be clear to the reader how this diagram represents the way in which the specification has been developed for store agents from components of the SMART framework defined in Chapter 2. While continuing to include such diagrams as the specification develops in order to provide a reference for interpreting future models, they will no longer be described in detail.

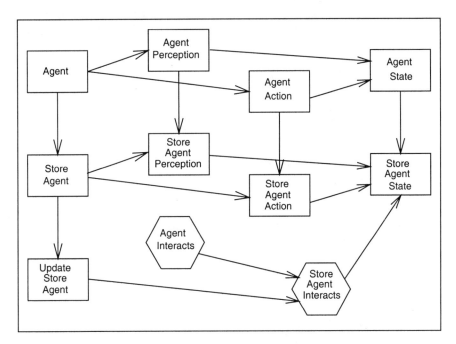

Fig. 5.1. Schema Structure for Specifying Store-Agents

The model of store-agents described in this section enables the description of agents at any level of abstraction depending on how the store is defined. At the most basic level, the store can be modelled as a series of binary digits, but it is more common to model it as containing information at the *knowledge-level* [96]. In this case, agents are referred to by Genesereth and Nilsson as *knowledge-level agents* [51], where an agent's mental actions are viewed as inferences on its database, so that prior experience and knowledge can be taken into account when determining which action to take. These agents can be reformulated by application of the store-agent model. However, before proceeding, *hysteretic* agents, which are strongly related to knowledge-level agents, but are more general, are considered

5.2.1 Applying SMART: Hysteretic Agents

Hysteretic agents are similar to store-agents in that they are both able to retain information internally. They have an internal store that can be in one of several states from the set I of all possible internal states. As with *tropistic agents*, (see Section 2.6), external perceptual capabilities are limited and partition the set S of external environments as described by *see*. In addition — but in contrast to modelling external perceptual abilities as limited — it is assumed that hysteretic agents are able to distinguish each possible internal state.

Hysteretic action-selection thus depends on the agent's internal state as well as the perceptions of the external environment; updating the internal state is determined by *internal*, which is a function of elements of I and T. The following tuple defines *hysteretic* agents.

$$(I, S, T, A, see : S \rightarrow T, do : A \times S \rightarrow S,$$
$$action : I \times T \rightarrow A, internal : I \times T \rightarrow I)$$

Recall that the functions defined in this section for store-agents are as follows. The two models can be related as shown below.

$storecanperceive : Environment \rightarrow \mathbb{P}\,Action \nrightarrow View$
$extcanperceive : Environment \rightarrow \mathbb{P}\,Action \nrightarrow View$
$updatestore : View \nrightarrow Environment \rightarrow \mathbb{P}\,Goal \rightarrow \mathbb{P}\,Action \rightarrow Environment$

The set of hysteretic agent internal states is defined to be the type *Environment* from the agent framework and the type definitions for tropistic agents defined in Chapter 2 still apply.

$$I == Environment \wedge S == Environment \wedge T == View \wedge A == Action$$

Hysteretic agents perceive each internal state completely and correctly at every step in the agent's cycle, which is is formalised by equating *storecanperceive* with the identity function. The possible external perceptions are defined in the same way as those for tropistic agents and the *willperceive* function is again equated to the identity function, since goals constrain neither the hysteretic agent's internal perceptions nor its external perceptions.

$\forall i : I \bullet (storecanperceive\ i\ internalperceivingactions) = i$
$\forall e : S \bullet see\ e = (extcanperceive\ e\ perceivinegactions)$
$willperceieve\ g = \{e : Environment \bullet (e, e)\}$

As described earlier in this section, the set of percepts perceived by a store-agent with goals gs, store, i, and environment, e is calculated as follows.

$willperceive\ gs\ ((extcanperceive\ e\ perceivingactions) \cup$
$(storecanperceive\ i\ internalperceivingactions))$

Using the definitions above, this simplifies to the following predicate, which states that for an internal store, i, and an external environment, e, the agent perceives i and a subset of the external environment, e, as determined by *extcanperceive*.

$\forall i : I, e : S \bullet actualpercepts = (extcanperceive\ gs\ s) \cup i$

The functions defining action selection and the updating of internal store are both reformulated simply below. Since the internal update function for hysteretic agents does not depend on the actions-performed, this parameter is fixed to the empty set in *updatestore*.

$\forall i : I, t : T \bullet action(i, t) = agentactions\ \{gs\}\ (i \cup t)\ \{\}$
$\forall v : View;\ i : Environment \bullet internal\ (v, i) = updatestore\ v\ i\ \{gs\}\ \{\}$

5.2.2 Applying SMART: Knowledge-Based Agents

The conceptualisation of store or hysteretic agents allows the description of agents at any level of detail, the most common of which is the *knowledge-level* [96] where, in many cases, the store consists entirely of formulae in first order predicate calculus. The tuple defining these agents is exactly the same as for hysteretic agents and is not presented here. Instead the representation of the internal store is considered, since many agents contain databases or knowledge bases that consist of predicate calculus formulae. This also demonstrates how the abstract SMART framework types can be refined to describe more practical and definite concepts.

A formula is often called an *atom* [104] and can be defined as a *predicate symbol* (denoted by the given set, [*PredSym*]), and an associated sequence of *terms* as its argument.

```
┌─ Atom ──────────────────────────────────────
│ head : PredSym
│ terms : seq Term
└─────────────────────────────────────────────
```

A *term* is defined as either a *constant*, a *variable*, or a *functor symbol* with a sequence of terms as a parameter. If the set of all constants, variables and functor symbols are all given sets, then the definition of a term is as follows.

[*Const, Var, FunSym*]

$Term ::= const\langle\!\langle Const \rangle\!\rangle$
$\qquad | \quad var\langle\!\langle Var \rangle\!\rangle$
$\qquad | \quad functor\langle\!\langle FunSym \times seq\ Term \rangle\!\rangle$

Now, agents whose internal store consists solely of predicates have been referred to as *knowledge-based* agents [51]. Sometimes, the predicates continued in the store of these agents contain *ground* atoms only; they do not contain variables. Ground atoms can be formalised using the auxiliary functions below, which return the set of variables for terms and atoms respectively.

$termvars : Term \rightarrow (\mathbb{P}\ Var)$
$atomvars : Atom \rightarrow (\mathbb{P}\ Var)$

$\forall\ at : Atom;\ c : Const;\ v : Var;\ f : FunSym;\ ts : seq\ Term \bullet$
$\qquad termvars\ (const\ c) = \varnothing \wedge$
$\qquad termvars\ (var\ v) = \{v\} \wedge$
$\qquad termvars\ (functor(f, ts)) = \bigcup(ran(map\ termvars\ ts)) \wedge$
$\qquad atomvars\ at = \bigcup(ran(map\ termvars\ at.terms))$

The generic higher-order function *map* used above takes another function as its argument and applies it to every element in a sequence.

$== [X, Y] ==$
$map : (X \rightarrow Y) \rightarrow (seq\ X) \rightarrow (seq\ Y)$

$\forall f : X \rightarrow Y;\ x : X;\ xs, ys : seq\ X \bullet$
$\qquad map\ f\ \langle\rangle = \langle\rangle \wedge$
$\qquad map\ f\ \langle x \rangle = \langle f\ x \rangle \wedge$
$\qquad map\ f\ (xs \frown ys) = map\ f\ xs \frown map\ f\ ys$

It is then a simple matter to define the set of ground atoms as those that contain no variables.

$BaseAtoms == \{a : Atom \mid atomvars\ a = \varnothing\}$

A semantic base can now be provided for the type, *Attribute*, defined originally as a given set, by specifying attributes as ground predicates.

$Attribute == BaseAtoms$

As when defining tropistic agents using the SMART framework, the store-agent model can be applied directly to reformulate agent architectures with an internal memory. The knowledge-level agent example also demonstrates how the framework specification types that were defined as abstractly as possible can be refined to any specific level of detail as required.

5.3 Agent Models

Attention now turns to the dimensions specifically required for an agent to function effectively in multi-agent systems. In order that agents can take advantage of the capabilities of others they will generally need models of them. Models are representations recorded in the internal store. (For example, the Acquaintance Models of ARCHON [66] and the modelling layer of TouringMachines [43] contain models of other entities encoded in an internal store.) Here agent models are constructed at this level of abstraction by application of the SMART models; in general, agents not only need models of others but also of the relationships between them in order to act effectively.

5.3.1 Entity Models

The ability to isolate components in a complex external environment and to perceive them as a whole is the first task of any situated agent that is required to operate effectively. Representations of models of entities are called *entity models*. The way in which agents group attributes together to form entity models is purely subjective, being constrained by their capabilities and goals. Formally, representations of the entities themselves are distinguished from representations of models of those entities by defining *EntityModel* as the representation of a model that an agent has of an entity and other model-types analogously as follows.

$EntityModel == Entity$
$ObjectModel == Object$
$AgentModel == Agent$
$AutonomousAgentModel == AutonomousAgent$
$NeutralObjectModel == NeutralObject$
$ServerAgentModel == ServerAgent$

Following the structure of the SMART agent framework, the most basic agents in this category are those that can distinguish entities. This kind of modelling is used by mechanisms such as a robot arm on a production line. The arm is only concerned with the perceptual stimuli needed for it to perform appropriate actions on an entity, and is not concerned with its capabilities and goals. The *AgentModelEntities* schema, which refines the *StoreAgent* schema, describes such an agent and includes the *modelentities* variable to represent its entity models.

$$\begin{array}{l} \underline{\quad AgentModelEntities \quad} \\ StoreAgent \\ AgentState \\ modelentities : \mathbb{P}_1\ EntityModel \end{array}$$

If an agent can associate capabilities with its models of an entity, then it can also model objects. The *AgentModelObjects* schema describes this increased capability, which, for example, describes a robot able to test components in a production line for specified capabilities.

AgentModelObjects _____

AgentModelEntities
modelobjects : $\mathbb{P}_1$ *ObjectModel*
___

modelobjects $\subseteq$ *modelentities*

Increasing the capability with which an agent can model its environment according to the framework, we proceed to specify agents able to distinguish agents from neutral-objects in the *AgentModelAgents* schema. The subsequent *AgentModels* schema specifies those agents which, in addition, are able to distinguish autonomous agents from server-agents. Agents that can model the autonomy of others can then, in theory, understand the origination of goals in a multi-agent system. This schema includes an optional *modelself* variable, which is the model an agent has of itself. The value of this variable will become clear later when mechanisms for reasoning about plans are investigated.

AgentModelAgents _____

AgentModelObjects
modelagents : $\mathbb{P}_1$ *AgentModel*
modelneutralobjects : $\mathbb{P}$ *NeutralObjectModel*
___

modelagents $\subseteq$ *modelobjects*
modelobjects $=$ *modelagents* $\cup$ *modelneutralobjects*

AgentModels _____

AgentModelAgents
modelautonomousagents : $\mathbb{P}_1$ *AutonomousAgentModel*
modelserveragents : $\mathbb{P}$ *ServerAgentModel*
modelself : *optional* [*AgentModel*]
___

modelautonomousagents $\subseteq$ *modelagents*
modelserveragents $=$ *modelautonomousagents* $\setminus$ *modelserveragents*

For reference the schema structure used to define agent models is presented in Figure 5.2.

5.3.2 Sociological Agents

In general, it is not enough for agents to model other entities such as objects, agents or autonomous agents in isolation; they must also model the agent relationships between them. A robot without this capability could not model the relationship between users and workstations, for example, and could not reason about negotiating with the user to release the workstation for its use. Agents must model the engagements, cooperations and engagement chains of the system in which they are situated.

Definition 5.3.1. *A* sociological agent *is an agent that models other agents and the set of agent relationships (cooperations, engagements and engagement chains) between them.*

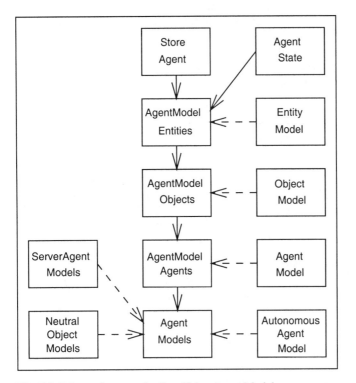

Fig. 5.2. Schema Structure for Specifying Agent Models

There are many definitions of what constitutes a social agent rather than a sociological agent. For example, Wooldridge states that any agent in a multi-agent system is necessarily social [133] and Moulin and Chaib-draa [93] take an agent to be social if it can model others. However, the term is more often associated with social *activity* such as provided by Wooldridge and Jennings [136] who refer to the process of interaction. We choose "sociological" since we are considering agents that can *model* their social environment rather than act in it socially. An agent must be sociological before it can be a generally effective social agent.

A sociological agent therefore views its environment as containing a collection of entities with engagements, engagement chains and cooperations between them. Such an agent is specified below in *SociologicalAgent*, which includes the schemas

DirectEngagementModel, *EngagementChainModel*, and *CooperationModel*, defining an agent's mental representations of agent relationships.

In addition, certain consistency requirements need to be specified as constraints on these mental representations of relationships and entities. Specifically, if a relationship is modelled by an agent, then the agents involved in that relationship must themselves be modelled. For example, the first predicate of the *SociologicalAgent* schema states that the client and server-agents for a modelled direct engagement must be contained in the set of modelled agents. The other schema predicates specify similar consistency constraints, which should be clear to the reader by now.

DirectEngagementModel

$modelclient : AgentModel$
$modelserver : ServerAgentModel$
$goal : Goal$

$modelclient \neq modelserver$
$goal \in modelclient.goals \cap modelserver.goals$

EngagementChainModel

$goal : Goal$
$modelautonomousagent : AutonomousAgentModel$
$modelagentchain : \text{seq}_1 \, ServerAgentModel$

$goal \in modelautonomousagent.goals$
$goal \in \bigcap\{s : ServerAgentModel \mid s \in \text{ran} \, modelagentchain \bullet s.goals\}$
$\#(\text{ran} \, modelagentchain) = \#modelagentchain$

CooperationModel

$goal : Goal$
$modelgeneratingagent : AutonomousAgentModel$
$modelcooperatingagents : \mathbb{P}_1 \, AutonomousAgentModel$

$goal \in modelgeneratingagent.goals$
$\forall a : modelcooperatingagents \bullet goal \in a.goals$
$modelgeneratingagent \notin modelcooperatingagents$

─── *SociologicalAgent* ───────────────────────────────
AgentState
AgentModels
modeldirectengagements : $\mathbb{P}$ *DirectEngagementModel*
modelengchains : $\mathbb{P}$ *EngagementChainModel*
modelcooperations : $\mathbb{P}$ *CooperationModel*
─────────────────────────────────────
$\forall$ *md* : *modeldirectengagements* •
     (*md.modelserver* $\in$ *modelserveragents*) $\wedge$
     (*md.modelclient* $\in$ *modelagents*)
$\forall$ *mch* : *modelengchains* •
     (ran *mch.modelagentchain* $\subseteq$ *modelserveragents*) $\wedge$
     (*mch.modelautonomousagent* $\in$ *modelautonomousagents*)
$\forall$ *mc* : *modelcooperations* •
     (*mc.modelgeneratingagent* $\in$ *modelautonomousagents*) $\wedge$
     (*mc.modelcooperatingagents* $\subseteq$ *modelautonomousagents*)
─────────────────────────────────────

Sociological agents can automatically derive the type of the relationship between two agents from these models as defined by the agent relationships taxonomy presented in Section 3.8. If, in a sociological agent's view, the only agent engaging the server-agent *s* is *c*, then the sociological agent models *c* as *owning s*. The relations *modelengages*, *modedengages*, *modelowns*, *modeldowns* and *modelcooperates* are formalised in the *ModelAgentRelationships* schema, and the other relations in the taxonomy can be defined similarly.

─── *ModelAgentRelationships* ────────────────────────
SociologicalAgent
modeldengages, modelengages, modelowns, modeldowns :
          AgentModel $\leftrightarrow$ *ServerAgentModel*
modelcooperates :
          AutonomousAgentModel $\leftrightarrow$ *AutonomousAgentModel*
─────────────────────────────────────
modeldengages =
     {*e* : *modeldirectengagements* •
          (*e.modelclient, e.modelserver*)}
modelengages =
     {*ec* : *modelengchains* •
          (*ec.modelautonomousagent, head ec.modelagentchain*)} $\cup$
               {*ec* : *modelengchains*; *c, s* : *AgentModel* |
                    ((*c, s*), *ec.modelagentchain*) $\in$ *before* • (*c, s*)}
modelcooperates =
     $\bigcup${*a*1, *a*2 : *AutonomousAgentModel* |
          ($\exists$ *c* : *modelcooperations* •
               *a*1 = *c.modelgeneratingagent* $\wedge$
               *a*2 $\in$ *c.modelcooperatingagents*) • {(*a*1, *a*2)}}
─────────────────────────────────────

Any recognised inter-agent relationships can then be exploited by intelligent sociological agents for more effective operation. Each agent must maintain information about the different entities in the environment, so that both existing and potential relationships between those entities may be understood and consequently manipulated as appropriate. For example, neutral-objects are not involved in relationships with agents, so that they can be engaged without affecting existing relationships. If an entity is viewed correctly as a server-agent, this must imply that it is *engaged* by another *autonomous* agent, either directly or through a chain of intermediate agents, grounded with an autonomous agent at the head of the chain. Knowledge of the agency of an entity allows viewing agents to reason about its role and the agents engaging it.

5.3.3 Modelling the Motivations of Others

Understanding the motivations that generated the goal of an inter-agent relationship provides further information. It is motivation that is the 'force' that causes engagement chains to be created, satisfying goals that mitigate the motivation. In attempting to understand the nature of the relationships between entities in a multi-agent system it is therefore necessary to be able to assess the relative strengths of motivation that caused the current set of relationships.

Consider, for example, the situation in which Anne is using a pencil, and Bill correctly views this pencil as Anne's agent satisfying her goal of writing notes. If Bill wishes to use the pencil, he must consider the strength of the motivations that generated Anne's goal, and his model may lead him to predict whether he will succeed in securing use of the pencil. Now, if Bill understands that Anne's goal was generated because of an imminent important deadline, then he may decide that an attempt to break the agent relationship will not be successful. Alternatively, if the motivation for using the pencil was weak, then Bill may rate his chances more highly.

In order to further illustrate how autonomous agents can use their models to make informed decisions about potential courses of action, a more general example is provided where one autonomous agent wishes to use the owned entity of another autonomous agent. This example requires the previous definition of the *motivational effect* on an agent of satisfying a goal, *satisfy*, defined in the *AssessGoals* schema in Section 3.3. The following conventions are also adopted.

- The expression $satisfy_B^A(gs)$ denotes the motivational effect on the autonomous agent, Anne, of satisfying the set of goals, gs, *according to Bill's model*.

- The expression $model_B^{A.goals}$ denotes Bill's model of Anne's goals.

- The expression $\overline{goal}$ denotes the goal to prevent *goal*.

Let us assume that Bill models Anne as being autonomous, having the goal, g_A, and directly owning the server-agent S, for the goal g_A. This can be written as follows.

$Anne \in Bill.modelautonomousagents$

$model_B^{A.goals} = \{g_A\}$

$MakeDirectEngagment(Anne, S, g_A) \in Bill.modeldirectengagements$

$(Anne, S) \in Bill.modeldowns$

The current motivational effect that Bill models Anne as having is represented by the following predicate.

$satisfy_B^A(\{g_A\})$

Now, if Bill wants to use S for some other goal g_B, there are several possible courses of action for him.

– Bill can persuade Anne to share S.
– Bill can persuade Anne to release S.
– Bill can attempt to take S by force without Anne's permission.
– Bill can give Anne priority and find an alternative.

Any decision as to which alternative Bill takes requires an analysis of both Bill's motivations and Bill's model of Anne's motivations.

– $satisfy_B^A\{g_B, g_A\} > satisfy_B^A\{g_A\}$. If g_B and g_A do not conflict, it is possible for S to adopt both of the goals of Bill and Anne without violating any motivational constraints. So long as the motivational effect on Anne of satisfying both goals is more than satisfying just her own, Anne will be disposed to share S.

– $satisfy_B^A\{g_B\} > satisfy_B^A\{g_A\}$. Bill understands that Anne stands to gain more from enabling Bill to satisfy his goal than from Anne satisfying her own goal. This is due to the effect that a positive change in Bill's motivations will have on Anne. This may require that Bill explains and persuades Anne of the degree of effect that g_B will have on him and hence on her. For example, if Anne is currently reading a book that Bill wants to borrow, his goal of borrowing the book may conflict with Anne's goal. However, if Anne wants to please Bill and does not need to read the book now, she may happily lend the book to him. Notice that this analysis might require an understanding of the nature of an object and whether it is disposed to being shared or owned. Clearly, if at some time a book is an server-agent, it is more likely that this book is be owned by one autonomous agent, rather than shared by many.

– $satisfy_B^B\{g_B\} > satisfy_B^B\{\overline{g_A}\}$. It may seem obvious that the motivational effect on Bill of satisfying his goal should be greater than the motivational effect on Bill of satisfying Anne's goal. However, if Anne's goal is not satisfied, then the motivational effect on Anne will be negative, resulting in a state which must be considered in terms of its effect on Bill. (In other words, a negative motivational effect on Anne, particularly if it was a consequence of some action of Bill, may result in a negative motivational effect on Bill.) Thus this alternative may be chosen if there is a positive motivational effect from Bill's goal being satisfied, *and* this is greater than the negative consequences of Anne's goal not being satisfied. Note that this relies on the relationship of Bill to Anne. Normally, Bill's motivations will be such that negative motivational effect on other agents will lead to some negative motivational effect on Bill himself. If, however, Bill is motivated by malicious concerns, then it is certainly possible that the consequences of Anne's goal not being satisfied may have a positive motivational effect on Bill. While we do not envisage such a situation arising regularly, and though this is a case typically not considered in related work, it ought to be possible within any formalism. By using motivations in the way described, the possibility of perverse configurations leading to such malicious behaviour is allowed, but appropriate design of motivations can ensure that this does not arise. Returning to the example where Anne is reading a book that Bill wants to borrow, he can simply take the book from her without permission as before. It only makes sense for him to do this, however, if the benefit he gains from having the book is more significant than the bad feeling caused in Anne by Bill having taken it forcibly.

– $satisfy_B^B\{g_B\} < satisfy_B^B\{\overline{g_A}\}$. Bill understands that the motivational effect of satisfying his goal will be less than the effect of causing a negative motivational effect on Anne through g_A not being satisfied. This affects Bill's behaviour, because his motivations are configured in such a way that he is concerned for Anne. In summary, the model captures normal social behaviour by which we act so as to avoid annoying others, but allows for situations where we may deliberately choose to annoy them as in the previous case.

5.3.4 Modelling the Models of Others

In some situations, agents may be designed not only to model other agents but also to model the *models of other agents*. This enables agents to consider the view of others on which they base their actions. As Durfee acknowledges [38], if agents are to coordinate their activities they may need to know not only about each other and about themselves but about how others view themselves and how others view others. For example, if Anne models Bill as a sociological agent then Anne assumes that Bill acts based on his current model of the current agent relationships. Such an agent is defined formally in the *ModelSociological* schema.

ModelSociological
SociologicalAgent
modelsociologicalagents : *Agent* $\nrightarrow$ *SociologicalAgent*

dom *modelsociologicalagents* $\subseteq$ *modelagents*

These agents can exploit their environment more effectively than agents described by the *SociologicalAgent* schema. As an example, consider the following situation:

– Bill is specified by *ModelSociological*;
– Anne is specified by *SociologicalAgent*;

- Bill desires to engage the entity E;
- E cannot be shared but must be owned;
- Anne owns E; and
- Bill's model of Anne's model of their shared environment includes the fact that Anne does not recognise the relationship between herself and E (Anne might be a very forgetful agent).

In this scenario Bill can forcibly use E, thus destroying its relationship with Anne, but in such a way as not to affect any relationship between himself and Anne. This level of reasoning is not possible for sociological agents, but only for those agents able to model *others* as sociological.

Extensions to describe agents able to model the models that agents have of others can be formalised easily reusing existing schemas as shown in the *ModelModels* schema.

ModelModels _____

ModelSociological
modelsociological : *Agent* $\nrightarrow$ *ModelSociological*

_____

dom *modelsociological* $\subseteq$ *modelagents*

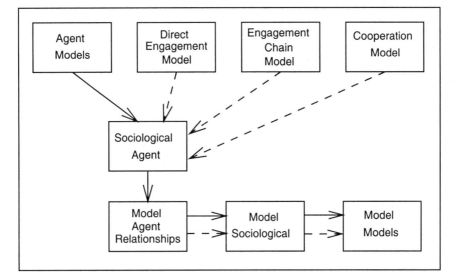

Fig. 5.3. Schema Structure for Specifying Sociological Agents

The specification structure presented in this section is illustrated in Figure 5.3; schemas can be further extended in this way to develop nested models such as those proposed in Recursive Agent Modelling [127]. This shows how the SMART framework models can be applied to the incremental development and subsequent analysis of the social capabilities of agents.

5.4 Agent Plans

5.4.1 Introduction

Sometimes, agents may select an action, or a set of concurrent actions, to achieve goals directly. At other times, however, there may not be such a simple correspondence between goals and actions, and appropriately designed agents may perform *sequences* of actions, or *plans*, to achieve their goals. In multi-agent systems, agents have at their disposal not only their own capabilities but, potentially, the capabilities of others. Agents with plans requiring actions outside their competence need models of others to consider making use of their capabilities. If these agents are sociological then they can evaluate plans with respect to their model of the current agent relationships. For example, agents can decide how much plans can exploit current relationships as well as consider how they may *impinge* on them. In general, agents must reason about how to exploit existing and potential relationships without inadvertently or unnecessarily destroying them.

The *process* of planning, which is the ability to construct sequences of actions that are executed in an attempt to bring about a goal [78], is not modelled, but the ways in which plans can be modelled, and then how agents can evaluate plans using these models, is considered. While some agent systems, including the Procedural Reasoning System [54], do not construct their plans in this sense, others do, such as the *partial global planning* of agents in the distributed vehicle monitoring testbed [39]. Clearly, a representation of plans is required before planning algorithms can be specified and this is the aim here.

There are many different notions of agent plans at both theoretical and practical levels and in order to substantiate the claim that the SMART framework can be generally applied, it is necessary for different representations of plans to be equally accommodated. While not every type of plan of which we are aware is specified, we do intend to show *how* the framework can be extended to describe familiar notions of plans, and to impress upon the reader how other models of plans can be included. This is achieved by specifying general theoretical plan representations, called *total* plans, *partial* plans and *tree* plans.

5.4.2 Plan-Agents

One methodological characteristic of this book is the *incremental* development of the models in it. Therefore, a high-level model of *plan-agents*, which applies equally well to reactive or deliberative, single-agent or multi-agent, planners, is constructed. It represents a high-level of abstraction because nothing is decided about the nature of the agent, the plan representation, or the agent's environment; it simply distinguishes *categories* of plan and possible relationships between an agent's plans and goals. Specifically, *non-active* plans are defined to be those which have not been identified as a means of achieving a current goal; *active* plans to be those identified as candidate plans not yet selected for execution; and *executable* plans to be those active plans that have been selected for execution (which may currently be executing).

In general, an agent has a repository of goals, and a repository of plans that have either been designed before the agent starts executing [53] or acquired and developed over the course of the agent's life [106]. In addition, plans may be associated with one or more goals, identifying the plan as a potential means of achieving those goals. Sugawara [123], for example, proposes a plan-reuse framework which maintains information that includes associations between plans and goals. Agents can then reuse plans that have successfully achieved their goal, by recording a relationship between the plan and goal. Similarly, in dMARS goals are associated with plans by means of the *invocation condition* of plans [53]. Finally, a set of *active* plans may be associated with a *current* goal signifying that they are alternatives for execution.

Formally, the set of all agent plans is initially defined to be a given set ([*Plan*]), thereby choosing a level of abstraction at which nothing is specified about the nature of plans themselves. The highest-level description of a *plan-agent* is formalised in the *PlanAgent* schema below. Since plans must be encoded as aspects of an internal store and, since active and executable plans are clearly aspects of the agent's *state*, the *StoreAgentState* schema is included. We choose to refer to *plan-agents* rather than 'planning' agents or 'planners' since we remain neutral on whether the agent has the ability to construct or modify its own plans. The variables *goallibrary*, *planlibrary*, *activeplans* and *executableplans* represent the agent's repository of goals, repository of plans, active plans and executable plans, respectively. Each active plan is necessarily associated with one or more of the agent's current goals, as specified by *activeplangoal*. For example, if the function contains the pair $(g, \{p_1, p_2, p_3\})$, it indicates that p_1, p_2 and p_3 are competing active plans for g. Whilst active plans must be associated with at least one active goal, the converse is not true since agents may have goals for which no plans have been considered. Analogously the *plangoallibrary* function relates the repository of goals, *goallibrary*, to the repository of plans, *planlibrary*. However, not all library plans and goals are necessarily related by this function. Here, three categories relating to the state of agent plans are distinguished. Others (such as, for example, the *suspended* plans of PRS [54]) can be added similarly.

```
┌─ PlanAgent ─────────────────────────────────────────────────
│ StoreAgentState
│ goallibrary : ℙ Goal
│ planlibrary, activeplans, executableplans : ℙ Plan
│ activeplangoal, plangoallibrary : Goal ↦ ℙ Plan
├─────────────────────────────────────────────────────────────
│ dom activeplangoal ⊆ goals
│ ⋃(ran activeplangoal) = activeplans
│ dom plangoallibrary ⊆ goallibrary
│ ⋃(ran plangoallibrary) ⊆ planlibrary
│ goals ⊆ goallibrary
│ executableplans ⊆ activeplans ⊆ planlibrary
└─────────────────────────────────────────────────────────────
```

Now, agents can be constrained in their design by including additional predicates. For example, it is possible to restrict the active plans of an agent (with respect to a current goal) to those which are related to that goal by the function *plangoallibrary*. This can be achieved in the specification of such an agent by including the following predicate.

$$\forall ag : PlanAgent;\ g : Goal;\ ps : \mathbb{P}_1\ Plan \bullet$$
$$(g, ps) \in ag.activeplangoal \Rightarrow$$
$$(\exists qs : \mathbb{P}\ Plan \mid qs \subset ag.planlibrary \bullet$$
$$(g, (ps \cup qs)) \in ag.plangoallibrary)$$

The actions performed by such agents are a function of their plans as well as their goals and perceptions, as described by the *PlanAgentAction* schema that refines the *AgentAction* schema, and specifies the selection of actions for a plan-agent. Other definitions formalising the perception of store-agents can be specified similarly.

```
┌─ PlanAgentAction ───────────────────────────────────────────
│ PlanAgent
│ AgentAction
│ planagentactions :
│     ℙ Goal → ℙ Plan → View → Environment → ℙ Action
├─────────────────────────────────────────────────────────────
│ ∀ gs : ℙ Goal; ps : ℙ Plan; v : View; env : Environment •
│     (planagentactions gs ps v env) ⊆ capabilities
│ dom planagentactions = {goals}
│ dom(planagentactions goals) = {executableplans}
└─────────────────────────────────────────────────────────────
```

5.4.3 Multi-Agent Plans

In order for agents to reason about plans involving others it is necessary to analyse the nature of the plans themselves. This involves defining first the *components* of a plan, and then the *structure* of a plan. The components, which are called *plan-actions*, each consist of a *composite-action* and a set of related entities as described below. The structure of plans defines the relationship of the component plan-actions to one another. For example, plans may be *total* and define a sequence of plan-actions, *partial* and place a partial order on the performance of plan-actions, or *trees* and, for example, allow choice between alternative plan-actions at every stage in the plan's execution.

Composite-Actions and Plan-Actions. Four types of action are identified that may be contained in plans, called *primitive, template, concurrent-primitive* and *concurrent-template*. There may be other categories and variations on those chosen, but not only do they provide a starting point for specifying systems, they also illustrate how different representations can be formalised and incorporated within the same model. A primitive action is simply a base action as defined in the framework, while an action template provides a high-level description of what is required by an action, defined as the set of all primitive actions that may result through an instantiation of that action-template. For example, in dMARS, template actions represent action formulae containing free variables, and become primitive actions when bound to values. A concurrent-primitive action is also defined as a set of primitive actions to be performed concurrently and a concurrent action-template as a set of template actions that are performed concurrently. Finally a new type, *ActionComp*, is defined as a *compound-action* to include all four of these types.

$$
\begin{aligned}
&Primitive && == Action \\
&Template && == \mathbb{P}\,Action \\
&ConcPrimitive && == \mathbb{P}\,Action \\
&ConcTemplate && == \mathbb{P}(\mathbb{P}\,Action) \\
&ActionComp && ::= Prim\langle\!\langle Primitive\rangle\!\rangle \\
&&& \mid\ Temp\langle\!\langle Template\rangle\!\rangle \\
&&& \mid\ ConcPrim\langle\!\langle ConcPrimitive\rangle\!\rangle \\
&&& \mid\ ConcTemp\langle\!\langle ConcTemplate\rangle\!\rangle
\end{aligned}
$$

Now, actions must be performed by entities, so every composite-action in a plan is associated with a set of entities, such that each entity in the set can potentially perform the action. At some stage in the planning process this set may be empty, indicating that no choice of entity has yet been made. A *plan-action* is defined as a set of pairs, where each pair contains a composite-action and a set of the entities that could potentially perform the action. Plan-actions are defined as a set of pairs rather than *single* pairs so that plans containing simultaneous actions can be represented.

$$PlanAction == \mathbb{P}(ActionComp \times \mathbb{P}\,EntityModel)$$

The following examples illustrate this representation. First, the a_1 action is to be performed by either the plan-agent itself or the entity, *entity1*. The second example describes the two separate actions, a_{2_1} and a_{2_2}, being performed simultaneously by the *entity1* and *entity2* respectively. Then, the third example states that the actions a_{3_1} and a_{3_2} are to be performed simultaneously. No entity has been established as a possibility to perform a_{3_1}, and a_{3_2} is to be performed by either *entity2* or *entity3*.

1. $\{(a_1, \{self, entity1\})\}$
2. $\{(a_{2_1}, \{entity1\}), (a_{2_2}, \{entity2\})\}$
3. $\{(a_{3_1}, \{\ \}), (a_{3_2}, \{entity2, entity3\})\}$

Three auxiliary functions, useful for analysing composite-actions and plan-actions are defined below: *actions* returns the set of actions from a composite-action; *actionsofPA* returns the set of actions of a plan-action; and *entitiesofPA* returns the set of entity-models of a plan-action.

$$actions : ActionComp \rightarrow \mathbb{P}\, Action$$
$$actionsofPA : PlanAction \rightarrow \mathbb{P}\, Action$$
$$entitiesofPA : PlanAction \rightarrow \mathbb{P}\, EntityModel$$

$\forall p : ActionComp \bullet$
$\quad (p \in \text{ran}\, Prim \Rightarrow actions\, p = \{Prim^{-1}p\}) \wedge$
$\quad (p \in \text{ran}\, Temp \Rightarrow actions\, p = Temp^{-1}p) \wedge$
$\quad (p \in \text{ran}\, ConcPrim \Rightarrow actions\, p = ConcPrim^{-1}p) \wedge$
$\quad (p \in \text{ran}\, ConcTemp \Rightarrow actions\, p = \bigcup(ConcTemp^{-1}p))$
$\forall pa : PlanAction \bullet$
$\quad actionsofPA\, pa = \bigcup\{aes : pa \bullet actions\,(first\ aes)\} \wedge$
$\quad entitiesofPA\, pa = \bigcup\{aes : pa \bullet second\ aes\}$

Plan Structure. Three commonly-found categories of plan are specified according to their structure as discussed earlier. Other types may be specified similarly.

– *Partial Plans* A partial plan imposes a partial order on the execution of actions, subject to two constraints. First, an action cannot be performed before itself and, second, if plan-action a is before b, b cannot be before a. Formally, a partial plan is a relationship between plan-actions such that the pair (a, a) is not in the transitive closure and, further, if the pair (a, b) is in the transitive closure of the relation then the pair (b, a) is not. The standard definition of the transitive closure of a relation can be found in Appendix A.2.2.
– *Total Plans* A plan consisting of a total order of plan-actions is a total plan. Formally, this is represented as a sequence of plan-actions.
– *Tree Plans* A plan that allows a choice between actions at every stage is a tree. In general, a tree is either
  1. a leaf node containing a plan-action, or
  2. a fork containing a node, and a (non-empty) set of branches each leading to a tree.

These are formalised as follows replacing the definition of *Plan* as a given set by a free-type definition to include the three plan categories thus defined.

$PartialPlan == \{ps : PlanAction \leftrightarrow PlanAction \mid \forall a, b : PlanAction \bullet$
$\qquad\qquad\qquad (a, a) \notin ps^+ \wedge (a, b) \in ps^+ \Rightarrow (b, a) \notin ps^+ \bullet ps\}$

$TotalPlan \quad == seq\ PlanAction$

$TreePlan \quad ::= Tip \langle\!\langle PlanAction \rangle\!\rangle$
$\qquad\qquad\quad \mid\ Fork \langle\!\langle \mathbb{P}_1(PlanAction \times TreePlan) \rangle\!\rangle$

$Plan \qquad\quad ::= Partial \langle\!\langle PartialPlan \rangle\!\rangle$
$\qquad\qquad\quad \mid\ Total \langle\!\langle TotalPlan \rangle\!\rangle$
$\qquad\qquad\quad \mid\ Tree \langle\!\langle TreePlan \rangle\!\rangle$

Next several auxiliary functions useful for analysing these plans are defined. The
planpairs function returns the plan-actions of a plan, *planactions* returns the set of
actions contained in a plan, and *planentities* returns the set of entities included in a
plan. These definitions invoke the function, *TreeNodes*, which takes a tree-plan and
returns all the action-plans in that tree. This, in turn, relies on *mapset*, which applies
a function to every element in a set.

$=[X, Y]=$

$mapset : (X \rightarrow Y) \rightarrow \mathbb{P}\,X \rightarrow \mathbb{P}\,Y$

$\forall f : X \rightarrow Y;\ xs : \mathbb{P}\,X \bullet mapset\,f\,xs = \{x : xs \bullet f\,x\}$

$treenodes : TreePlan \rightarrow \mathbb{P}\,PlanAction$

$\forall p : Plan;\ pa : PlanAction;\ ps : \mathbb{P}(PlanAction \times TreePlan) \bullet$
$\quad treenodes\,(Tip\,pa) = \{pa\}\ \wedge$
$\quad treenodes\,(Fork\,(ps)) = \bigcup(mapset\ treenodes\ (mapset\ second\ ps))$

$planpairs : Plan \rightarrow \mathbb{P}\,PlanAction$
$planentities : Plan \rightarrow \mathbb{P}\,EntityModel$
$planactions : Plan \rightarrow \mathbb{P}\,Action$

$\forall p : Plan \bullet$
$p \in ran\,Partial \Rightarrow$
$\quad planpairs\,p = dom(Partial^{-1}p) \cup ran(Partial^{-1}p)\ \wedge$
$\quad planentities\,p =$
$\qquad \bigcup(entitiesofPA(\!|\ (dom(Partial^{-1}p) \cup ran(Partial^{-1}p))\ |\!))\ \wedge$
$\quad planactions\,p =$
$\qquad \bigcup(actionsofPA(\!|\ (dom(Partial^{-1}p) \cup ran(Partial^{-1}p))\ |\!))\ \wedge$
$p \in ran\,Total \Rightarrow$
$\quad planpairs\,p = ran(Total^{-1}p)\ \wedge$
$\quad planentities\,p = \bigcup(entitiesofPA(\!|\ ran(Total^{-1}p)\ |\!))\ \wedge$
$\quad planactions\,p = \bigcup(actionsofPA(\!|\ ran(Total^{-1}p)\ |\!))\ \wedge$
$p \in ran\,Tree \Rightarrow$
$\quad planpairs\,p = treenodes(Tree^{-1}p)\ \wedge$
$\quad planentities\,p = \bigcup(entitiesofPA(\!|\ treenodes(Tree^{-1}p)\ |\!))\ \wedge$
$\quad planactions\,p = \bigcup(actionsofPA(\!|\ treenodes(Tree^{-1}p)\ |\!))$

5.4.4 Multi-Agent Plan-Agents

For *single*-agent systems all the actions of an executable plan must be within its capabilities specified in the predicate below.

$$\forall \, sap : PlanAgent; \; plan : Plan \; | $$
$$plan \in sap.planlibrary \; \bullet$$
$$planactions \, plan \subseteq sap.capabilities$$

By contrast, plan-agents in *multi* agent systems can consider executing plans containing actions not within their capabilities as long as they can model the capabilities of others. However, agents only able to model entities at the object level cannot make informed decisions about plan suitability, since they would attempt to involve other entities without regard to their agency or autonomy. However, if agents can distinguish agency and autonomy, they can identify neutral-objects as most appropriate for using in plans. Such agents are referred to as *multi-agent plan-agents* since they are able to evaluate the potential of involving other agents to execute their plans. This is similar to existing descriptions such as that proposed by Lux and Steiner [86], who describe multi-agent plans as plans that are executed by more than one agent.

Clearly, any entity included in an agent's plan must be modelled by that agent. Furthermore, an entity must be able to perform the actions with which it is associated in a plan *according to the models of the plan-agent*. Of course it may be that, for example, Anne thinks that Bill can help her lift a table when, due to a recent injury unknown to Anne, in fact he cannot. This problem is likely to occur frequently in multi-agent systems in which agents only have partial knowledge of the plans, goals and abilities of others. However, asserting internal consistency constraints is quite different, since they could, and should, be adhered to by any agent system design.

The precise relationship of a plan-action to an entity depends on the type of plan-action.

- If the action is a primitive action then it must be an element of the capabilities of the associated entities.
- If the action is a concurrent-primitive action then the set of actions must be a subset of the capabilities of the associated entities.
- If the action is a template-action, then at least one of the actions that belong to this set must be within the capabilities of the associated entities.
- If the action is a concurrent-template action then each of the template-actions must contain at least one action in the capabilities of any associated entity.

The schema below refines *PlanAgent*, includes *AgentModels*, and formalises these constraints.

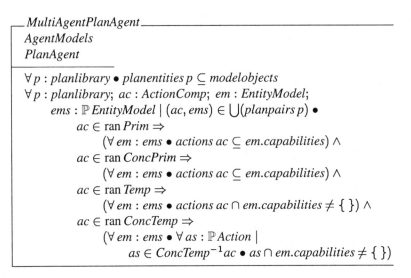

$\_\_MultiAgentPlanAgent_____$
AgentModels
PlanAgent
___

$\forall\, p : planlibrary \bullet planentities\, p \subseteq modelobjects$
$\forall\, p : planlibrary;\ ac : ActionComp;\ em : EntityModel;$
$\quad ems : \mathbb{P}\, EntityModel \mid (ac, ems) \in \bigcup(planpairs\, p) \bullet$
$\quad\quad ac \in \mathrm{ran}\, Prim \Rightarrow$
$\quad\quad\quad (\forall\, em : ems \bullet actions\, ac \subseteq em.capabilities) \wedge$
$\quad\quad ac \in \mathrm{ran}\, ConcPrim \Rightarrow$
$\quad\quad\quad (\forall\, em : ems \bullet actions\, ac \subseteq em.capabilities) \wedge$
$\quad\quad ac \in \mathrm{ran}\, Temp \Rightarrow$
$\quad\quad\quad (\forall\, em : ems \bullet actions\, ac \cap em.capabilities \neq \{\,\}) \wedge$
$\quad\quad ac \in \mathrm{ran}\, ConcTemp \Rightarrow$
$\quad\quad\quad (\forall\, em : ems \bullet \forall\, as : \mathbb{P}\, Action \mid$
$\quad\quad\quad\quad as \in ConcTemp^{-1}ac \bullet as \cap em.capabilities \neq \{\,\})$

5.4.5 Sociological Plan-Agents

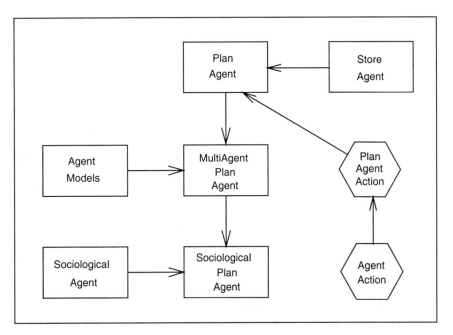

Fig. 5.4. Schema Structure for Specifying Sociological Plan-Agents

If multi-agent plan-agents are also *sociological* agents then they can make more informed choices about plan selection. Such agents are *sociological plan-agents* as defined very simply in the *SociologicalPlanAgent* schema below that includes the previous schema definitions illustrated in Figure 5.4.

```
__ SociologicalPlanAgent _____
  SociologicalAgent
  MultiAgentPlanAgent
```

To illustrate the greater reasoning capacity of sociological agents over their non-sociological counterparts, the following categories of plans and goals that can be determined only by sociological plan-agents are defined. Note that all these categories are defined with respect to the models of the sociological agent.

− A *self-sufficient plan* is any plan that involves only neutral-objects, server-agents the plan-agent owns, and the plan-agent itself. Self-sufficient plans can therefore be executed without regard to other agents, and can exploit existing agent relationships. Formally, this category is defined in the *SelfSufficientPlan* schema where *selfsufficientplans* represents the self-sufficient plans of an agent. This schema uses the relational image operator defined in the Appendix A.2.2. In general, the relational image $R(\!| \ S \ |\!)$ of a set S through a relation R is the set of all objects y to which R relates to some member x of S.

```
__ SelfSufficientPlan _____
  ModelAgentRelationships
  SociologicalPlanAgent
  selfsufficientplans : ℙ Plan
 _____
  selfsufficientplans = {p : planlibrary | planentities p ⊆
      modelneutralobjects ∪ modelself ∪ modelowns(| modelself |) • p}
```

− A *self-sufficient goal* is any goal in the goal library that has an associated self-sufficient plan. These goals can then, according to the agent's model, be achieved independently of the existing social configuration. Formally, a goal is self-sufficient if, according to the function, *plangoallibrary*, there is an associated self-sufficient plan.

```
__ SelfSufficientGoal _____
  SelfSufficientPlan
  selfsufficientgoals : ℙ Goal
 _____
  selfsufficientgoals = {g : goallibrary |
      (∃p : Plan | p ∈ plangoallibrary g • p ∈ selfsufficientplans) • g}
```

− A *reliant-goal* is any goal that has a non-empty set of associated plans that are not self-sufficient. Formally, a goal is reliant if no plan in the non-empty set of associated plans as determined by *plangoallibrary* is self-sufficient.

$\quad$ _ReliantGoal_ _____

SelfSufficientGoal
reliantgoal : $\mathbb{P}$ _Goal_

---
reliantgoal = {_g_ : _goallibrary_ | _plangoallibrary g_ ≠ { } ∧
$\quad$ ¬ (∃_p_ : _Plan_ | _p_ ∈ _plangoallibrary g_ •
$\qquad\qquad$ _p_ ∈ _selfsufficientplans_) • _g_}

For each plan that is not self-sufficient, a sociological plan-agent can establish those autonomous agents that may be affected by its execution. The number of such agents is an important criterion when a plan needs to be selected from competing alternative active plans. An autonomous agent may be affected by a plan in one of two ways: either it is required to perform an action directly, or it is engaging a server-agent required by the plan. In this latter case, a sociological plan-agent can reason about either persuading Anne to share or release _S_, taking _S_ without permission, or finding an alternative server-agent or plan as discussed in the previous section. In order that sociological agents can analyse their plans in more detail, further definitions are introduced.

- The _cooperating autonomous agents_ of a plan are those autonomous agents, other than the plan-agent itself, that are involved in performing actions of that plan. These agents will need to cooperate with the plan-agent for the plan to be executed. Formally, an agent is a cooperating autonomous agent with respect to a plan if it is contained in the set of entities required for the plan.

$\quad$ _CooperatingAgents_ _____

ModelAgentRelationships
SociologicalPlanAgent
cooperatingagents : _Plan_ → $\mathbb{P}$ _AutonomousAgentModel_

∀_p_ : _Plan_ • _cooperatingagents p_ =
$\quad$ {_a_ : _modelautonomousagents_ | _a_ ∈ _planentities p_ • _a_} \ _modelself_

- The _affected autonomous agents_ of a plan are those autonomous agents, other than the plan-agent itself, that are engaging an entity required in the plan. Formally, an autonomous agent is _affected_ with respect to a plan if there exists a server-agent contained in the set of entities required by the plan that is currently engaged by the autonomous agent. These agents _may_ need to cooperate with the plan-agent. Notice that the affected autonomous agents do not include the cooperating agents.

```
┌─ AffectedAutonomousAgents ──────────────────────────────────
│ ModelAgentRelationships
│ SociologicalPlanAgent
│ affectedautonomousagents : Plan → ℙ AutonomousAgentModel
├──────────────────────────────────────────────────────────────
│ ∀ p : Plan • affectedautonomousagents p =
│     {a : modelautonomousagents |
│         (∃ s : ServerAgent • s ∈ planentities p ∧
│             (a, s) ∈ modelengages) • a} \ modelself
└──────────────────────────────────────────────────────────────
```

– The *least-direct-fuss plans* for any reliant-goal are those plans that require the fewest number of cooperating agents.

```
┌─ LeastDirectFuss ───────────────────────────────────────────
│ ReliantGoal
│ CooperatingAgents
│ leastdirectfuss : Goal → ℙ Plan
├──────────────────────────────────────────────────────────────
│ ∀ g : reliantgoal • leastdirectfuss g =
│     {p : Plan | (p ∈ plangoallibrary g) ∧
│         ¬ (∃ q : Plan | q ∈ plangoallibrary g •
│             #(cooperatingagents q) <
│                 #(cooperatingagents p)) • p}
└──────────────────────────────────────────────────────────────
```

– The *least-fuss plans* for any reliant-goal are those plans affecting the fewest number of affected autonomous agents.

```
┌─ LeastFussPlan ─────────────────────────────────────────────
│ ReliantGoal
│ AffectedAutonomousAgents
│ leastfuss : Goal → ℙ Plan
├──────────────────────────────────────────────────────────────
│ ∀ g : reliantgoal • leastfuss g =
│     {p : Plan | (p ∈ plangoallibrary g) ∧
│         ¬ (∃ q : Plan | q ∈ plangoallibrary g •
│             #(affectedautonomousagents q) <
│                 #(affectedautonomousagents p)) • p}
└──────────────────────────────────────────────────────────────
```

The schema structure used to define these categories of plans, goals and agents is illustrated in Figure 5.5.

5.4.6 An Illustrative Example

To illustrate the value to a sociological plan-agent of being able to analyse plans using the categories above, consider an autonomous sociological plan-agent, Anne, and suppose that it models the agent relationships in its environment as follows. Autonomous agent Bill directly owns the server-agent *S*2 and directly engages *S*3, autonomous agent Claire directly engages *S*3, and Anne directly owns *S*1. In addition, in Anne's view, *O*1 and *O*2 are neutral-objects. This agent configuration can be seen in Figure 5.6 and would be represented in Anne's models as follows.

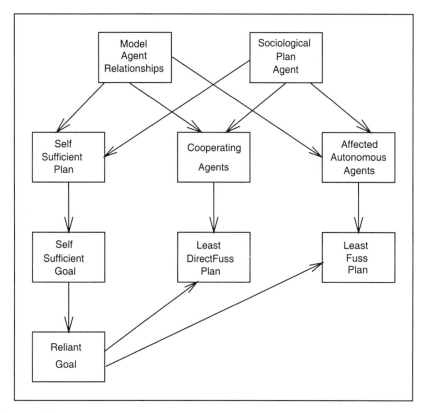

Fig. 5.5. Schema Structure for Specifying Sociological Plan Categories

$\{Anne, Bill, Claire\} \subseteq modelautonomousagents$
$\{Anne\} = modelself$
$\{S1, S2, S3\} \subseteq modelserveragents$
$\{O1, O2\} \subseteq modelneutralobjects$
$\{(Anne, S1), (Bill, S2), (Bill, S3), (Claire, S3)\} \subseteq modeldirectengagements$
$\{(Anne, S1), (Bill, S2)\} \subseteq modeldowns$

Consider also that Anne generates the goal, g_A, and activates four *total* plans p_1, p_2, p_3 and p_4 to achieve g_A as follows. The four plans are then in the set of active plans, and the pair $(g_A, \{p_1, p_2, p_3, p_4\})$ is in the function *activeplangoal* relating current goals to candidate active plans.

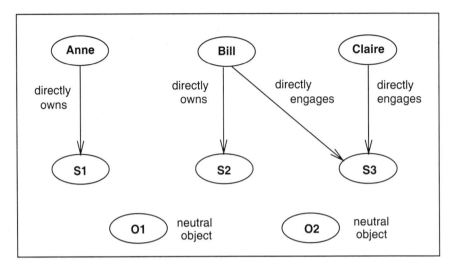

Fig. 5.6. Example: A Sociological Agent's Model

$\{g_4\} \subseteq goals$
$\{p_1, p_2, p_3, p_4\} \subseteq activeplans$
$(g_A, \{p_1, p_2, p_3, p_4\}) \in activeplangoal$

In addition, suppose the plans are as follows.

$p_1 = Total \{\{(a_1, \{Bill, Claire\}), (a_2, \{Anne\})\}, \{(a_3, \{S2, S3\})\}\}$
$p_2 = Total \{\{(a_{11}, \{O1\}), (a_1, \{Anne\})\}, \{(a_{12}, \{S1\}), (a_2, \{Anne\})\},$
$\qquad\qquad \{(a_{13}, \{O1\}), (a_3, \{Anne\})\}, \{(a_{14}, \{S1\}), (a_4, \{Anne\})\},$
$\qquad\qquad\qquad \{(a_{15}, \{O1\}), (a_5, \{Anne\})\}\}$
$p_3 = Total \{\{(a_1, \{Anne\})\}, \{(a_2, \{S3\})\}\}$
$p_4 = Total \{\{(a_1, \{Anne\})\}, \{(a_2, \{S2\})\}\}$

Notice that since in the plan p_1, the action a_1, can be performed by either the agents, Bill or Claire, and the action a_3 by either $S2$ or $S3$, there are four possible ways of executing this plan. These can be represented by p_{1_1}, p_{1_2}, p_{1_3} and p_{1_4} as follows.

$p_{1_1} = \{\{(a_1, \{Bill\}), (a_2, \{Anne\})\}, \{(a_3, \{S2\})\}\}$
$p_{1_2} = \{\{(a_1, \{Bill\}), (a_2, \{Anne\})\}, \{(a_3, \{S3\})\}\}$
$p_{1_3} = \{\{(a_1, \{Claire\}), (a_2, \{Anne\})\}, \{(a_3, \{S2\})\}\}$
$p_{1_4} = \{\{(a_1, \{Claire\}), (a_2, \{Anne\})\}, \{(a_3, \{S3\})\}\}$

The agent then has seven alternative plans for execution selection. Now, by inspection, the entities required by plan p_2 are Anne, $S1$ and $O1$.

$planentities \, p_2 = \{Anne, S1, O1\}$

The previous definition of a self-sufficient plan for an agent Anne is any plan that only requires neutral-objects, agents owned by Anne, and Anne herself. In this case the union of the set of neutral-objects, owned agents and Anne is simple to calculate.

$$modelneutralobjects \cup modelself \cup modelowns(modelself) =$$
$$\{O1, O2, Anne, S1\}$$

The set of entities required by the plan is a subset of this set which means that the plan p_2 is self-sufficient as is the associated goal g_A.

$$\{Anne, S1, O1\} \subseteq \{O1, O2, Anne, S1\} \Rightarrow p_2 \in selfsufficientplans$$
$$p_2 \in selfsufficientplans \Rightarrow g_A \in selfsufficientgoals$$

Plan	p_{1_1}	p_{1_2}	p_{1_3}	p_{1_4}	p_3	p_4
cooperating agents	{Bill}	{Bill}	{Claire}	{Claire}	{ }	{ }
affected autonomous agents	{Bill}	{Bill, Claire}	{Bill}	{Bill, Claire}	{Bill, Claire}	{Bill}

Table 5.1. Sociological Plan Evaluation Example

Anne is thus able to achieve g_A without affecting other autonomous agents and can act without regard to them, while exploiting the current set of agent relationships. However, she may decide that, even though p_2 is a self-sufficient plan, it is too costly, dismisses this possibility, and evaluates the six other alternatives to give the information shown in Table 5.1. It can be seen that the least-fuss and least-direct-fuss plans are as follows. Each of the least fuss plans affects only the one autonomous agent (in fact Bill in each case) as a result of requiring the server-agent S2 which is engaged by Bill. Both the direct least fuss plans require no cooperating agent.

$$leastfuss\ g_A = \{p_{1_1}, p_{1_3}, p_4\} \wedge leastdirectfuss\ g_A = \{p_3, p_4\}$$

Based on this analysis, p_4 may seem like the best candidate plan for execution since it does not involve the direct cooperation of other entities, and only affects one autonomous agent, Bill. The plan-agent can then analyse options concerning how to engage S2, as discussed previously. Clearly, the final decision about plan selection will be based on other considerations also such as the motivations of the plan-agent, and its models of the motivations of others affected by plans. Nevertheless, this brief example illustrates just how sociological agents can use the plan, goal and agent categories defined in this section as important criteria in evaluating alternative active plans.

5.4.7 Modelling the Plans of Others

If agents can model the plans of others, or produce agreed *multi-agent plans*, then they can *coordinate* their actions in order to achieve their local goals more effectively. In fact, many authors argue that agents *must* model the plans of others for effective coordination to occur [64, 122]. Agents can then take advantage of the plans of others to avoid duplication of effort and to avoid *conflict*, which arises, for example, when two agents require direct ownership of the same entity at the same time.

Once agents are designed with the ability to reason about the plans of other agents, bargaining can take place between agents able to help each other in their plans. As an example, suppose agent Anne has a plan that necessarily involves the cooperation of Bill. It may be appropriate for Anne to consider the plans of Bill that involve Anne's cooperation since Anne may then realise that Bill has a high-priority plan that can only be achieved with Anne's cooperation. In this case Anne would consider herself to be in a strong bargaining position. This level of modelling, where agents can model the plans of others, has been mapped out in the work of Social Dependence Networks, which are considered in detail in Chapter 8.

The actual level at which other agents are modelled is clearly critical in directing behaviour. For example, a sociological agent with models of other agents as non-sociological may realise that these agents are unable to recognise any agent relationship. The sociological agent may then be concerned that these other agents may use entities that destroy their own existing agent relationships.

Again, models of increasingly more sophisticated agents can developed incrementally. For example, a sociological agent able to model the plans of others is defined below in *SociologicalPlanAgentModelsPlanAgent*. Finally, the schema that defines agents able to model others as sociological plan-agents is given as *SociologicalPlanAgentModelsSociologicalPlanAgent*.

```
┌─ SociologicalPlanAgentModelsPlans ────────────────────────
│ SociologicalAgent
│ modelplanagents : Agent ⇸ PlanAgent
├────────────────────────────────────────────────────────────
│ dom modelplanagents ⊆ modelagents
└────────────────────────────────────────────────────────────
```

```
┌─ SociologicalPlannerModelsSociologicalPlanAgent ──────────
│ SociologicalAgent
│ modelsociologicalplanagents : Agent ⇸ SociologicalPlanAgent
├────────────────────────────────────────────────────────────
│ dom modelsociologicalplanagents ⊆ modelagents
└────────────────────────────────────────────────────────────
```

5.5 Summary

Having identified a set of inter-agent relationships that underlie all multi-agent systems, this chapter has provided models of the requisite agent dimensions for effective social functioning in such systems. We have incrementally developed the SMART framework to specify agents that:

– have an internal store;
– can model others in their environment;
– can model the agent relationships in their environment; and
– can evaluate competing plans with respect to their model of the current agent relationships.

Models are critical because effective social agents need to represent the inter-agent relationships in the environment in which they are situated. Such agents are able to reason about acting to exploit these relationships without inadvertently or unnecessarily affecting them. They can then make more enlightened choices between alternative plans based, not only on the entities involved, but the current agency obligations of the entities involved.

In general, it has been shown that computational agents able to recognise the agent relationships in their environment can reason with much more sophistication than those agents only able to model other agents. These *sociological* agents have shown their increased functionality, and it can be argued that effective agents must necessarily be sociological.

Our model of deliberative, sociological agents has been developed by extending the SMART framework, justifying the claim that it can accommodate both deliberative and reflexive agents equally. Indeed, the models of deliberative agents developed in this chapter are still generally applicable. For example, the representation of plans can be applied, and easily extended where necessary, to existing theories and systems as will be demonstrated in the remaining chapters.

Not only have the schemas of SMART been refined to develop a model of sociological agents, but it has been shown how it necessarily impacts on the design of effective agents. Similarly, it has been shown that the agent relationships previously identified affect the development of generally effective social agents who must recognise, exploit and manipulate them. The models developed in this book can, therefore, not only be used to reason about agents and their relationships, but, significantly, to develop formal descriptions of the agents themselves.

6. The Contract Net as a Goal Directed System

6.1 Introduction

The models defined in SMART provide a structure that can be applied directly to describe and analyse multi-agent systems and theories, and to derive models that highlight relevant aspects. In this chapter, the path from the initial SMART framework to the modelling of such specific systems is completed by describing a mechanism for implementing the contract net protocol.

Thee contract net protocol [24, 118, 119] is chosen as the first system to which the SMART framework is applied because it is one of the most common models of agent interaction in both real applications and simulations [101]. Equally, it has been used extensively to demonstrate the applicability of new theories and models [46, 89, 94], yet is very firmly situated in the practical and experimental camp. It is relatively well-defined and understood, and is hence very suitable to be used as an exemplar for the kind of work described here. In addition, several extensions of the contract net protocol [100, 109] have been proposed and there have also been several attempts at its formalisation [129, 133]. In specifying the contract net protocol, we build a bridge between the formality on the one hand and the practical work on the other.

Essentially, the contract net provides a mechanism by which nodes can dynamically enter into relationships in response to current needs. It has been used in manufacturing, transport systems and assembly problems, all described in more detail elsewhere (e.g. [101]).

6.2 Contract Net Protocol

In this book, a *contract net* is taken to be any system that uses the contract net protocol for *opportunistic task allocation*. A contract net is thus a collection of components, or equally, nodes that are able to take on *roles* dynamically according to *contracts*, with no pre-determined control hierarchy. A contract is an agreement between a *manager* node and a *contractor* node, resulting from contractor's successfully *bid* for the contract. In essence, the contractor agrees by this to perform a task for the manager.

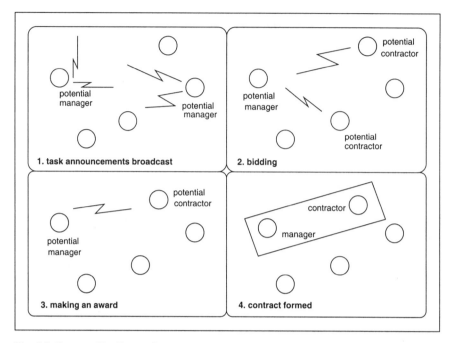

Fig. 6.1. Contract Net Protocol

Contracts are established by mutual agreement between two nodes after an ex-change of information, the structure of which is determined beforehand by the con-tract net protocol as illustrated in Figure 6.1, which is based on a diagram presented in the protocol's original description [119]. The protocol is initiated when a node is given the responsibility to undertake and satisfy a newly generated task. These tasks are decomposed into sub-tasks and, when there may be inadequate knowledge or data to undertake these sub-tasks directly, they are offered for bidding by other agents. This is achieved by a *task announcement* message that is broadcast advertis-ing this task to other nodes. The message includes information relating to the task that enables other nodes to evaluate whether or not they are suited to perform it. For example, when the contract net protocol is applied to the simulation of a distributed sensing system a task announcement includes three types of information [117].

- *Task abstraction slots* specify the identity and position of the manager that enables potential contractors to reply to the task announcement.
- *Eligibility specifications* specify the location and capabilities required by bidders.
- *Bid specifications* indicate a bidder's position and sensing capabilities.

In response to the current task announcements, nodes can evaluate their interest using *task evaluation procedures* specific to the problem at hand. If a node has suf-ficient interest in a task announcement, it will submit a bid to undertake to perform the task. The owner of the task announcement (the *manager*) selects nodes using *bid evaluation procedures* based on the information supplied in the bid. It sends *award* messages to successful bidders which then become *contractors* to the manager. These contractors may in turn subcontract parts of their task by announcing their own task announcements, and the contract net protocol is repeated with the contractor eventually becoming a manager for these sub-contracts. This leads to a hierarchical configuration in the contract net. The contractors issue reports to the manager that may be *interim* reports or *final* reports containing a result description. Finally, the manager finally terminates a contract with a *termination* message.

A key feature of the case study in this chapter is the ease with which the contract net can be accommodated in the SMART models. First, an analysis of contract net components and the inter-agent relationships between them is presented. The additional functionality required by agents to engage in the protocol, including the ability of nodes to analyse *task announcements* and make bids for *contracts* is then considered, so that the *state* of a contract net during the protocol can be modelled. The protocol itself is then defined using operations that apply to this system state; they describe how bids and task announcements are made and how contracts are awarded and terminated.

6.3 Contract Net Components

The SMART framework is refined to arrive at a formal specification of the contract net that retains the structure of the framework. The first task is to specify the different kinds of component that can be found in a system employing the contract net protocol. Next the five categories of contract net entity based on the SMART framework components are specified.

6.3.1 Nodes

A node in the contract net has capabilities and attributes such as its processing potential and physical location. A contract net node is therefore simply an object. Formally, it is defined in *ContractNetNode* that simply includes the *Object* schema.

```
┌─ ContractNetNode ─────────────────────────────────
│ Object
│
└───────────────────────────────────────────────────
```

6.3.2 Agents

A contract net agent is a node that performs a task or, equally, can be ascribed a set of goals. Such agents are defined by *ContractNetAgent*, which includes the *ContractNetNode* and *Agent* schemas.

```
┌─ ContractNetAgent ────────────────────────────────
│ ContractNetNode
│ Agent
│
└───────────────────────────────────────────────────
```

6.3.3 Monitor Agents

Davis and Smith [24] also describe a single-processor node in a distributed sensing example, called a monitor node, which starts the initialisation as the first step in the contract net operation. If this is just a node that passes on information to another, then it is no different from the manager specified above. However, if it generated the goal or task to perform, then it is autonomous. In this case monitors are defined in the *MonitorAgent* schema, which includes the *AutonomousAgent* and *ContractNetAgent* schemas.

```
┌─ CNMonitoAgent ─────────────────────────────────
│ AutonomousAgent
│ ContractNetAgent
│
└─────────────────────────────────────────────────
```

6.3.4 Idle Nodes

An *idle node* is modelled as a neutral-object. Formally, it is defined by *CNIdleNode* and includes the schemas *ContractNetNode* and *NeutralObject*.

```
┌─ CNIdleNode ─────────────────────────────────────
│ ContractNetNode
│ NeutralObject
│
└─────────────────────────────────────────────────
```

6.3.5 Server-Agents

Contract net server-agents are agents that are not autonomous. Such agents are defined by *ContractServerAgent*, which includes the schemas *ContractNetAgent* and *ServerAgent*.

```
┌─ ContractServerAgent ────────────────────────────
│ ContractNetAgent
│ ServerAgent
│
└─────────────────────────────────────────────────
```

A contract net thus comprises a set of nodes of which at least two are agents, and at least one of these is a monitor agent. Nodes in the net are either idle or agents, and agents are either monitors or server-agents. The union of *monitors* and *contractserveragents* is equal to *contractagents* and the union of *idlenodes* and *contractagents* is equal to *nodes*.

```
┌─ ContractNetEntities ──────────────────────────────────
│ nodes : ℙ ContractNetNode
│ contractagents : ℙ ContractNetAgent
│ monitors : ℙ CNMonitoAgent
│ idlenodes : ℙ CNIdleNode
│ contractserveragents : ℙ ContractServerAgent
├────────────────────────────────────────────────────────
│ monitors ⊂ contractagents ⊆ nodes
│ contractagents = monitors ∪ contractserveragents
│ nodes = idlenodes ∪ contractagents
│ #contractagents ≥ 2
│ #monitors ≥ 1
└────────────────────────────────────────────────────────
```

This schema is analogous to *MultiAgentSystem* in Section 3.2, which defines the set of entities in a multi-agent system. This analogy can be exploited directly in Z, which allows the renaming of schema components. Thus, it is possible to rename the components of the *MultiAgentSystem* schema to define the *ContractNetEntities* schema, so that the schema below is identical to the one above. The sole predicate included in the schema states that a contract net includes non-autonomous agents.

```
┌─ ContractNetEntities ──────────────────────────────────
│ MultiAgentSystem[nodes/objects,
│                  contractagents/agents,
│                  monitors/autonomousagents,
│                  idlenodes/neutralobjects,
│                  contractserveragents/serveragents]
├────────────────────────────────────────────────────────
│ monitors ⊂ contractagents
└────────────────────────────────────────────────────────
```

This completes the description of the components in a contract net, and we proceed to an analysis of the inter-agent relationships in it in terms of node dependencies by application of the relevant models from SMART.

6.4 Contract Net Relationships

When a node is awarded a contract by another, the first node is *engaged* by the second, and they become the contractor, and the manager of the contract respectively. The contractor then performs the task of the contract for the manager and sends back progress reports and results. Tasks specify states of affairs to be achieved, and have the same type as the SMART type for goals.

Task == *Goal*

Thus, a contract can be represented as a task with two distinct nodes, the manager and the contractor, both of which must be ascribed the task of the contract.

Formally, a contract is defined by the *Contract* schema below, which includes the variables, *task*, *manager* and *contractor*, such that *task* is included in the intersection of the goals of the manager and contractor. While the manager of a contract may be autonomous, the contractor must be a server-agent.

Contract

task : *Task*
manager : *ContractNetAgent*
contractor : *ContractServerAgent*

---
manager ≠ *contractor*
task ∈ (*manager.goals* ∩ *contractor.goals*)

A contract is thus a specific type of *direct engagement* in which the client of the engagement is the manager of the contract, the server is the contractor, and the goal of the engagement is the task of the contract. In this way, contracts can be defined by renaming the components of a direct engagement.

Contract

DirectEngagement[*manager*/*client*,
                contractor/*server*,
                task/*goal*]

The configuration of a contract net is the result of the set of all contracts between agents. An example of a possible configuration is shown in Figure 6.2. in which node *C* has been awarded a contract by *A* and, in turn, has awarded a contract to *I*. Formally, the set of contracts is modelled in the *ContractNetRelationships* schema: the set of managers comprises those nodes that are managing a current contract, and the set of contractors are defined similarly. The predicate part asserts that the combination of all contractors and managers from all contracts within the contract net is equal to the set of all contract net agents.

ContractNetRelationships

ContractNetEntities
contracts : ℙ *Contract*
managers : ℙ *ContractNetAgent*
contractors : ℙ *ContractServerAgent*

---
managers = {*c* : *Contract* | *c* ∈ *contracts* • *c.manager*}
contractors = {*c* : *Contract* | *c* ∈ *contracts* • *c.contractor*}
managers ∪ *contractors* = *contractagents*

Again, this schema can be derived by renaming the components of the schema, *SystemEngagements*, defined in Section 3.5.

Engagement chains as well as engagements arise naturally in a contract net. For example, in Figure 6.2, while *H* may be engaging *N* with a task that is unrelated to

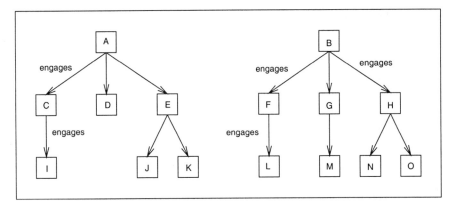

Fig. 6.2. Example: Contract Net Configuration I

the contract between B and H, it is also possible that the sequence of nodes $\langle B, H, N \rangle$ is an *engagement chain*. This arises when the contract between H and N is a direct consequence of the relationship between B and H. In fact, modelling the contract net as engagement chains is exactly right, since they reveal the inter-node dependencies for any task, and also reveal the *flow* of contracts as they are formed between agents. Moreover, if A and B are autonomous monitor nodes then A may adopt the task of B to *cooperate* with B as illustrated in Figure 6.3. It is therefore possible that cooperations as well as engagements can exist in a contract net depending on the autonomy of the agents involved. Naturally, all these can be modelled in SMART, enabling the exact relationship between any two nodes (such as direct ownership, for example) to be determined using the relationship taxonomy of Section 3.8.

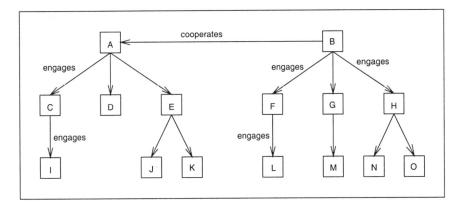

Fig. 6.3. Example: Contract Net Configuration II

6.5 Contract Net State

The model is now developed further to describe the state of the CN which, as well as including the components and their relationships, also includes the set of task announcements and bids.

6.5.1 Task Announcements

A node intending to become the manager of a contract for one of its tasks, first makes a *task announcement* that includes information relating to the task. In particular, it provides an *eligibility* specification that states the attributes and capabilities required to perform that task. A node is only *eligible* for a task if its actions and attributes satisfy the eligibility of the task announcement. Formally, *Eligibility* is a type comprising a set of actions and attributes and therefore has the same type as an object.

$Eligibility == Object$

A task announcement is issued by a *sender* to a set of *recipients* to request bids for a particular *task* from agents that match *eligibility* requirements. The sender must be an agent, whereas the recipients can be any CN node.

$Sender == ContractNetAgent$
$Recipient == ContractNetNode$

A task announcement is defined below, and comprises the prospective manager, *sender*, the non-empty set of recipients that do not include the sender, *recipients*, the task to be performed, *task*, and an eligibility requirement, *eligibility*. Notice that the combination of a task together with an eligibility is, in fact, an *agency* requirement since it specifies attributes, capabilities and goals.

$$
\begin{array}{|l}
\_\_ CNTaskAnnouncement _____ \\
sender : Sender \\
recipients : \mathbb{P}_1\,Recipient \\
task : Task \\
eligibility : Eligibility \\
\hline
sender \notin recipients \\
\end{array}
$$

6.5.2 Bids

In response to a task announcement, agents can evaluate their interest in the task by using *task evaluation procedures*. If there is sufficient interest after evaluation, agents will submit a *bid* to undertake to perform the task. Now, a bid involves a node describing a subset of itself in response to an eligibility specification that will be used in evaluating the bid. Bids are formalised by the *Bid* schema below, which includes the associated node and its eligibility.

```
__ CNBid _____
  bidnode : Recipient
  eligibility : Eligibility
  _____
  eligibility.capabilities ⊆ bidnode.capabilities
  eligibility.attributes ⊆ bidnode.attributes
```

6.5.3 System State

The state of the contract net can now be represented as the current set of nodes, contracts, task announcements and bids. Each task announcement will have associated with it a set of bids that are just eligibility specifications as described above. The following schema defines the state and includes the set of entities, contracts, task announcements and bids. Every bid is associated with a task announcement, and must have been made by a node that is in the list of recipients of that task announcement. The *taskannouncements* variable defines the current set of system task announcements.

```
__ ContractNetState _____
  ContractNetRelationships
  bids : CNTaskAnnouncement ⇸ ℙ CNBid
  taskannouncements : ℙ CNTaskAnnouncement
  _____
  taskannouncements = dom bids
  ∀ t : CNTaskAnnouncement; b : CNBid; bs : ℙ CNBid | b ∈ bs •
                    (t, bs) ∈ bids ⇒ b.bidnode ∈ t.recipients
```

6.6 Contract Net Protocol

The contact net protocol is specified as changes to the state of the contract net as the protocol progresses. Before this task is undertaken, however, some axiomatic definitions that are necessary for determining those tasks that nodes may be interested in, and how bids are ranked must be specified.

6.6.1 Axiomatic Definitions

First, each node has a means of deciding whether it is capable of, and interested in, performing certain tasks given certain eligibilities. This determines whether nodes bid for these tasks. The predicate, *interested*, holds whenever a node can bid for a task with a specific eligibility. Second, each node has a means of rating bids for the task announcements it has broadcast. This is achieved by the *rating* function, which maps the node making the rating, its task announcement and associated bid to a natural number.

$$
\begin{array}{|l}
\mathit{interested} \ \_ : \mathbb{P}(\mathit{ContractNetNode} \times \mathit{Task} \times \mathit{Eligibility}) \\
\mathit{rating} : \mathit{ContractNetNode} \nrightarrow \mathit{CNTaskAnnouncement} \nrightarrow \mathit{CNBid} \rightarrow \mathbb{N}
\end{array}
$$

In addition, it is a simple matter to define a contract net node being instantiated with a new task, and an agent removing one of its goals in terms of the SMART framework functions, *EntityAdoptGoals* and *EntityRemoveGoals*, respectively.

$$
\begin{array}{l}
\mathit{ContractNodeNewTask} == \mathit{EntityAdoptGoals} \\
\mathit{ContractNodeRemoveTask} == \mathit{EntityRemoveGoals}
\end{array}
$$

The former of these is used in the *auxiliary* function, *makecontract*, which forms a contract from its constituent components as long as the manager has the task as a goal and the contractor does not. A contract is then formed to include the newly instantiated contractor agent.

$$
\begin{array}{|l}
\mathit{makecontract} : \\
\quad \mathit{Task} \nrightarrow \mathit{ContractNetAgent} \nrightarrow \mathit{ContractNetNode} \nrightarrow \mathit{Contract} \\
\hline
\forall t : \mathit{Task}; \ m : \mathit{ContractNetAgent}; \\
\quad c : \mathit{ContractNetNode}; \ con : \mathit{Contract} \mid \\
\qquad t \in (m.\mathit{goals}) \wedge \\
\qquad t \notin (m.\mathit{goals}) \wedge \\
\qquad m \neq c \ \bullet \\
\qquad \mathit{makecontract} \ t \ c \ m = con \Leftrightarrow \\
\qquad\qquad con.\mathit{task} = t \wedge \\
\qquad\qquad con.\mathit{manager} = m \wedge \\
\qquad\qquad con.\mathit{contractor} = \mathit{ContractNodeNewTask}(c, \{t\})
\end{array}
$$

6.6.2 Making Task Announcements

When a node makes a task announcement, there is no change to the node dependencies, so that the components and contracts remain unaltered. Any node that issues a task announcement must be an agent since it must have a current task. In addition, both the recipients and the sender must be nodes, the task must be in the goals of the sender, and the sender must not be able to satisfy the eligibility requirements of the task alone. As a result of this operation, a new system task announcement is created that is associated with an empty set of bids, since at this time none will have been offered for it. The operation is defined formally in the next schema, which changes *ContractNetState* but not *ContractNetRelationships*. The preconditions of the operation ensure that the task announcement is well-defined, and that the announcing agent does not have the eligibility to perform the associated task.

CNMakeTaskAnnouncement _____
$\Delta ContractNetState$
$\Xi ContractNetRelationships$
$an?$: $ContractNetAgent$
$ta?$: $CNTaskAnnouncement$

$an? \in nodes$
$ta?.recipients \subseteq nodes$
$ta?.sender = an?$
$ta?.task \in an?.goals$
$\neg \, (ta?.eligibility.capabilities \subseteq an?.capabilities \, \wedge$
$\qquad\qquad ta?.eligibility.attributes \subseteq an?.attributes)$
$bids' = bids \cup \{(ta?, \{\})\}$
$taskannouncements' = taskannouncements \cup \{ta?\}$

6.6.3 Making Bids

In response to a task announcement, a node may make a bid as long as it is both eligible for, and interested in, the task. This bid is then added to the set of previous bids received in response to the task announcement, but again the state of the inter-node relationships is unaffected by this operation. Formalised in the schema below, it includes preconditions to ensure that nodes can only bid for task announcements for which they are recipients. As a result of a node making a bid, the set of task announcements does not change, but the bids associated with the task announcement are updated to include the new bid. The final predicate defining this update to the *bids* function uses the relational override operator which is defined in Appendix A.2.2. Essentially, the relation $R \oplus S$ relates everything in the domain of S to the same objects as S alone does, and everything else in the domain of R to the same objects as R alone.

$MakeBid$ _____
$\Delta ContractNetState$
$\Xi ContractNetRelationships$
$biddingnode? : ContractNetNode$
$bid? : CNBid$
$ta? : CNTaskAnnouncement$

$bid?.bidnode = biddingnode?$
$biddingnode? \in nodes$
$ta? \in taskannouncements$
$biddingnode? \in ta?.recipients$
$ta?.eligibility.capabilities \subseteq bid?.eligibility.capabilities$
$ta?.eligibility.attributes \subseteq bid?.eligibility.attributes$
$interested\ (biddingnode?, ta?.task, ta?.eligibility)$
$taskannouncements' = taskannouncements$
$bids' = bids \oplus \{(ta?, bids\ ta? \cup \{bid?\})\}$

6.6.4 Awarding Contracts

After receiving bids, the issuer of a task announcement awards the contract to the highest rated bid. In order to choose the best bid with respect to a task announcement, the *rating* function is used to select the bid with the highest rating and form a contract with that node. Since a new contract is formed, the set of relationships is updated to include a contract for the task with the issuer of the task announcement as manager, and the awarded bidder as contractor.

In the following schema, which describes the owner of the task announcement awarding a contract to a bidder, the set of agent relationships in the contract net is altered as well as the state. Here, the new contract, formed between the owner (as manager) and the contract server-agent that results from instantiating the bidding node with the additional task, is added to the set of system contracts. If the bidding agent was an idle node prior to the operation, then it must be removed from the set of idle nodes. Similarly, if the node was previously an agent then it must be removed from the set of agents. In both cases, the set of agents is updated to include the newly instantiated contractor. Finally, the task announcement is removed from the set of task announcements and from the domain of the *bids* function using the anti-domain restriction operator defined in Appendix A.2.2.

__CNAwardContract_____
Δ*ContractNetState*
man? : *ContractNetAgent*
ta? : *CNTaskAnnouncement*
bid? : *CNBid*

---
man? $=$ *ta?.sender*
bid? $\in$ *bids ta?*
$\forall\, b : CNBid \mid b \in bids\ ta?\ \bullet$
    rating man? ta? bid? $\geq$ *rating man? ta? b*
contracts' $=$ *contracts* $\cup$
    $\{makecontract\ ta?.task\ man?\ bid?.bidnode\}$
contractagents' $=$ *contractagents* $\cup$
    $\{ContractNodeNewTask(bid?.bidnode, \{ta?.task\})\}$
bid?.bidnode $\in$ *idlenodes* $\Rightarrow$
    idlenodes' $=$ *idlenodes* $\setminus \{bid?.bidnode\}$ $\wedge$
    contractagents' $=$ *contractagents* $\cup$
            $\{ContractNodeNewTask(bid?.bidnode, \{ta?.task\})\}$
bid?.bidnode $\in$ *contractserveragents* $\Rightarrow$
    contractagents' $=$ $(contractagents \setminus \{bid?.bidnode\}) \cup$
            $\{ContractNodeNewTask(bid?.bidnode, \{ta?.task\})\}$
taskannouncements' $=$ *taskannouncements* $\setminus \{ta?\}$
bids' $=$ $\{ta?\} \lhd bids$

6.6.5 Terminating Contracts

Finally, a manager can terminate a contract with one of its contractors. Here, the task of the contract is removed from the contractor's goals and this (former) contractor may revert to being an agent with fewer goals, or to an idle node. Here, the situation where the manager retains the task of the contract is specified, though it may be possible that in some situations the task is also dropped by the manager. In the following schema, if the formerly contracted node is still an agent, then it remains in the set of agents. However, if the node had one task only, it is removed from the set of agents and added to the set of idle nodes.

_CNTerminateContract_____

Δ_ContractNetState_
man?, con? : _ContractNetAgent_
_t?_ : _Task_
contract? : _Contract_

_____

contract?.task = t?
contract?.manager = man?
contract?.contractor = con?
contract? $\in$ _contracts_
contracts' = contracts \ {contract?}
ContractNodeRemoveTask (con?, {t?}) $\in$ _ContractNetAgent_ $\Rightarrow$
    contractagents' = (contractagents \ {con?}) $\cup$
        {ContractNodeRemoveTask(con?, {t?})}
ContractNodeRemoveTask (con?, {t?}) $\notin$ _ContractNetAgent_ $\Rightarrow$
    contractagents' = contractagents \ {con?} $\wedge$
    idlenodes' =
        idlenodes $\cup$ _{ContractNodeRemoveTask (con?, {t?})}_

The schemas describing the award and termination of contracts are analogous to the _SystemEngage_ and _SystemDisengage_ schemas describing the making and breaking of engagements presented in Chapter 4.

6.7 Summary

Structurally, the specification describing the components and relationships of a system that employs the contract net protocol is shown in Figure 6.4. Both the contract net components and the relationships between them are derived from the SMART framework. At run-time, the state of the contract net is defined by including the set of bids and task announcements which, in turn, are all defined using SMART components, and is modelled by four operation schemas on the system state, as shown in Figure 6.5.

By applying SMART to the contract net protocol a formal specification has been produced that serves to make precise both the operation of nodes in the contract net and the state of the contract net at various points during the protocol. The nature of the dependencies between the nodes in the contract net can be readily explicated according to the agent relationships model. Indeed, the contract net protocol provides exemplars of the engagements and engagement chains described earlier.

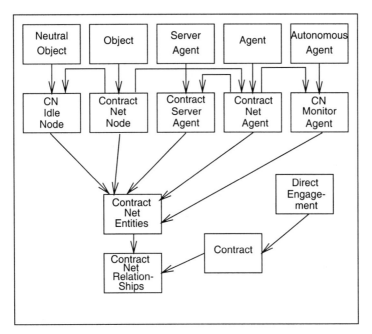

Fig. 6.4. Schema Structure for Specifying Contract Net Components and Relationships

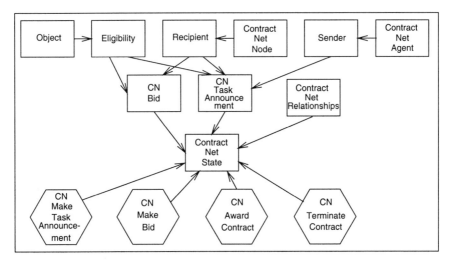

Fig. 6.5. Schema Structure for Specifying Contract Net Protocol

7. Computational Architecture for BDI Agents

7.1 Introduction

While many different and contrasting single-agent architectures have been proposed, perhaps the most successful are those based on the belief-desire-intention (BDI) framework. There is a wealth of research that has accumulated on both the formal and theoretical aspects of BDI agents through the use and development of various logics, for example, on the one hand, and on the practical aspects through the development of implementations of BDI agents on the other. Indeed, so many deliberative agent architectures and systems are based on the BDI framework that it is viewed as being as central to single-agent systems as the contract net is to multi-agent systems.

However, there is a fragmentation between the theoretical and practical BDI camps. In response to this the agent programming language AgentSpeak(L) was developed to provide an abstraction for implemented BDI systems such as PRS and dMARS. This example is chosen for the following reasons: it is a representative of a large family of systems inspired by the BDI framework that figure so predominantly in agent-based work; it is an attempt to integrate theoretical and practical concerns; and it demonstrates how specific agent architectures may be incorporated into SMART. Part of this latter issue has already demonstrated by applying the SMART models to *tropistic* and *hysteretic* agents. However, the SMART framework ought to apply as equally to more sophisticated architectures such as AgentSpeak(L).

In this chapter, a computational architecture that implements the agent language AgentSpeak(L) is developed by application of the generic skeletal architectures of SMART. A complete specification of a working architecture is not provided here as we only wish to show how the main components can be readily and simply accommodated within the framework. A complete specification, together with a more detailed exposition, can be found elsewhere [35].

7.2 AgentSpeak(L)

The basic operation of agents in AgentSpeak(L) is constructed around their beliefs, desires and intentions. An agent has beliefs (about itself and the environment), desires (in terms of the states it wants to achieve in response) and intentions as adopted plans. In addition, agents also maintain a repository of available plans, known as the *plan library*. Agents respond to changes in their goals and beliefs, which result from perception, and which are packaged into data structures called *events*, representing either new beliefs or new goals. They respond to these changes by selecting plans from the plan library for each change and then instantiating one of these plans as an intention. These intentions comprise plans which, in turn, comprise actions and goals to be achieved, with the latter possibly giving rise to the addition of new plans to that intention.

The operation of an AgentSpeak(L) agent can be summarised as follows.

− If there are more events to process, select one.
− Retrieve from the plan library all the plans *triggered* by this event that can be executed in the current circumstances.
− Select for execution one of the plans thus generated, and generate an *instance* of that plan, known as the *intended means*.
− Add the intended means to the appropriate intention. This will be a new intention in the case of an external event arising through changes to beliefs, and an existing intention in the case of an internal event resulting from attempting to satisfy a goal in that intention.
− Select an intention and consider the next step in its top plan. If this is an action, perform it, and if it is a goal, add a corresponding event to the set of events yet to be processed.
− If the top plan is complete, consider the next plan; if the intention is empty, then it has succeeded and can be removed from the set of intentions.

This description captures the essential operation of AgentSpeak(L) agents. More detail will be added to the description, however, when the operation cycle is elaborated further with the formal specification that follows.

7.3 Types

Designing an AgentSpeak(L) agent consists of building its plan library. The agent is initialised with a set of *beliefs* and *events*, which are processed during run-time by manipulating a set of *intentions*. Therefore, the store of an AgentSpeak(L) agent comprises plans (which are fixed), beliefs, events and intentions (which are all are in flux). As when defining the knowledge-level agents in Section 5.2, we provide a semantics for the SMART attributes type. An AgentSpeak(L) attribute is either a plan, intention, event or belief.

$$Attribute ::= plan\langle\!\langle ASPlan \rangle\!\rangle$$
$$| \quad intention\langle\!\langle ASIntention \rangle\!\rangle$$
$$| \quad event\langle\!\langle ASEvent \rangle\!\rangle$$
$$| \quad belief\langle\!\langle ASBelief \rangle\!\rangle$$

Next, each of these four different attribute types is specified.

7.3.1 Beliefs

Beliefs are either *belief literals* or conjunctions of two beliefs.

ASBelief ::= *ASliteral*⟨⟨*ASLiteral*⟩⟩ | *and*⟨⟨*ASBelief* × *ASBelief*⟩⟩

A belief literal is either an *atom* or the *negation* of an atom, where atoms are defined in Section 5.2.

ASLiteral ::= *pos*⟨⟨*Atom*⟩⟩ | *not*⟨⟨*Atom*⟩⟩

For example, if the type, *Atom*, contained only the elements $P(X, Y)$ and $Q(Y)$, then the type, *ASLiteral*, would be equal to the following set.

$\{not\ P(X, Y), pos\ P(X, Y), not\ Q(Y), pos\ Q(Y)\}$

7.3.2 Events

Events are the addition or deletion of a *trigger*, which is either a belief or a *goal*, and may also be associated with an *intention*. In AgentSpeak(L), events result either from an external source, in which case they are just external triggering events unrelated to an intention, or from the execution of a current intention, in which case they are (subgoal) triggering events with an explicit connection to an intention. Thus, the *Event* type is defined as follows, where *int* represents an *optional* intention. (The definitions of *optional* and related concepts, *defined*, *undefined* and *the*, can be found in Section 4.2).

ASEvent
trig : *ASTriggerEvent*
int : *optional* [*ASIntention*]

ASTrigger ::= *bel*⟨⟨*ASBelief*⟩⟩ | *goal*⟨⟨*ASGoal*⟩⟩
TriggerSymbol ::= *add* | *remove*
ASTriggerEvent == *TriggerSymbol* × *ASTrigger*

As stated above, in an external event, the intention is not defined, while in an internal event, it is defined.

ASExternalEvent
ASEvent
---
undefined int

ASInternalEvent
ASEvent
---
defined int

Goals are defined as either *achieving* an atom (making some predicate true) or *querying* an atom (testing whether some predicate is true).

$ASGoal ::= achieve\langle\!\langle Atom\rangle\!\rangle \mid query\langle\!\langle Atom\rangle\!\rangle$

7.3.3 Plans

Plans in AgentSpeak(L) comprise three components. The *invocation condition* details the circumstances, in terms of beliefs or goals, that have caused a plan to be triggered. Similarly, a *context* specifies the beliefs of the agent that must hold for the plan to be selected for execution. Finally, the part of the plan that specifies the sequence of *formulae* the agent needs to perform is known as the plan *body*. This determines what the agent must *do*.

```
__ASPlan_____
 inv : ASTriggerEvent
 context : ℙ ASBelief
 body : seq ASFormula
```

A formula is either an *action* to be executed, an 'achieve goal' to be satisfied, or a test goal to be answered.

$ASFormula ::= actionformula\langle\!\langle ASAction\rangle\!\rangle \mid goalformula\langle\!\langle ASGoal\rangle\!\rangle$

Actions are represented by an *action symbol* and a sequence of terms.

[*ActionSym*]

```
__ASAction_____
 name : ActionSym
 terms : seq Term
```

Consider a very simple example of a plan, given below, which is triggered whenever a compulsive robot car-thief finds itself next to a car. In order to select this plan, the robot must believe that the car is empty. The plan body, which details how to gain control of the car, consists of a sequence of formulae. In this case, the robot must first perform the primitive action to move to the car, then the primitive action to get in the car, and then achieve the subgoal to start the car. The actual achievement of this subgoal may require further plans.

$inv = (+, belief \; \texttt{adjacent(Robot, Car)})$
$context = \{literal \; (pos \; \texttt{empty(Car)})\}$
$body = \langle actionformula \; \texttt{MoveTo(Car)}, actionformula \; \texttt{GetIn(Car)},$
$\qquad\qquad\qquad goalformula \; (achieve \; \texttt{Start(Car)})\rangle$

7.3.4 Intentions

Intentions are simply non-empty sequences of plans that need to be executed in order.

$$ASIntention \; == \; \text{seq}_1 \, ASPlan$$

7.4 AgentSpeak(L) Agents

Now that formal descriptions of the mental components and data structures of AgentSpeak(L) agents have been developed, it is now possible to consider how they can be incorporated to define the agents themselves. Specifically, this can be achieved by refining the SMART model of a store-agent, defined in Section 5.2, because the agent will need an internal repository to store its library of plans as defined below.

$$
\begin{array}{|l}
\underline{ASAgent} \\
\; StoreAgent \\
\; planlibrary : \mathbb{P} \, ASPlan \\
\hline
\; store = plan(\!| \; planlibrary \;|\!) \\
\end{array}
$$

The *state* of an agent at run-time includes the agent's beliefs, intentions and events as well as its plan library. In addition, the set of attributes the agent can perceive from its *internal* store is defined by the current value of the variable *events*. If *events* is non-empty, the agent chooses an event to process as determined by the function *eventselect*, specified below. The function *storecanperceive* is thus the identity function since it can perceive all its events, and the function *willperceive*, which is independent of the agent's goals, is simply equal to the function *eventselect*. According to the SMART models, the possible percepts of an AgentSpeak(L) agent at any time are simply the set of events in its store. (The *posspercepts* variable is defined in the *ASAgentState* schema in Section 2.4).

Although this is not mentioned in Rao's original description, it is also necessary to record the *status* of each current intention, in order to ensure that when intentions become *suspended* they are not selected for execution.

$$
\begin{array}{|l}
\; eventselect : \mathbb{P}_1 \, ASEvent \rightarrow ASEvent \\
\end{array}
$$

$$Status ::= active \mid suspended$$

┌─ *ASAgentState* ───
│ *StoreAgentState*
│ *ASAgent*
│ *beliefs* : $\mathbb{P}\,ASBelief$
│ *intentions* : $\mathbb{P}\,ASIntention$
│ *events* : $\mathbb{P}\,ASEvent$
│ *status* : $ASIntention \nrightarrow Status$
├──
│ $store = plan(\!|\,planlibrary\,|\!) \cup intention(\!|\,intentions\,|\!) \cup$
│ $event(\!|\,events\,|\!) \cup belief(\!|\,beliefs\,|\!)$
│ $\forall\,as : \mathbb{P}\,Attribute;\ gs : \mathbb{P}\,Goal \mid as \subseteq (\mathrm{ran}\,event) \bullet$
│ $storecanperceive\ as\ internalperceivingactions = as \wedge$
│ $willperceive\ gs\ as =$
│ $\{event\ (eventselect\ \{a : as \bullet event^{-1}\,a\})\}$
│ $posspercepts = \{s : store \mid s \in (\mathrm{ran}\,event) \bullet s\}$
│ $\mathrm{dom}\,status = intentions$
└──

The beliefs and events are supplied when the agent is initialised, at which time the set of intentions is empty.

┌─ *ASStartAgent* ───
│ $\Delta ASAgentState$
│ *beliefs?* : $\mathbb{P}\,ASBelief$
│ *events?* : $\mathbb{P}\,ASEvent$
├──
│ $store' = store \cup event(\!|\,events?\,|\!) \cup belief(\!|\,beliefs?\,|\!)$
│ $store' \cap (\mathrm{ran}\,intention) = \{\}$
└──

Now that the AgentSpeak(L) agent has been defined, as well as its general and initial state, it is possible to specify its actual operation.

7.5 AgentSpeak(L) Agent Operation

At any time an agent may receive a new *external* event that is added to the store, but agents have no choice about the events they receive from the external environment. This is modelled by defining the SMART function *extcanperceive* (which has so far left unspecified for the AgentSpeak(L) agent) as the identity function.

$\underline{\quad ASNewExternalEvent \quad\underline{\qquad\qquad\qquad\qquad\qquad\qquad\qquad}}$
attribute? : *Attribute*
ΔASAgentState

---

attribute? ∈ (ran *event*)
store' = *store* ∪ {*attribute?*}
∀ *as* : ℙ *Attribute* | *as* ⊆ (ran *event*) •
    extcanperceive as externalperceivingactions = *as*

While the perception of an AgentSpeak(L) agent is straightforward and amounts to an agent processing an event, the mechanism by which it selects its actions through executing intentions is not. The former is illustrated in Figure 7.1 and is described below.

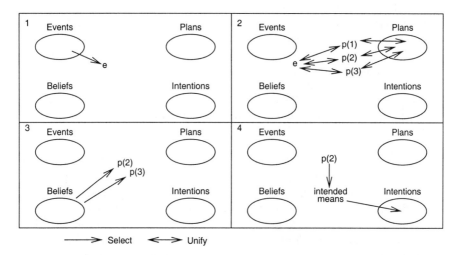

Fig. 7.1. Updating Intentions in Response to a Perceived Event in AgentSpeak(L)

1. The agent selects an event (*e*).
2. The agent generates all the plans whose invocation condition matches[1] this event. These plans are known as the *relevant* plans ({*p*(1), *p*(2), *p*(3)}) and are generated using the function *genrelplans* which is applied to the selected event and the plan library. Only the signature of this function is presented here.

$$\mid genrelplans : ASEvent \to \mathbb{P} ASPlan \to \mathbb{P} ASPlan$$

---

[1] Defining this 'matching' requires a detailed specification of the standard aspects of unification. This is not provided here since it is unnecessary for the treatment of agent architecture in this chapter. Details can be found in [51], pages 66-67.

3. From these relevant plans, the agent identifies those with pre-conditions that are currently satisfied with respect to the agent's beliefs. These plans are called *applicable* plans ($\{p(2), p(3)\}$) and are generated using the function *genapplplans*, which is applied to the relevant plans and the current set of beliefs.

$$\mid \quad genapplplans : \mathbb{P}\, ASPlan \rightarrow \mathbb{P}\, ASBelief \rightarrow \mathbb{P}\, ASPlan$$

4. If there are several plans that are applicable, one is chosen nondeterministically (by applying the function *planselect* specified below). The set of bindings used to unify the trigger and context with the selected event and current beliefs is called a *unifier*, and is found by applying the function *unify* to the selected plan, beliefs and selected event. The unifier is applied to the selected plan using the function *ApplySub*, and the resulting plan (the intended means), is therefore a partially instantiated copy of the plan chosen from the plan library. The agent's intentions are then updated in the following way: if the selected event is external, a new intention is generated with an active status; if the selected event is internal, the plan is added to the head of the intention that posted it, and the status of this intention is reset to active.

$$\begin{aligned}
&planselect : \mathbb{P}_1\, ASPlan \rightarrow ASPlan \\
&ApplySub : Substitution \rightarrow ASPlan \rightarrow ASPlan \\
&unify : ASPlan \rightarrow \mathbb{P}\, ASBelief \rightarrow ASEvent \rightarrow Substitution
\end{aligned}$$

The schema below specifies an AgentSpeak(L) agent processing an event (*selectedevent*), generating the relevant plans (*relevantplans*) and the applicable plans (*applicableplans*), selecting one of these (*selectedplan*), and applying the unifier (*applicableunifier*) that was used to match this plan with the selected event and current beliefs to generate the intended means (*intendedmeans*). The way in which the intentions are updated then depends on whether the selected event is internal or external as described above. The pre-condition simply states that the operation can only occur when there are events to process.

___ASProcessEvent_____
| $\Delta ASAgentState$
|_____
| $events \neq \varnothing$
| **let** $selectedevent == eventselect\ events\ \bullet$
| **let** $relevantplans == genrelplans\ selectedevent\ planlibrary\ \bullet$
| **let** $applicableplans == genapplplans\ relevantplans\ beliefs\ \bullet$
| **let** $selectedplan == planselect\ applicableplans\ \bullet$
| **let** $applicableunifier == unify\ selectedplan\ selectedevent\ beliefs\ \bullet$
| **let** $intendedmeans == ApplySub\ applicableunifier\ selectedplan\ \bullet$
| $selectedevent \in ASExternalEvent \Rightarrow$
| $(intentions' = intentions \cup \{\langle intendedmeans \rangle\} \wedge$
| $status' = status \cup \{(\langle intendedmeans \rangle, active)\}) \wedge$
| $selectedevent \in ASInternalEvent \Rightarrow$
| (**let** $oldintention == (\ the\ selectedevent.int)\ \bullet$
| **let** $newintention == \langle intendedmeans \rangle \frown oldintention\ \bullet$
| $(intentions' = (intentions \setminus \{oldintention\}) \cup \{newintention\} \wedge$
| $status' = (\{oldintention\} \lhd status) \cup \{(newintention, active)\}))$

The agent's other mode of operation is the execution of intentions. During this phase the agent selects an intention (*selectedintention*) and attempts to execute the next formula (*executingformula*) in the topmost plan (*executingplan*). There are three cases depending on whether the formula is an achieve goal, a query goal or an action.

First, if the formula is an achieve goal, it is assumed that it cannot immediately be achieved, and a goal event (sometimes called an internal event) is created. This event is added to the set of events in the store for future processing, and it alerts the agent to finding a plan to achieve the goal so that the execution of the current intention stack can continue. The schema below includes a reference to the auxiliary function *MakeEvent*, which simply constructs an element of type *Event* from its constituent components.

___ASPostAchieveGoal_____
| $\Delta ASAgentState$
|_____
| $executingformula \in ran\ goalformula$
| $(goalformula^{-1}\ executingformula) \in ran\ achieve$
| **let** $achievegoal == goalformula^{-1}\ executingformula\ \bullet$
| $events' = events \cup$
| $\{MakeEvent\ ((add, goal\ achievegoal), \{selectedintention\})\}$

In this case, the intention becomes suspended so that it cannot be chosen for execution until the newly-posted subgoal has been achieved.

```
__ ASSuspendIntention _____
  ΔASAgentState
 _____
  status' = status ⊕ {(selectedintention, suspended)}
```

Second, if the formula is a query goal that can be unified (matched) with the set of current beliefs, then the substitution that achieves this unification is applied to the rest of the executing plan. In the following schema, *querygoal* represents the query goal and *mgu* represents the substitution that unifies the query goal with the beliefs, found by applying *mguquery* to *querygoal* and *beliefs*. The *executingplan'* variable, which represents the state of the executing plan after the operation, is the result of applying the bindings in *mgu* to the variables in *executingplan*.

```
__ ASAchieveQueryGoal _____
  ΔASAgentState
 _____
  executingformula ∈ ran goalformula
  goalformula⁻¹ executingformula ∈ ran query
  let querygoal == goalformula⁻¹ executingformula •
  let mgu == mguquery(querygoal, beliefs) •
       executingplan' = ApplySub mgu executingplan
```

In the third case, the formula is an action that is posted for future performance to a buffer called *actionbuffer* as described in the schema below.

```
__ ASPostAction _____
  actionbuffer, actionbuffer' : ℙ Action
  ΔASAgentState
 _____
  executingformula ∈ ran actionformula
  actionbuffer' = actionbuffer ∪ {actionformula⁻¹ executingformula}
```

In the last two of these cases, the executing formula is removed from the executing plan. If there is then no next formula in the executing plan, but a next plan in the selected intention, the unifier of the invocation condition of the *second plan* on the stack and the invocation of the *executing plan* is found, and this substitution is applied to the second plan in the stack. If there is no next formula and no next plan, then the intention has succeeded since it is empty, and can be removed from the set of intentions. (Note that this latter possibility is not addressed in Rao's original operational semantics [104], but is an important case that demands explicit consideration. Though this case and the previous one are not specified here, a formal treatment of both can be found elsewhere [35].)

In addition, according to SMART, there are aspects of the general operation of an agent that are not considered by AgentSpeak(L). First, it does not specify the performance of the actions contained in the agent's buffer and second, it does not detail how actions change the state of the environment (defined by the framework functions *agentactions* and *effectinteraction*). It is thus possible to identify omissions in the scope of the language which need to be addressed before it can provide a comprehensive definition of the operation of an agent in practice.

7.6 Summary

In this chapter, it has been shown how the set of generic templates from the SMART store-agent model can be applied to formalise the specific architecture of AgentSpeak(L) agents. First, the representation of attributes required to model the mental and data components of the store of an AgentSpeak(L) agent are defined. These are then incorporated to define the architecture of the AgentSpeak(L) agent by refining the schemas of the SMART model for store-agents, which specify perception and action capabilities. Finally, after the agent's state at run-time is described, the operation of the agent is specified.

This reformalisation has revealed a number of errors and omissions in the original formulation, including some relating to the specification of aspects of binding and plans, an omission of one possible case in the agent operation cycle, and the incorrect assertion that an intention stack can only be executed if the event queue is non-empty, which is inappropriate. In developing the specification, we add to the original work of Rao, and progress beyond the description of a particular language, by giving a formal specification of a general belief-desire-intention architecture that can be used as the basis for providing such formal specifications of more sophisticated systems. By using the standard Z specification language, the problem is tackled from a software engineering perspective and make the specification accessible and amenable to implementation by providing a clean and explicit representation of the state and operations on state (including identifying data structures required for operation) that must underlie any implementation.

8. Evaluating Social Dependence Networks

8.1 Introduction

Social dependence networks [112] (SDNs) are structures that form the basis of a computational model of *social power theory* as originally proposed by Castelfranchi [10]. Essentially, they are taxonomies of social relationships that can be derived from the 'power' agents have over one another as a result of their ability to achieve each other's goals. Based on these taxonomies, *social reasoning mechanisms* have been developed by which agents can reason about inter-agent dependencies.

In this chapter SDNs are reformulated for two key reasons. First, in contrast to the lower-level concerns of practical implemented systems of particular relevance in industrial applications (such as the contract net and BDI systems), SDNs have not been applied or evaluated in the same way. The SMART framework is equally applicable to both implemented systems and theoretical models, and social dependence networks provide a suitable counterpoint to the case-studies of the previous chapters. Second, the SDN model is of particular relevance to this book since it provides a taxonomy of inter-agent relationships similar in spirit to our own. It is therefore appropriate to analyse the model in terms of SMART.

8.2 Social Dependence Networks

Social power theory (SPT) is relevant to multi-agent systems because it attempts to provide an explanation of why autonomous agents adopt the goals of others. The theory is proposed by Castelfranchi, partly as a reaction against the assumption of *benevolence* in the design of agents in distributed agent architectures [8, 12], which requires that agents always adopt the goals of others whenever they are able to do so. Castelfranchi states that benevolence severely limits the behavioural possibilities of agents and argues for accounts of more *autonomous* goal adoption. SPT is proposed as a mechanism for determining why non-benevolent agents adopt each other's goals.

The theory is based on notions of *dependence* and *reciprocation*, which arise because agents have limited capabilities and resources and may therefore depend on others to achieve their goals. If an agent depends on another for one of its goals, then the latter agent has *power* over the former. This power provides an explanation of why the former agent may autonomously adopt the goals of the latter. For example, suppose that agent A has the goal g_A, which requires the action a to achieve it. If a is not in the capabilities of A, but in the capabilities of another agent B, then B is said to have power over A. In this situation, B may be able to persuade A to adopt another goal because of this power, and the autonomous agents can *reciprocate*. Now, based on these notions, the Social Dependence Network (SDN) model was developed, relying on the following premises.

- Each agent has goals, actions, resources and plans.
- Goals are achieved by plans.
- Goals are associated with a set of plans to achieve that goal.
- Plans are sequences of actions.
- Each action in a plan may require resources.
- Each plan may require resources.
- Some resources are owned by agents.
- Agents maintain a model, called an *external description*, of the goals, actions, resources and plans of all system agents. An example of an external description can be found in Table 8.1, taken from Sichman et al. [112].

ag_j	$G(ag_j)$	$A(ag_j)$	$R(ag_j)$	$P(ag_j)$
jamie	$g1$	$a1$	$r1$	$g1 := a3(r1).$
	$g2$			$g2 := a6(r1), a7(r2).$
	$g3$			$g3 := a1(r1), a7(r2).$
	$g4$			$g4 := a1(r1), a4(r5), a5(r4).$
rosaria	$g1$	$a2$	$r2$	$g1 := a2(r2).$
cristiano	$g5$	$a3$	$r3$	$g5 := a3(r3).$
vittorio	$g4$	$a4$	$r4$	$g4 := a4(r5), a5(r4).$
maria	$g4$	$a5$	$r5$	$g4 := a1(r1), a5(r7).$
amedea	$g3$	$a6$	$r6$	$g3 := a6(r6).$
paola	$g2$	$a7$	$r7$	$g2 := a5(r1), a7(r2).$
	$g3$			$g3 := a1(r2), a6(r3).$

Table 8.1. Example: An External Description

In this table, Jamie has four goals ($g1$, $g2$, $g3$ and $g4$), is able to perform one action ($a1$), owns one resource ($r1$), and has a plan for achieving each of the four goals. The plan for achieving $g1$, for example, consists of performing the action $a3$ using resource $r1$. However, since Cristiano is the only agent capable of performing $a1$, in the situation where Jamie wishes to achieve $g1$, Cristiano is said to have "social power" over Jamie.

– Any two agents have the same external description of any other agent including themselves.

All subsequent inter-agent relationships in the SDN model are defined with respect to the external descriptions of agents analysing their situation with respect to *the set of plans of an agent to achieve a goal*. These plans can either belong to the reasoning agent or to any other agent in the system. The presentation of the SDN model falls readily into three aspects discussed below.

8.2.1 Action and Resource Autonomy

An agent can establish its autonomy with respect to a goal and any set of plans an agent has to achieve that goal. Specifically, agents are *a-autonomous* with respect to a set of plans to achieve a goal if there is a plan in the set that has actions within the agent's capabilities. Similarly, agents are *r-autonomous* if they own all the resources required in a plan, and *s-autonomous* if they are both *a-autonomous* and *r-autonomous*. It is important to note that these categories, and the ones that follow, are determined with respect to the set of plans of *any* agent to achieve that goal. An agent A can determine whether B has the capabilities and resources to achieve its goal, according to the plans of either A, B, or some other agent, C.

8.2.2 Dependence Relations

If agents are not autonomous with respect to a goal according to a set of plans as described above, they will depend on other agents for actions or resources in order to achieve it. Such situations are modelled using *dependence relations*. Agents either *a-depend*, *r-depend* or *s-depend* according to whether the dependence is for actions, resources or both.

8.2.3 Dependence Situations

The entire set of dependence relations between agents provides a *dependence network*, which can be used to establish the *dependence situations* for any two agents. Depending on whether agent A depends on B, or whether B depends on A, for either the same or for different goals, four dependence situations can be established. An agent A can be either *independent*, *unilaterally dependent*, *mutually dependent* or *reciprocally dependent* on another agent B.

In the rest of the chapter SDN model is reformulated using SMART.

8.3 External Descriptions

8.3.1 Introduction

The original formalisation of external descriptions can be found in Table 8.2. An agent, ag_i, has a set of external descriptions of the other agents and itself, as formalised in the first definition. Each external description that agent ag_i has of ag_j is denoted by $Ext_{ag_i}(ag_j)$, formalised in the next definition, and consisting of the goals, actions, resources and plans that ag_i believes ag_j possesses. Goals, actions and resources are defined textually as those an agent "wants to achieve", those an agent is "able to perform" and those over which an agent has "control". Plans, which are formalised in terms of these notions, are described as those that "an agent has using any actions and resources to achieve a goal". The expression $P_{ag_i}(ag_j, g_k)$ represents the *set* of plans that agent ag_i believes that agent ag_j possesses in order to achieve the goal g_k. Each plan within this set is denoted by $p_{ag_{i_l}}$, where $R(p_{ag_{i_l}})$ represents the set of resources required for the plan, and the expression $I(p_{ag_{i_l}})$ represents a *sequence* of instantiated actions used in this plan. Finally, each instantiated action within a plan is defined by the action itself and the set of resources used in the instantiation of the action.

$$
\begin{array}{rcl}
Ext_{ag_i} & \stackrel{def}{\equiv} & \bigcup_{j=1}^{n} Ext_{ag_i}(ag_j) \\
Ext_{ag_i}(ag_j) & \stackrel{def}{\equiv} & \{G_{ag_i}(ag_j), A_{ag_i}(ag_j), R_{ag_i}(ag_j), P_{ag_i}(ag_j)\} \\
p_{ag_{i_l}}(ag_j, g_k) & \stackrel{def}{\equiv} & \{g_k, R(p_{ag_{i_l}}(ag_j, g_k)), I(p_{ag_{i_l}}(ag_j, g_k))\} \\
i_m(p_{ag_{i_l}}(ag_j, g_k)) & \stackrel{def}{\equiv} & \{a_m, R_{a_m}(p_{ag_{i_l}}(ag_j, g_k))\}
\end{array}
$$

Table 8.2. Original Definition of External Descriptions

The *hypothesis of external description compatibility*, which states that any two agents agree on their external descriptions is adopted in the SDN model. For any two agents i and j, i's external description entry for i is the same as j's external description for i and i's external description for j is the same as j's external description for j. This is formalised below.

$$Ext_{ag_i}(ag_i) = Ext_{ag_j}(ag_i) \wedge Ext_{ag_i}(ag_j) = Ext_{ag_j}(ag_j)$$

8.3.2 SDN in SMART

There are several issues concerned with external descriptions that arise directly from comparison with SMART.

Agents and Resources.
In SMART, no distinction is made between agents and resources, and instead only agents are considered with different functionalities. As a result, plan-agents need only to consider the set of *agents* required in a plan. Plans can therefore be represented as sets of actions, where each action is associated with a set of agents, each one potentially capable of performing the action. Crucially, the distinction between a resource and an agent in SDN is not clear and, presumably, an arbitrary distinction between agents and resources must be made for SDN to be applied. The distinction is important because the nature of a plan assumes that while all the *resources* required by an action have already been identified, the agents that might perform that

action have not. In this respect, incomplete plans, where the resources required *have not yet been considered*, cannot be represented. Equally, a plan where the agent that is to perform an action *has been established* cannot be represented. Thus the SDN formalism is inflexible in this respect, and too critically influenced by whatever distinction is chosen to differentiate between resources and agents. By allowing agents with different functionalities in SMART, the restriction on SDN plans that requires the resources needed for each action to be selected but not the agents, can be removed.

Simultaneous and Concurrent Actions.
According to the SMART model of plans and plan-agents in Section 5.4, agents may plan to perform concurrent actions and, further, plans can comprise several actions that need to be performed simultaneously by different agents. In the SDN model, the assumption is that actions are neither simultaneous nor concurrent.

Ownership.
The notion of ownership in SDN is critical but not defined, and detracts from definitions that rely on it. In SMART, an agent *owns* another entity if it is not engaged by any other agent and can be used as required without regard to others. Furthermore, sociological agents are able to understand and reason about such relationships, enabling them to determine the interaction possibilities available. No such analysis is apparent in SDN, and there is a strong indication of an underlying simplification that resources cannot be shared. This restrictive issue is addressed using SMART later.

Agent Perspective.
The SDN *hypothesis of external description compatibility* used in the development of SDNs ensures that any two agents will agree on their external description entry for a given agent. In SMART, agents are more general and may have different and conflicting views of their environment; they can never *know* about the plans, goals and capabilities of others.

We can now apply SMART to model SDNs. Without any loss of generality we equate SDN actions and goals to be SMART actions and goals. As the meaning of a *resource* is not clear, and in order that this reformulation makes no limiting assumptions, we take a resource to be an entity, the most general type possible. Thus the relationship of SDN plans to SMART plans is more complicated and is discussed below.

– All SDN plans are SMART *total* plans (see Section 5.4).

– SDN plans contain only primitive actions.

– In SMART, the associated entities of a primitive action must have the necessary capabilities to perform that action. This is clearly an underlying assumption of the SDN model.

– Plans in SMART consist of plan-actions, which are sets of ordered pairs. The first element of each ordered pair is a compound-action, and the second is the set of entities that may perform that action. Sets of pairs are used in order to represent simultaneous actions. In the SDN model, no two entities can simultaneously perform actions so that plan-actions contain only one pair containing a primitive action. Actions in SDN plans are associated with a set of entities used to perform that action. Since, in SMART, an action in a plan is also associated with a set of entities, this representation of a plan can be directly applied.

– SDN goals are associated with sets of plans to achieve them, where each plan is considered as a potential means of achieving a goal. In SMART, this association is represented by the functions, *activeplangoal* or *plangoallibrary*, in the *PlanAgent* schema depending on whether the goal is a current one.

– The resources required by an action in a plan, as well as the resources required by a plan, are represented in the SDN model. However, if the resources required by each action within a plan are known, then the set of all the resources required by the plan must also be known, and this latter information is therefore not included in this reformulation.

8.3.3 Formalising External Descriptions

According to the discussion above, the schema formalising external descriptions is a refinement of the *PlanAgent* schema introduced in Section 5.4. One additional variable is included to represent the set of resources owned by an agent. The schema predicates make *explicit*, assumptions that are *implicit* in SDN as discussed above, which assert that plan-actions are sets containing only one pair, any action in a plan-action is primitive, and all plans are total. The feature to notice here is how easily the set of premises and implicit assumptions on which SDN is built can be illustrated in SMART.

$$
\begin{array}{|l|}
\hline
\_\,SDNExternalDescription\,_____ \\
PlanAgent \\
ownedresources : \mathbb{P}\, Entity \\
\hline
\forall pa : PlanAction \bullet \forall p : Plan \mid \\
\quad p \in planlibrary \land pa \subseteq \bigcup(planpairs\, p) \bullet \\
\quad\quad \#pa = 1 \land \\
\quad\quad \mathrm{dom}\, pa \subseteq \mathrm{ran}\, Prim \land \\
\quad\quad p \in \mathrm{ran}\, Total \\
\hline
\end{array}
$$

We can now define multi-agent system comprising of SDN agents. Each such agent has an external description of every other agent according to the *hypothesis of external description compatibility*, which states that any two agents have the same external description for each agent. To model this, we simply associate an external description with each agent.

```
┌── SDNMultiAgentSystemExternalDescriptions ──────────────────
│  MultiAgentSystem
│  extdes : Agent ⇸ SDNExternalDescription
├──────────────────────────────────────────────────────────
│  dom extdes = agents
└──────────────────────────────────────────────────────────
```

Then, according to the external description of an agent, A,

$(extdes\ A).planlibrary$ is its set of library plans,

$(extdes\ A).activeplan$ is its set of active plans,

$(extdes\ A).capabilities$ is its set of actions,

$(extdes\ A).ownedresources$ is its set of resources,

$(extdes\ A).goals$ is its set of current goals, and

$(extdes\ A).goallibrary$ is its set of library goals.

If resources cannot be shared, there is a further restriction on the state that can be expressed explicitly using the SMART relationship taxonomy. Specifically, if an agent *directly engages* an entity then it must *directly own* that entity. This is a restriction placed on the environment itself, not on the way in which agents model the environment and can be formalised using the *AgentRelationsTaxonomy* schema first introduced in Section 3.7.

$$\forall\ system : AgentRelationshipsTaxonomy;\ A : Agent;\ S : ServerAgent \bullet$$
$$(A, S) \in system.dengages \Rightarrow (A, S) \in system.downs$$

8.4 Action and Resource Autonomy

```
┌──────────────────────────────────────────────────────────┐
│  An agent $ag_i$ will be *a_autonomous* for a given goal $g_k$, *according to a set of*   │
│  *plans* $P_{qk}$ if there is a plan that achieves this goal in this set and every action │
│  appearing in this plan belongs to $A(ag_i)$.                                            │
│                                                                                          │
│  An agent $ag_i$ will be *r_autonomous* for a given goal $g_k$, *according to a*          │
│  *set of plans* $P_{qk}$ if there is a plan that achieves this goal in this set and every │
│  resource appearing in this plan belongs to $R(ag_i)$.                                   │
│                                                                                          │
│  An agent $ag_i$ will be *s_autonomous* for a given goal $g_k$, *according to a*          │
│  *set of plans* $P_{qk}$ if he is both *a_autonomous* and *r_autonomous* for this goal.   │
└──────────────────────────────────────────────────────────┘
```

Table 8.3. Original Definition of Action and Resource Autonomy

Using external descriptions, three distinct categories of autonomy referred to as *a_autonomous*, *r_autonomous* and *s_autonomous* are identified. According to these

$$a_{aut}(ag_i, g_k, P_{qk}) \overset{\text{def}}{\equiv} \exists g_k \in G(ag_i) \exists p_{lk} \in P_{qk} \forall i_m \in (p_{lk}) \in I(p_{lk}) a_m \in A(ag_i)$$

$$r_{aut}(ag_i, g_k, P_{qk}) \overset{\text{def}}{\equiv} \exists g_k \in G(ag_i) \exists p_{lk} \in P_{qk} \forall r_m \in R(p_{lk}) r_m \in R(ag_i)$$

$$s_{aut}(ag_i, g_k, P_{qk}) \overset{\text{def}}{\equiv} a_{aut}(ag_i, g_k, P_{qk}) \wedge r_{aut}(ag_i, g_k, P_{qk})$$

Table 8.4. Original Formalisation of Action and Resource Autonomy

definitions agents are autonomous if they have the necessary capabilities and resources to achieve a goal and so do not need the help of others. The original definitions and their formal representations can be found in Table 8.3 and Table 8.4.

It is not clear in these definitions whether agents can reason with respect just to their current goals or to any goal in their goal library. The distinction is important, since it has ramifications for subsequent SDN categorisations as will be discussed later. However, we formalise two possible interpretations of the meaning of goals. First, agents that can reason with respect to any goal in any agent's goal library using the *libraryachieves* relation are defined. It holds between an agent, a goal and a set of plans from the plan library if the plans are non-empty, and related to the goal according to the function *plangoallibrary* from the *PlanAgent* schema.

libraryachieves $(A, g, ps) \Leftrightarrow$
$\quad (g, ps) \in (extdes\ A).plangoallibrary \wedge ps \neq \{\ \}$

Alternatively, agents may only be able to reason with respect to *current* goals. This scenario is formalised by the predicate, *achieves* (A, g, ps), which holds precisely when an agent, A, has goal g, and the non-empty set of *active* plans ps associated with g in order to achieve it, according to the external description of A.

achieves $(A, g, ps) \Leftrightarrow$
$\quad (g, ps) \in (extdes\ A).activeplangoal \wedge ps \neq \{\ \}$

Consider the definition of the category *s_autonomous*. An agent is in this category if, within the set of plans being analysed, there is one plan that contains actions within the agent's capabilities, and another plan that involves resources all owned by the agent. However, there is no stipulation that these plans are the same. In other words, an agent can be *s_autonomous* for a goal, and still not be able to achieve it, since there may be no *specific* plan that requires just the capabilities *and* resources of that agent. This is easy to rectify and in the following schema, these three classes of autonomy using the *achieves* relation are defined. The second predicate states that an agent, A, is *a_autonomous* with respect to a current goal, g, according to some (non-empty) set of plans, ps, if and only if there is some agent, C, with goal, g, and plans, ps, to achieve g such that some plan, p in ps, contains actions all in the capabilities of A. Similar predicates are specified for *r_autonomous*.

SDNAutonomyRelations

SDNMultiAgentSystemExternalDescriptions
achieves _ : $\mathbb{P}(Agent \times Goal \times \mathbb{P} \, Plan)$
a_autonomous _, r_autonomous _, s_autonomous _ :
$\qquad\qquad\qquad\qquad\qquad \mathbb{P}(Agent \times Goal \times \mathbb{P} \, Plan)$

$\forall A : Agent; \; g : Goal; \; ps : \mathbb{P} \, Plan \bullet$
achieves $(A, g, ps) \Leftrightarrow$
$\qquad (g, ps) \in (extdes \, A).activeplangoal \, \wedge$
$\qquad ps \neq \{ \} \wedge$
a_autonomous $(A, g, ps) \Leftrightarrow$
$\qquad (\exists \, C : Agent \bullet$ achieves $(C, g, ps)) \, \wedge$
$\qquad (\exists \, p : ps \bullet (planactions \, p \subseteq (extdes \, A).capabilities)) \, \wedge$
r_autonomous $(A, g, ps) \Leftrightarrow$
$\qquad (\exists \, C : Agent \bullet$ achieves $(C, g, ps)) \, \wedge$
$\qquad (\exists \, p : ps \bullet ((planentities \, p \subseteq (extdes \, A).ownedresources))) \, \wedge$
s_autonomous $(A, g, ps) \Leftrightarrow$
$\qquad (\exists \, C : Agent \bullet$ achieves $(C, g, ps)) \, \wedge (\exists \, p : ps \bullet$
$\qquad\qquad ((planentities \, p \subseteq (extdes \, A).ownedresources) \, \wedge$
$\qquad\qquad (planactions \, p \subseteq (extdes \, A).capabilities)))$

Note that it is the quantification of the specific plan p in the set ps, in the formal definition for *s_autonomous*, that ensures that the agent is both *a_autonomous* and *r_autonomous* with respect to the same plan.

8.5 Dependence Relations

An agent ag_i *a_depends* on another agent ag_j for a given goal g_k, according to a set of plans P_{qk} if he has g_k in his set of goals, he is not s-autonomous for g_k and there is a plan in P_{qk} that achieves g_k and at least one action used in this plan is in ag_i's set of actions.

An agent ag_i *r_depends* on another agent ag_j for a given goal g_k, according to a set of plans P_{qk} if he has g_k in his set of goals, he is not r-autonomous for g_k and there is a plan in P_{qk} that achieves g_k and at least one resource used in this plan is in ag_i's set of resources.

An agent ag_i *s_depends* on another agent ag_j for a given goal g_k, according to a set of plans P_{qk} if he either *a_depends* or *r_depends* on this latter agent.

Table 8.5. Original Definition of Dependence Networks

$$
\begin{aligned}
a_{dep}(ag_i, ag_j, g_k, P_{qk}) &\overset{\mathrm{def}}{\equiv} \exists\, g_k \in G(ag_i)\, \neg a_{aut}(ag_i, g_k, P_{qk}) \wedge \\
&\quad \exists\, p_{lk} \in P_{qk}\, \exists\, i_m(p_{lk}) \in I(p_{lk}) a_m \in A(ag_j) \\
r_{dep}(ag_i, ag_j, g_k, P_{qk}) &\overset{\mathrm{def}}{\equiv} \exists\, g_k \in G(ag_i)\, \neg r_{aut}(ag_i, g_k, P_{qk}) \wedge \\
&\quad \exists\, p_{lk} \in P_{qk}\, \exists\, r_m \in R(p_{lk}) r_m \in Rag_j \\
s_{dep}(ag_i, ag_j, g_k, P_{qk}) &\overset{\mathrm{def}}{\equiv} a_{dep}(ag_i, ag_j, g_k, P_{qk}) \vee r_{dep}(ag_i, ag_j, g_k, P_{qk})
\end{aligned}
$$

Table 8.6. Original Formalisation of Dependence Networks

If agents are not autonomous they are dependent on others to achieve their goals, and
the dependencies in the SDN model are defined in Table 8.5 and Table 8.6. These
relations can be readily formalised in the *DependenceRelations* schema below. As
an example, the first predicate states that for two distinct agents, *A* and *B*, a goal, *g*,
and a set of plans *ps*, *A a_depends* on *B* for *g* with respect to *ps*, if and only if *g* is a
goal of *A*, *A* is not *a_autonomous* with respect to *g* and *ps*, and there is some agent,
C, with the goal, *g*, and plans to achieve *g*, *ps*, such that at least one plan in *ps* has
an action in the capabilities of *B*.

SDNDependenceRelations
SDNAutonomyRelations
$a\_depends\,\_, r\_depends\,\_, s\_depends\,\_ :$
$$\mathbb{P}(Agent \times Agent \times Goal \times \mathbb{P}\,Plan)$$

$\forall A, B : Agent;\ g : Goal;\ ps : \mathbb{P}\,Plan \mid A \neq B \bullet$
$a\_depends\,(A, B, g, ps) \Leftrightarrow$
   $(g \in (extdes\ A).goals) \wedge$
   $\neg\ a\_autonomous\,(A, g, ps) \wedge$
   $(\exists\, C : Agent \bullet achieves\,(C, g, ps) \wedge$
      $(\bigcup\{p : ps \bullet planactions\ p\} \cap$
            $(extdes\ B).capabilities \neq \{\,\})) \wedge$
$r\_depends\,(A, B, g, ps) \Leftrightarrow$
   $(g \in (extdes\ A).goals) \wedge \neg\ r\_autonomous\,(A, g, ps) \wedge$
   $(\exists\, C : Agent \bullet achieves\,(C, g, ps) \wedge$
      $(\exists\, p : ps \bullet (planentities\ p) \cap$
            $(extdes\ B).ownedresources \neq \{\,\})) \wedge$
$s\_depends\,(A, B, g, ps) \Leftrightarrow$
   $a\_depends\,(A, B, g, ps) \vee r\_depends\,(A, B, g, ps)$

According to the SDN model, *A* depends on *B* if and only if there is a plan to
achieve a goal of *A* that involves an action in the capabilities of *B*. However, in this
situation it makes little sense to say that *A* depends on *B* for a goal if the actions that
achieve that goal are also in *A*'s capabilities. In other words, the SDN formalisation
of *a_depends* does not define dependence at all; rather it indicates the existence of a
plan where there is a potential for *B* to help *A*. Similarly, it makes little sense to say
that *A* depends on another agent for a resource if that resource is owned (in the SDN

sense) by both. A better definition of A depending on B, which allows for agents having common actions, is that there is a plan to achieve A's goal that requires an action in the capabilities of B but *not in the capabilities* of A. This interpretation of dependence is defined below.

An agent, A, *a_depends* on another agent, B, for a given goal, g, according to some set of plans of some agent, C, to achieve g, if g is a goal of A, A is not *a_autonomous* for g, and there is a plan in ps containing an action in B's capabilities that is not in A's capabilities. This is formalised by the following predicate.

$$a\_depends\ (A, B, g, ps) \Leftrightarrow (g \in (extdes\ A).goals) \land$$
$$\neg\ a\_autonomous\ (A, g, ps) \land$$
$$(\exists\, C : Agent \bullet achieves\ (C, g, ps) \land$$
$$(\exists\, action : (\bigcup\{p : ps \bullet planactions\ p\} \bullet$$
$$action \in (extdes\ B).capabilities \land$$
$$action \notin (extdes\ A).capabilties)))$$

However, even when B is capable of an action of which A is not, but which is required in a plan to achieve A's goal, it still makes little sense to say there is a *dependence*, because there may be other plans that do not require B's assistance. It is more appropriate to say that there is a possibility of B being able to help A in achieving her goal because there happens to be a plan where A needs B's help. A better notion of actual *dependence* between A and B with respect to a goal and a *set* of plans would be if *every* plan in the set of plans associated with A's goal required B's assistance. In this respect A would have a real dependence on B in order to achieve her goal, since the goal could not be achieved without B's help. This notion of dependence is defined and formalised below.

An agent, A, *a_depends* on another agent, B, for a given goal, g, according to some set of plans of some agent, C, to achieve g, if g is a goal of A, A is not *a_autonomous* for g, and every plan in ps contains an action in B's capabilities that is not in A's capabilities.

$$a\_depends\ (A, B, g, ps) \Leftrightarrow (g \in (extdes\ A).goals) \land$$
$$\neg\ a\_autonomous\ (A, g, ps) \land$$
$$(\exists\, C : Agent \bullet achieves\ (C, g, ps) \land$$
$$(\forall\, p : ps \bullet \exists\, action : planactions\ p \bullet$$
$$action \in (extdes\ B).capabilities \land$$
$$action \notin (extdes\ A).capabilities)))$$

The key point here is to show how it is possible to generalise the SDN model and remove the need for limiting assumptions so that the model can be used to describe systems containing shared resources, and agents having actions in common. By reformulating SDN it has been shown that several options exist for a range of different types of dependencies. These definitions can easily be modified or updated, depending on which assumptions about the nature of the multi-agent system under investigation are chosen.

8.6 Dependence Situations

The entire set of dependence relations produces a *dependence network* that can be used to classify distinct *dependence situations* between two agents, as shown in Table 8.7.

---

mutual dependence is a situation where an agent ag_i infers that he and [an]other agent ag_j a-depend on each other for the *same goal* g_k, according to a set of plans P_{qk}.

reciprocal dependence is a situation where an agent ag_i infers that he and [an]other agent ag_j a-depend on each other, but for *different goals* g_k and g_l according to the sets of plans P_{qk} and P_{ql} (both sets belonging to the same external description entry).

independence is a situation where, using his own plans, ag_i infers that he does not a-depend on ag_j for g_k.

unilateral dependence is a situation where, using his own plans, ag_i infers that he a-depends on ag_j for g_k, but this latter does not a-depend on him for any of his goals.

Table 8.7. Original Definition of Dependence Situations

These categories might be more appropriately named if they were based on dependencies for actions outside the capabilities of an agent, as considered previously. For example, the SDN definition of A's independence of B implies that it is not possible for B to *help* A in performing an action. A more intuitive definition of *independence* would be that A does not *need* B to perform any action.

Consider the definition of mutual dependence between A and B. This states that A and B both have a goal g, and according to A's plans, ps to achieve g, there is some plan in which B could perform an action, and some plan (not necessarily the same plan) in which A could perform an action. Rather than mutual dependence, this categorisation describes a potential for cooperation (if the agents are autonomous), or mutual engagement otherwise. This SDN category simply identifies situations where a single plan, or possibly two plans, can involve both A and B. A more appropriate definition of mutual dependence might be that *every* plan in the set, ps, *needs* both agents to act as discussed previously. A further alternative would be to define mutual dependence with respect to a *single* plan rather than a set of plans. Agents could then be mutually dependent with respect to a plan if the plan required the capabilities of both agents.

Reciprocal dependence occurs when, according to two sets of plans, A could help B achieve some goal g_B, and B could help A achieve some goal g_A. The mechanism is described as *social exchange*. However, if agents can only reason with respect to sets of plans associated with a *current* goal, and since the definition is given with respect to A's plans, A must currently *desire* both g_A and g_B. This is restrictive since bargaining can occur (for example, when A and B have different single goals) in order for each to adopt the other's goal.

In order to resolve these problems, consider a situation with two agents, A and B, where A is not *a_autonomous* for some goal, g_A, according to A's plans, ps_A, to achieve g_A. The following situations can then be identified.

- A is *independent* (*IND*) with respect to B for g if, according to ps_A, it infers that it does not *a_depend* on B for g.
- A is *unilaterally dependent* (*UD*) on B for g_A if, according to ps_A, A *a_depends* on B, but there is no goal for which B *a_depends* on A.
- Two agents are *mutually dependent* (*MD*) if they *a_depend* on each other for the same goal g_A according to ps_A.

If, in addition, B is not *a_autonomous* for some other goal, g_B, according to A's plans ps_B to achieve g_B then the following can be written.

- Two agents are *reciprocally dependent* (*RD*) if they *a_depend* on each other for g_A and g_B, according to two sets of plans, ps_A and ps_B, respectively.

We can now map these textual definitions onto formal ones. Given two agents, A and B, where A is not *a_autonomous* for some goal, g, we define the dependence situations in the schema below. As an example, reciprocal dependence is defined as follows. For any two agents, A and B, any two goals g_A and g_B and any two plans ps_A and ps_B such that A and B are distinct, g_A and g_B are distinct, ps_A is A's set of plans to achieve the goal g_A, A is not *a_autonomous* with respect to g_A according to ps_A, A is reciprocally dependent on B according to the goals g_A and g_B and the plans ps_A and ps_B if and only if ps_B are A's plans to achieve g_B and, according to ps_A, A *a_depends* on B for g_A, and according to ps_B, B *a_depends* on B for g_B.

SDNDependenceSituations _____

SDNDependenceRelations
$IND \_, UD \_ : \mathbb{P}(Agent \times Agent \times Goal)$
$MD \_ : \mathbb{P}(Agent \times Agent \times Goal \times \mathbb{P}\,Plan)$
$RD \_ : \mathbb{P}(Agent \times Agent \times Goal \times Goal \times \mathbb{P}\,Plan \times \mathbb{P}\,Plan)$

_____

$\forall A, B : Agent;\ g_A, g_B: Goal;\ ps_A, ps_B : \mathbb{P}\,Plan \mid (A \neq B) \wedge (g_A \neq g_B) \wedge$
$\quad\quad achieves\ (A, g_A, ps_A) \wedge \neg\ a\_autonomous\ (A, g_A, ps_A) \bullet$
$\quad IND\ (A, B, g_A) \Leftrightarrow$
$\quad\quad\quad \neg\ a\_depends\ (A, B, g_A, ps_A) \wedge$
$\quad UD\ (A, B, g_A) \Leftrightarrow$
$\quad\quad\quad a\_depends\ (A, B, g_A, ps_A) \wedge$
$\quad\quad\quad \neg(\exists g : Goal;\ ps : \mathbb{P}\,Plan \mid$
$\quad\quad\quad\quad\quad achieves\ (A, g, ps) \bullet a\_depends\ (B, A, g, ps)) \wedge$
$\quad MD\ (A, B, g_A, ps_A) \Leftrightarrow$
$\quad\quad\quad a\_depends\ (A, B, g_A, ps_A) \wedge$
$\quad\quad\quad a\_depends\ (B, A, g_A, ps_A) \wedge$
$\quad RD\ (A, B, g_A, g_B, ps_A, ps_B) \Leftrightarrow$
$\quad\quad\quad achieves\ (A, g_B, ps_B) \wedge$
$\quad\quad\quad \neg\ a\_autonomous\ (B, g_B, ps_B) \wedge$
$\quad\quad\quad a\_depends\ (A, B, g_A, ps_A) \wedge$
$\quad\quad\quad a\_depends\ (B, A, g_B, ps_B)$

8.7 Summary

This chapter has applied the SMART models to evaluate social dependence networks, enabling limiting assumptions on which SDNs are built to be isolated. The reformulation has enabled a stronger, more consistent formal model to be constructed of which there are three important aspects. First, *implicit* assumptions can be isolated and made explicit. Any theoretical developments are then more strongly underpinned and in a well-defined context. Second, restrictive assumptions about agents, such as no shared resources or no agents having actions in common, can be removed. This allows the model to be applied in more general systems. Third, relevant issues overlooked in SDN can be addressed. Specifically, SDNs do not provide analyses of key agent relationships, nor of how agents model their environments before forming dependence networks.

This last point can be appreciated by referring to Figure 8.1, which shows that the SMART schemas, *MultiAgentSystem* and *PlanAgent*, have been used as the basis from which to reformalise SDNs. It also shows that the schemas *AgentSociety* and *SociologicalAgent* were *not* used, highlighting what has been neglected in the original SDN analysis: first, no analysis of the key social relationships was presented; and second, no model was developed to show how agents would interpret them.

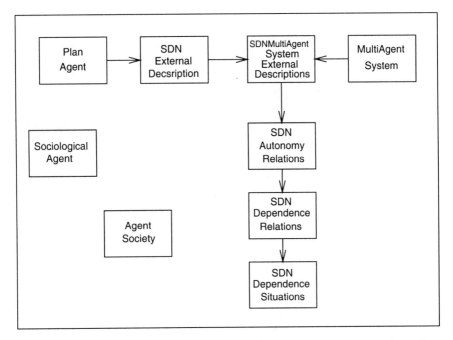

Fig. 8.1. Schema Structure for Specifying Reformulation of Social Dependence Networks

9. Conclusions

9.1 Summary

9.1.1 The SMART Framework

This book has described a generally applicable notion of agenthood that is not an attempt to create yet another agent definition, but one that relates to existing concepts and attempts to encompass them. In the definitions provided, we set up a sound conceptual base on which to elaborate more sophisticated definitions and architectures, while at the same time constructing a framework that can accommodate all types of agent, be they non-computational, reflexive, or deliberative.

In the view we propose, agents and autonomous agents are distinguished from each other, as well as from non-autonomous entities, with clear and precise distinctions being made. Agents are defined as objects that can be ascribed goals, while the definition of autonomous agents as agents that can generate their own goals arises as a consequence. The hierarchy thus constructed is clean and simple, but embodies a sufficient set of concepts to provide a firm grounding for subsequent development and analysis.

In particular, the definitions of agency and autonomy are presented in base abstract architectures. Thus, even at the definition stage, the models have a direct link to issues involved in system design, since they detail the interdependence of the various aspects of an agent's data components and activity. This interdependence is described in these architectures using a functional model, which relates actions, goals, motivations (where appropriate) and perceptions. Once an agent is situated in an environment, the parameters of functions are available, and they can be evaluated to describe the agent's state at run-time. Importantly, the book includes an operational model that details the interaction of an agent with its environment as changes to the agent's state.

The SMART framework is thus universally applicable, since it does not specify any internal architectural, design or implementation biases. All that is required of agent systems is a minimal adherence to the set of basic action and perception functionalities that are specified as part of the model.

9.1.2 Agent Relationships

The analysis of fundamental inter-agent relationships has arisen neatly and naturally out of the SMART framework. This results from the definition of agents as objects with an ascribed set of goals, since it necessitates not only the existence of autonomous agents who can generate their own goals, but the need for goal adoption as the mechanism by which non-autonomous entities can become agents. Goal adoption is the key process underlying multi-agent systems, and once an agent has adopted the goal of another, an essential relationship is created between the two, with one entity acting on behalf of the other. Thus agency necessitates goal adoption, which in turn creates and defines the universal relationships of multi-agent systems.

This model allows us to reason about how and why goal adoption takes place, a mechanism previously not generally investigated as an integral aspect of multi-agent systems. Agent relationships depend on the entities involved; while autonomous agents enter into relationships voluntarily, non-autonomous agents do not have this choice. Cooperation is therefore distinguished from engagement; while autonomous agents cooperate in voluntary relationships, non-autonomous agents are engaged in compulsory ones. The framework provides an understanding of the origin of these relationships, how and when they are initiated, manipulated, or broken and, perhaps more importantly, how any changes may impact on other relationships.

Cooperation and engagement relationships can also be analysed further to define a taxonomy of the different ways in which two agents can be related. This information is important, not only since it is possible to understand the precise dependence of any two agents according to goal adoption, but also since it highlights the different interaction possibilities that are available to participating agents.

9.1.3 Agent Architectures

This book has shown that in order to be generally effective in multi-agent systems, agents need to be sociological. In other words, they need to have access to information about agent relationships, and recognise them in the system of which they are a part. This is not only so that they can reason about taking advantage of the current social configuration of agents, but also so that they can avoid unnecessarily affecting this structure in any potentially harmful or damaging way. The book has provided an abstract architecture for such agents and demonstrated how their increased reasoning capabilities enable them to make more informed social decisions in relation to multi-agent *plans* containing actions to be performed by others. *En route* to demonstrating the effectiveness of sociological agents, it established a taxonomy of multi-agent plans, based on the current social obligations of the agents involved, and providing basic information to these agents.

9.2 Evaluation

The models in the book can be evaluated under three different headings: *generality*, *application* and *methodology*. First, we discuss how the models have been structured and organised so that they are encompassing with respect to the field in general.

Second, we show the way in which they have been applied to both existing and new artifacts and ideas so as to demonstrate its practical benefits. Finally, we consider the methods employed.

9.2.1 Generality

The ability to conceptualise systems at different levels of abstraction is generally acknowledged as crucial in the design of software systems. This is particularly true in many agent-based approaches that provide the means for abstracting out internal system features and interpreting or designing systems at higher levels such as the mentalistic or intelligent level. In this book, every model is related to every other model according to the level of abstraction at which it is described. We thus have a complete hierarchy of abstraction levels where each subsequent level is a refinement of the previous one.

One of the principal aims of this book has been to determine and analyse fundamental relationships in multi-agent systems. In order to undertake an analysis of this kind it is first important to understand the nature of the agents themselves. However, if we are to build models of agents, it is important that they are *general*, and not biased towards any theory, architecture, design or implementation. This is not only so that the agent models can themselves be generally applied without prejudice to the range of existing agent systems, but also so that the subsequent analysis of inter-agent relationships is also universally applicable. Developing generally applicable models of agents using generic abstract architectures has enabled us to use them as the basis from which to determine the key inter-agent relationships that arise naturally in multi-agent systems.

9.2.2 Application

One issue that has hampered the progress and development of the field of multi-agent systems is the relative lack of retrospective integration. As we have already suggested, existing ideas are often presented as new ones simply because a new conceptual foundation, research agenda or formal language is being employed. This arises because conceptual or theoretical foundations are are often uniquely tailored to the specific requirements of individual research agendas; agent frameworks are seldom built for application to other work.

To demonstrate that the models in this book are generally applicable to existing research formal models of two different multi-agent mechanisms have been constructed, and it has been shown how these can be structured within the SMART agent framework so that the nature of their sociological relationships can be highlighted. In addition, the framework has been applied to produce specifications of several single-agent architectures. Through this approach, the systems themselves can be evaluated by directly applying the theoretical models to build specifications of both implemented and theoretical single-agent architectures and multi-agent system mechanisms. In this way, theory and practice are brought together in a very strong and coherent way.

The first of the two multi-agent system case-studies is the contract net protocol, a mechanism for dynamic task allocation in distributed systems. It is one of the most common techniques employed in implemented multi-agent systems and there is a great deal of literature on its use in industrial applications. The second case-study covers the social reasoning mechanism based on social dependence networks, which provide agents with a means for determining the interdependence of agents to achieve their goals. In contrast with the contract net protocol, the social dependence models are are a theoretical development arising out of related work on social interaction in sociology and psychology. It is therefore situated at the other end of the spectrum from the contract net protocol in terms of its nature, its origin and its use in deployed systems. The third case study is AgentSpeak(L), which falls within the single-agent category. AgentSpeak(L) is important since it is an attempt to build a theoretical language that captures the essential operation of systems based on the belief-desire-intention (BDI) model, of which there are many. Indeed this model is seen by some as the best example of deliberative intelligent agent architecture.

9.3 Concluding Remarks

The lack of an agreed terminology or structure within which to pursue research in multi-agent systems is set to hamper the further development of the field if efforts are not made to address it. This book has described one such effort which has provided a framework that allows the development of diverse definitions, architectures, designs, theories and systems to be related within a single coherent whole. It has provided simple and encompassing definitions of agency and autonomy and explicated the relationship between them. These definitions are encapsulated in abstract general architectures that can be applied to analyse inter-agent relationships and refined to provide more detailed architectures for the deliberative dimensions required by more practical agents. The usefulness of the models has been demonstrated by elaboration and refinement to the point where we have been able to present descriptions, stated in terms of our formal models, of both implemented systems and theoretical models.

There is currently a high financial investment in agent products and it is becoming a mature technology. We must therefore address the need to develop agent-based tools, supported by a strong conceptual foundation, which can be used to design, specify and implement such systems. This book seeks to provide just such a tool that spans a range of levels of definition and abstraction, in order to provide a common integrated framework within which different levels of reasoning, behavioural and interaction tasks can be related and considered through design and specification.

A. The Z Specification Language

A.1 Introduction to Z

In this appendix, we introduce the syntax of the Z language by way of example. Much of this will be intuitive to many, but for a more detailed exposition, the authors recommend consulting one of the many texts cited in Chapter 1.

Z, developed in the late 1970s, is based on set theory and first order predicate calculus. The key syntactic element of Z is the schema, which allows specifications to be structured into manageable modular components. Z schemas consist of two parts: the upper declarative part, which declares variables and their types; and the lower predicate part, which relates and constrains those variables. It is therefore appropriate to liken the semantics of a schema to that of Cartesian products. For example, suppose we define a schema as follows.

$$
\begin{array}{|l}
\hline
\_Pair\_ \\
\hline
first : \mathbb{N} \\
second : \mathbb{N} \\
\hline
\end{array}
$$

This is very similar to the following Cartesian product type.

$$Pair == \mathbb{N} \times \mathbb{N}$$

The difference between these forms is that there is no notion of order in the variables of the schema type. In addition, a schema may have a predicate part that can be used to constrain the state variables. Thus, we can state that the variable, *first*, can never be greater than *second*.

$$
\begin{array}{|l}
\hline
\_Pair\_ \\
\hline
first : \mathbb{N} \\
second : \mathbb{N} \\
\hline
first \leq second \\
\hline
\end{array}
$$

Modularity is facilitated in Z by allowing schemas to be included within other schemas. We can select a state variable, *var*, of a schema, *schema*, by writing *schema.var*. For example, it should be clear that *Pair.first* refers to the variable *first* in the schema *Pair*.

Now, operations in a state-based specification language are defined in terms of *changes to the state*. Specifically, an operation relates variables of the state after the operation (denoted by dashed variables) to the value of the variables before the operation (denoted by undashed variables). Operations may also have inputs (denoted by variables with question marks), outputs (exclamation marks) and preconditions. In the *GettingCloser* schema below, there is an operation with an input variable, *new*?; if *new*? lies between the variables *first* and *second*, then the value of *first* is replaced with the value of *new*?. The value of *second* does not change, and the output *old*! is equal to the value of the variable *first* as it was before the operation occurs. The $\Delta Pair$ symbol, is an abbreviation for *Pair* $\wedge$ *Pair'* and, as such, includes in this operation schema all the variables and predicates of the state of *Pair* before and after the operation.

```
┌─ GettingCloser ──────────────────────────────────
│ new? : ℕ
│ ΔPair
│ old! : ℕ
├──────────────────────────────────────────────────
│ first ≤ new?
│ new? ≤ second
│ first' = new?
│ second' = second
│ old! = first
└──────────────────────────────────────────────────
```

To introduce a type in Z when no information about the elements within that type is specified, a *given set* is used. This is an important abstraction mechanism that allows us to model things at the higest possible level. For example, we can write [*TREE*] to represent the set of all trees without stating anything about the nature of the individual elements within the type. If we wish to state that a variable takes on a value, a set of values, or an ordered pair of values of this type, we write $x : TREE$, $x : \mathbb{P}\,TREE$ and $x : TREE \times TREE$. If we have $xs : TREE \times TREE$ then the expressions *first xs* and *second xs* denote the first and second elements of the ordered pair *xs*.

Perhaps the most important type is the *relation* type, expressing a mapping between *source* and *target* sets. The type of a relation with source X and target Y is $\mathbb{P}(X \times Y)$, and any element of this type (or *relation*) is simply a set of ordered pairs.

The definition of functions is also standard: relations are functions if no element from the source is related to more than one element in the target set. If every element in the source set is related to one on the target, then the function is *total* (denoted by $\rightarrow$); *partial* functions ($\nrightarrow$) do not relate every source set element. If no two elements in the source relate to the same element in the target set then the function is injective ($\rightarrowtail$). Further, if all elements in the target set are related then the function is surjective ($\twoheadrightarrow$).

Sequences are simply special types of function where the domain consists of contiguous natural numbers.

By way of illustration, we introduce two examples of relations, *Fun*1 and *Seq*1, which define a *function* between trees, and a *sequence* of trees, respectively. The size of the source set determines whether *Fun*1 is a partial or a total function; if the only elements of the source set are *tree*1, *tree*2 and *tree*3, then the function is total, otherwise it is partial.

$$Fun1 = \{(tree1, tree2), (tree2, tree3), (tree3, tree2)\}$$
$$Seq1 = \{(3, tree3), (2, tree2), (1, tree4)\}$$

The sequence *Seq*1 is more usually written in Z as $\langle tree4, tree2, tree3 \rangle$. Operations on sequences include taking the head, tail and concatenation.

$$head\ Seq1 = tree4$$
$$tail\ Seq1 = \langle tree2, tree3 \rangle$$
$$Seq1 \frown Seq1 = \langle tree4, tree2, tree3, tree4, tree2, tree3, \rangle$$

The *domain* of a relation or function (dom) is the set of source elements, while the *range* (ran) is the set of target set elements. The *inverse* of a relation is obtained by reversing each of the ordered pairs so that the domain becomes the range and the range becomes the domain. A relation can be restricted to a particular subset of its range using *range restriction* ($\triangleright$). Similarly a relation can be domain anti-restricted by a set in such a way that the resulting relation does not contain any ordered pairs whose first element is in the restricting set. This is known as *anti-domain restriction* ($\triangleleft$). Finally, one relation can be updated by another relation using *relational overriding*. The second relation can be thought of as 'new' information about its domain elements, overwriting any pairs in the relation whose first element is in the domain of the second relation. Examples of these operators can be seen below.

$$\text{dom}\ Fun1 = \{tree1, tree2, tree3\}$$
$$\text{ran}\ Fun1 = \{tree2, tree3\}$$
$$\text{dom}\ Seq1 = \{1, 2, 3\}$$
$$\text{ran}\ Seq1 = \{tree2, tree3, tree4\}$$
$$Fun1^{-1} = \{(tree2, tree1), (tree3, tree2), (tree2, tree3)\}$$
$$Fun1 \triangleright \{tree3\} = \{(tree2, tree3)\}$$
$$\{tree1\} \triangleleft Fun1 = \{(tree2, tree3), (tree3, tree2)\}$$
$$Fun1 \oplus \{(tree1, tree3), (tree2, tree2), (tree2, tree3)\} =$$
$$\{(tree1, tree3), (tree2, tree2), (tree2, tree3), (tree3, tree2)\}$$

In the following examples we show how sets of elements can be defined using set comprehension, and how predicates are written. In addition, the final expression selects the unique element from the type A that satisfies the predicate P.

$$\{x : \mathbb{N} \mid x < 4 \bullet x * x\} = \{0, 1, 4, 9\}$$

$$\forall n : \mathbb{N} \mid n > 10 \bullet n * n > 100$$

$$\mu a : A \mid P$$

A summary of the notation that is used in this paper is given in Table A.1.

Table A.1. Summary of Z Notation

Definitions and declarations		Functions	
a, b	Identifiers	$A \nrightarrow B$	Partial function
p, q	Predicates	$A \rightarrow B$	Total function
s, t	Sequences	$A \nrightarrow\!\!\!\rightarrow B$	Total Surjection
x, y	Expressions	$A \rightarrowtail B$	Partial Injection
A, B	Sets	$A \rightarrowtail\!\!\!\rightarrow B$	Bijection
$a == x$	Abbreviated definition	**Sequences**	
$[a]$	Introduction of given set	$\langle x, y, \ldots \rangle$	Sequence
$a ::= b \langle\!\langle B \rangle\!\rangle$		$\mathrm{seq}\, A$	Finite sequences
$\quad \| \; c \langle\!\langle C \rangle\!\rangle$	Free type declaration	$\mathrm{seq}_1 A$	Non-empty seqs
$\mu d \mid P$	Definite description	$\mathrm{iseq}\, A$	Injective seqs
Logic		$\mathrm{iseq}_1 A$	Non-empty inj seqs
$\neg p$	Logical negation	$s \frown t$	Concatenation
$p \wedge q$	Logical conjunction	*head s*	First element of seq
$p \vee q$	Logical disjunction	*last s*	Last element of seq
$p \Rightarrow q$	Logical implication	$s \,\mathrm{in}\, t$	Subsequence
$p \Leftrightarrow q$	Logical equivalence	**Schema notation**	
$\forall X \bullet q$	Universal quantification		
$\exists X \bullet q$	Existential quantification		
Sets			
$x \in y$	Set membership		Vertical schema
$x \notin y$	Non-membership		
$\{\,\}$	Empty set		
$A \subseteq B$	Set inclusion		
$A \subset B$	Strict set inclusion		Axiomatic definition
$\{x, y, \ldots\}$	Set of elements		
$(x, y, \ldots)$	Ordered tuple		
$A \times B \times \ldots$	Cartesian product		
$\mathbb{P} A$	Power set		
$\mathbb{P}_1 A$	Non-empty power set		Schema inclusion
$A \cap B$	Set intersection		
$A \cup B$	Set union		
$A \setminus B$	Set difference		
$\bigcup A$	Generalised union		
$\bigcap A$	Generalised intersection		Operation schema
$\#A$	Size of finite set		
Relations			
$A \leftrightarrow B$	Relation	$z.a$	Component inclusion
$\mathrm{dom}\, R$	Domain of relation	**Conventions**	
$\mathrm{ran}\, R$	Range of relation	$a?$	Input to an operation
R^{-1}	Inverse of relation	$a!$	Output from an op
$R \rhd A$	Range restriction	a	Variable before op
$A \lhd R$	Anti-domain restriction	a'	Variable after op
R^{-1}	Relational Inverse	S	Schema before op
R^+	Transitive Closure	S'	Schema after op
$R (\!\| A \|\!)$	Relational Image	ΔS	Change of state
$R_1 \oplus R_2$	Relational Overriding	ΞS	No change of state

Schema notation diagrams:

$$
\begin{array}{|l}
\underline{\;S\;} \\
d \\
\hline
p
\end{array}
\qquad \text{Vertical schema}
$$

$$
\begin{array}{|l}
d \\
\hline
p
\end{array}
\qquad \text{Axiomatic definition}
$$

$$
\begin{array}{|l}
\underline{\;S\;} \\
T \\
d \\
\hline
p
\end{array}
\qquad \text{Schema inclusion}
$$

$$
\begin{array}{|l}
\underline{\;\Delta S\;} \\
S \\
S'
\end{array}
\qquad \text{Operation schema}
$$

A.2 Generic Z Definitions

Below, we provide the standard library of mathematical definitions that are used in this book. A complete set of definitions can be found in The Z Handbook [121] on which the definitions below are based.

A.2.1 Sets

A set, S, is a subset of another set, T, if whenever an element is contained in S, it is also contained in T. S is a strict subset of T if it S is a subset of T but S is not equal to T.

$$
\begin{array}{|l}
\hline
[X] \\
\_ \subseteq \_ : \mathbb{P}X \leftrightarrow \mathbb{P}X \\
\hline
\forall S, T : \mathbb{P}X \bullet \\
\quad (S \subseteq T \Leftrightarrow (\forall x : X \bullet x \in S \Rightarrow x \in T)) \wedge \\
\quad (S \subset T \Leftrightarrow S \subseteq T \wedge S \neq T) \\
\end{array}
$$

For any set X, $\mathbb{P}_1 X$ is the set of all subsets of X which are non-empty.

$$\mathbb{P}_1 X == \{S : \mathbb{P}X \mid S \neq \{\}\}$$

$S \cup T$ denotes those objects that are members of S or T or both; $S \cap T$ denotes those objects that are members of both S and T; and $S \setminus T$ denotes those objects that are members of S but not of T.

$$
\begin{array}{|l}
\hline
[X] \\
\_ \cap \_, \_ \cup \_, \_ \setminus \_ : (\mathbb{P}X \times \mathbb{P}X) \rightarrow \mathbb{P}X \\
\hline
\forall S, T : \mathbb{P}X \bullet \\
\quad S \cup T = \{x : X \mid x \in S \vee x \in T\} \wedge \\
\quad S \cap T = \{x : X \mid x \in S \wedge x \in T\} \wedge \\
\quad S \setminus T = \{x : X \mid x \in S \wedge x \notin T\} \\
\end{array}
$$

The generalised union of a set of sets contains every object that is in at least one of the sets. The generalised intersection of a set of sets contains those objects that are contained in every set.

$$
\begin{array}{|l}
\hline
[X] \\
\bigcap, \bigcup : \mathbb{P}(\mathbb{P}X) \rightarrow \mathbb{P}X \\
\hline
\forall A : \mathbb{P}(\mathbb{P}X) \bullet \\
\quad \bigcup A = \{x : X \mid (\exists S : A \bullet x \in S)\} \wedge \\
\quad \bigcap A = \{x : X \mid (\forall S : A \bullet x \in S)\} \\
\end{array}
$$

The functions *first* and *second* return the first and second element of an ordered pair.

$$
\begin{array}{|l}
\hline
[X, Y] \\
\hline
first : X \times Y \to X \\
second : X \times Y \to Y \\
\hline
\forall x : X;\ y : Y \bullet \\
\quad first(x, y) = x \land \\
\quad second(x, y) = y \\
\hline
\end{array}
$$

A.2.2 Relations

The domain of a relation, R, with source set X and target set Y comprises all the elements of X that are related to at least one element of Y. The range of a relation, R, with source set X and target set Y comprises all the elements of Y that are related to at least one element of X.

$$
\begin{array}{|l}
\hline
[X, Y] \\
\hline
\mathrm{dom} : (X \leftrightarrow Y) \to \mathbb{P}\,X \\
\mathrm{ran} : (X \leftrightarrow Y) \to \mathbb{P}\,Y \\
\hline
\forall R : X \leftrightarrow Y \bullet \\
\quad \mathrm{dom}\,R = \{x : X;\ y : Y \mid (x, y) \in R \bullet x\} \land \\
\quad \mathrm{ran}\,R = \{x : X;\ y : Y \mid (x, y) \in R \bullet y\} \\
\hline
\end{array}
$$

The range restriction of a relation, R, with source set X and target set Y, with respect to a set S of type $\mathbb{P}\,Y$, comprises all the pairs of R whose second element is a member of the set S. The anti-range restriction of a relation, R, with source set X and target set Y, with respect to a set S of type $\mathbb{P}\,Y$, comprises all the pairs of R whose second element is not a member of the set S.

$$
\begin{array}{|l}
\hline
[X, Y] \\
\hline
\_ \rhd \_ : (X \leftrightarrow Y) \times (\mathbb{P}\,Y) \to (X \leftrightarrow Y) \\
\_ \lhd \_ : (\mathbb{P}\,X) \times (X \leftrightarrow Y) \to (X \leftrightarrow Y) \\
\hline
\forall S : \mathbb{P}\,Y;\ T : \mathbb{P}\,X;\ R : X \leftrightarrow Y \bullet \\
\quad R \rhd S = \{x : X;\ y : Y \mid y \in S \land (x, y) \in R \bullet (x, y)\} \land \\
\quad T \lhd R = \{x : X;\ y : Y \mid x \notin T \land (x, y) \in R \bullet (x, y)\} \\
\hline
\end{array}
$$

An object y is related to an object x by the relation inverse R^{-1} of R if and only if x is related to y by R.

$$
\begin{array}{|l}
\hline
[X, Y] \\
\hline
\_^{-1} : (X \leftrightarrow Y) \to (Y \leftrightarrow X) \\
\hline
\forall R : X \leftrightarrow Y \bullet \\
\quad R^{-1} = \{x : X;\ y : Y \mid (x, y) \in R \bullet (y, x)\} \\
\hline
\end{array}
$$

The relational image $R(\!|\ S\ |\!)$ of a set through a relation R is the set of all objects y to which R relates some member x of S.

$$
\begin{array}{|l}
\underline{=[X, Y]=\!=\!=\!=\!=\!=\!=\!=\!=\!=\!=\!=\!=\!=\!=\!=\!=\!=\!=\!=} \\
\quad \_(\!|\ \_\ |\!) : (X \leftrightarrow Y) \times \mathbb{P}X \to \mathbb{P}Y \\
\hline
\forall R : X \leftrightarrow Y;\ S : \mathbb{P}X\ \bullet \\
\quad R(\!|\ S\ |\!) = \{x : X;\ y : Y \mid x \in S \wedge (x, y) \in R \bullet y\}
\end{array}
$$

A homogeneous relation is a relation whose source set equals the target set. The transitive closure of a homogeneous relation R is the smallest relation containing R that is transitive.

$$
\begin{array}{|l}
\underline{=[X]=\!=} \\
\quad \_^{+} : (X \leftrightarrow X) \to (X \leftrightarrow X) \\
\hline
\forall R : X \leftrightarrow X\ \bullet \\
\quad R^{+} = \bigcap\{Q : X \leftrightarrow X \mid R \subseteq Q \wedge Q \mathbin{\substack{\circ\\\circ}} Q \subseteq Q\}
\end{array}
$$

The relation $Q \oplus R$ relates everything in the domain of R to the same objects as R does, and everything else in the domain of Q to the same objects as Q does.

$$
\begin{array}{|l}
\underline{=[X, Y]=\!=} \\
\quad \_\oplus\_ : (X \leftrightarrow Y) \times (X \leftrightarrow Y) \to (X \leftrightarrow Y) \\
\hline
\forall R, S : X \leftrightarrow Y\ \bullet \\
\quad R \oplus S = (\operatorname{dom} S) \mathbin{\lhd\!\!\!-} R \cup S
\end{array}
$$

A.2.3 Functions

A partial function is a relation such that no element in the domain maps to more than one element in the range. A total function is defined for every element in the source set. A partial (or total) injection is a partial (or total) function such that no two elements in the domain map to the same element in the range. A partial (or total) surjection is a partial (or total) function that is defined for every element in the target set. Finally, a bijection is a function that is total, injective and surjective.

$$
\begin{aligned}
X \nrightarrow Y &== \{R : X \leftrightarrow Y \mid \forall x : X;\ y, z : Y \bullet (x, y) \in R \wedge (x, z) \in R \Rightarrow y = z\} \\
X \to Y &== \{f : X \nrightarrow Y \mid \operatorname{dom} f = X\} \\
X \rightarrowtail Y &== \{f : X \nrightarrow Y \mid (\forall x_1, x_2 : X \bullet f\, x_1 = f\, x_2 \Rightarrow x_1 = x_2)\} \\
X \rightarrowtail Y &== (X \to Y) \cap (X \nrightarrowtail Y) \\
X \twoheadrightarrow Y &== \{f : X \nrightarrow Y \mid \operatorname{ran} f = Y\} \\
X \twoheadrightarrow Y &== (X \to Y) \cap (X \twoheadrightarrow Y) \\
X \rightarrowtail\!\!\!\twoheadrightarrow Y &== (X \rightarrowtail Y) \cap (X \twoheadrightarrow Y)
\end{aligned}
$$

A.2.4 Sequences

The expression $m \ldots n$ defines the set of all numbers from m to n inclusive.

$$\begin{array}{|l}
\_\ldots\_ : \mathbb{N} \times \mathbb{N} \to \mathbb{P}\,\mathbb{N} \\\hline
\forall m, n : \mathbb{N} \bullet \\
\quad m \ldots n = \{a : \mathbb{N} \mid m \le a \le n\}
\end{array}$$

A sequence of type X is represented as a partial function from natural numbers to X such that the domain is a set of contiguous numbers from 1 up to the number of elements in the sequence. An injective sequence has no repeated elements. The set of non-empty sequences and non-empty injective sequences are also defined.

$$\text{seq}\,X == \{f : \mathbb{N} \nrightarrow X \mid \text{dom}\,f = 1 \ldots \#f\}$$
$$\text{seq}_1\,X == \{s : \text{seq}\,X \mid \#s > 0\}$$
$$\text{iseq}\,X == \text{seq}\,X \cap (\mathbb{N} \nrightarrowtail X)$$
$$\text{iseq}_1\,X == \text{iseq}\,X \cap \text{seq}_1\,X$$

The concatenation of two sequences s and t contains the elements of s followed by the elements of t.

$$\begin{array}{|l}
[X] \\\hline
\_\frown\_ : \text{seq}\,X \times \text{seq}\,X \to \text{seq}\,X \\\hline
\forall s, t : \text{seq}\,X \bullet \\
\quad s \frown t = s \cup \{n : 1 \ldots \#t \bullet ((n + \#s), t(n))\}
\end{array}$$

The *head* and *last* of a non-empty sequence are the first and last elements of that sequence.

$$\begin{array}{|l}
[X] \\\hline
head, last : \text{seq}_1\,X \to X \\\hline
\forall s : \text{seq}_1\,X \bullet \\
\quad head\ s = s(1)\ \wedge \\
\quad last\ s = s(\#s)
\end{array}$$

One sequence is a subsequence of another if the latter contains the former.

$$\begin{array}{|l}
[X] \\\hline
\_\text{in}\_ : \text{seq}\,X \leftrightarrow \text{seq}\,X \\\hline
\forall s, t : \text{seq}\,X \bullet \\
\quad s \text{ in } t \Leftrightarrow (\exists u, v : \text{seq}\,X \bullet u \frown s \frown v = t)
\end{array}$$

References

1. K. Arnold, B. O'Sullivan, R. W. Scheifler, J. Waldo, and A. Wollrath. *The Jini Specification*. Addison-Wesley, 1999.
2. R. Aylett and M. Luck. Applying artificial intelligence to virtual reality: Intelligent virtual environments. *Applied Artificial Intelligence*, 14(1):3–32, 2000.
3. J. Bowen. *Formal Specification and Documentation using Z: A Case Study Approach*. International Thomson Computer Press, 1996.
4. J. P. Bowen, S. Dunne, A. Galloway, and S. King, editors. *ZB 2000: Formal Specification and Development in Z and B, First International Conference of B and Z Users, Lecture Notes in Computer Science*, volume 1878. Springer-Verlag, 2000.
5. J. P. Bowen, S. Fett, and M. G. Hinchey, editors. *ZUM'98: The Z Formal Specification Notation, 11th International Conference of Z Users, Lecture Notes in Computer Science*, volume 1493. Springer-Verlag, 1998.
6. R. A. Brooks. A robust layered control system for a mobile robot. *IEEE Journal of Robotics and Automation*, 2(1):14–23, 1986.
7. J. A. Campbell and M. d'Inverno. Knowledge interchange protocols. In Y. Demazeau and J.-P. Müller, editors, *Decentralized AI: Proceedings of the First European Workshop on Modelling Autonomous Agents in a Multi-Agent World*, pages 63–80. Elsevier, 1990.
8. C. Castelfranchi. Social power. In Y. Demazeau and J.-P. Müller, editors, *Decentralized AI — Proceedings of the First European Workshop on Modelling Autonomous Agents in a Multi-Agent World*, pages 49–62. Elsevier Science Publishers B.V.: Amsterdam, The Netherlands, 1990.
9. C. Castelfranchi. Commitments: from individual intentions to groups and organizations. In *Proceedings of the First International Conference on Multi-Agent Systems*, pages 41–48, San Francisco, CA, 1995.
10. C. Castelfranchi. Guarantees for autonomy in cognitive agent architecture. In M. Wooldridge and N. R. Jennings, editors, *Intelligent Agents: Theories, Architectures, and Languages, Lecture Notes in Artificial Intelligence*, volume 890, pages 56–70. Springer-Verlag, 1995.
11. C. Castelfranchi. Distributed artificial intelligence and social science: Critical issues. In G. M. P. O'Hare and N. R. Jennings (eds), editors, *Foundations of Distributed Artificial Intelligence*. John Wiley and Sons, 1996.
12. C. Castelfranchi, M. Miceli, and A. Cesta. Dependence relations among autonomous agents. In E. Werner and Y. Demazeau, editors, *Decentralized AI 3 — Proceedings of the Third European Workshop on Modelling Autonomous Agents in a Multi-Agent World*, pages 215–231. Elsevier Science Publishers B.V.: Amsterdam, The Netherlands, 1992.
13. B. Chaib-draa. Industrial applications of distributed AI. *Communications of the ACM*, 38(11):49–53, 1995.
14. B. Chellas. *Modal Logic: An Introduction*. Cambridge University Press: Cambridge, England, 1980.
15. D. Chess, B. Grosof, C. Harrison, D. Levine, C. Parris, and G. Tsudik. Itinerant agents for mobile computing. *IEEE Personal Communications*, 2(5):34–49, 1995.

16. P. R. Cohen and C. R. Perrault. Elements of a plan based theory of speech acts. *Cognitive Science*, 3:177–212, 1979.

17. B. P. Collins, J. E. Nicholls, and I. H. Sørensen. Introducing formal methods: The CICS experience with Z. In B. Neumann et al., editors, *Mathematical Structures for Software Engineering*. Oxford University Press, 1991.

18. D. Connah and P. Wavish. An experiment in cooperation. In Y. Demazeau and J.-P. Müller, editors, *Decentralized AI — Proceedings of the First European Workshop on Modelling Autonomous Agents in a Multi-Agent World*, pages 197–214. Elsevier Science Publishers B.V.: Amsterdam, The Netherlands, 1990.

19. R. Conte, M. Miceli, and C. Castelfranchi. Limits and levels of cooperation. In Y. Demazeau and J.-P. Müller, editors, *Decentralized AI 2 — Proceedings of the Second European Workshop on Modelling Autonomous Agents in a Multi-Agent World*, pages 147–160. Elsevier Science Publishers B.V.: Amsterdam, The Netherlands, 1991.

20. A. Covrigaru and R. Lindsay. Deterministic autonomous systems. *AI Magazine*, 12(3):110–117, 1991.

21. B. Crabtree. What chance software agents? *Knowledge Engineering Review*, 13(2):131–136, 1998.

22. I. D. Craig. *The Formal Specification of Advanced AI Architectures*. Ellis Horwood, 1991.

23. D. Craigen, S. L. Gerhart, and T. J. Ralston. An international survey of industrial applications of formal methods. Technical Report NIST GCR 93/626-V1 & 2, Atomic Energy Control Board of Canada, US National Institute of Standards and Technology, and US Naval Research Laboratories, 1993.

24. R. Davis and R. G. Smith. Negotiation as a metaphor for distributed problem solving. *Artificial Intelligence*, 20(1), 1983.

25. Y. Demazeau and J.-P. Müller. Decentralized artificial intelligence. In Y. Demazeau and J.-P. Müller, editors, *Decentralized AI — Proceedings of the First European Workshop on Modelling Autonomous Agents in a Multi-Agent World*, pages 3–17. Elsevier Science Publishers B.V.: Amsterdam, The Netherlands, 1990.

26. M. d'Inverno, M. Fisher, A. Lomuscio, M. Luck, M. de Rijke, M. Ryan, and M. Wooldridge. Formalisms for multi-agent systems. *Knowledge Engineering Review*, 12(3):315–321, 1997.

27. M. d'Inverno, K. Hindriks, and M. Luck. A formal architecture for the 3APL agent programming language. In *ZB2000: First International Conference of B and Z Users, Lecture Notes in Computer Science*, volume 1878, pages 168–187. Springer-Verlag, 2000.

28. M. d'Inverno, D. Kinny, and M. Luck. Interaction protocols in Agentis. In *ICMAS'98 Proceedings of the Third International Conference on Multi-Agent Systems*, pages 112–119, Paris, France, 1998. IEEE Computer Society.

29. M. d'Inverno, D. Kinny, M. Luck, and M. Wooldridge. A formal specification of dMARS. In *Intelligent Agents IV: Proceedings of the Fourth International Workshop on Agent Theories, Architectures and Languages, Lecture Notes in Artificial Intelligence*, volume 1365, pages 155–176. Springer-Verlag, 1998.

30. M. d'Inverno and M. Luck. A formal view of social dependence networks. In C. Zhang and D. Lukose, editors, *Distributed Artificial Intelligence Architecture and Modelling: Proceedings of the First Australian Workshop on Distributed Artificial Intelligence, Lecture Notes in Artificial Intelligence*, volume 1087, pages 115–129. Springer-Verlag, 1996.

31. M. d'Inverno and M. Luck. Formalising the contract net as a goal directed system. In W. Van de Velde and J.W. Perram, editors, *Agents Breaking Away: Proceedings of the Seventh European Workshop on Modelling Autonomous Agents in a Multi Agent World, Lecture Notes in Artificial Intelligence*, volume 1038, pages 72–85. Springer-Verlag, 1996.

32. M. d'Inverno and M. Luck. Understanding autonomous interaction. In W. Wahlster, editor, *ECAI'96 - Proceedings of the 13th European Conference on Artificial Intelligence*, pages 529–533. John Wiley and Sons, Ltd, 1996.

33. M. d'Inverno and M. Luck. Development and application of a formal agent framework. In M. G. Hinchey and L. Shaoying, editors, *ICFEM'97: Proceedings of the First IEEE International Conference on Formal Engineering Methods*, pages 222–231. IEEE Computer Society, 1997.

34. M. d'Inverno and M. Luck. Making and breaking engagements: An operational analysis of agent relationships. In C. Zhang and D. Lukose, editors, *Multi-Agent Systems Methodologies and Applications: Proceedings of the Second Australian Workshop on Distributed Artificial Intelligence, Lecture Notes in Artificial Intelligence*, volume 1286, pages 48–62. Springer-Verlag, 1997.

35. M. d'Inverno and M. Luck. Engineering AgentSpeak(L): A formal computational model. *Journal of Logic and Computation*, 8(3), 1998.

36. M. d'Inverno, M. Luck, and M. Wooldridge. Cooperation structures. In *Proceedings of the Fifteenth International Joint Conference on Artificial Intelligence*, pages 600–605, Nagoya, Japan, 1997.

37. M. d'Inverno, M. Priestley, and M. Luck. A formal framework for hypertext systems. *IEE Proceedings – Software Engineering*, 144(3):175–184, 1997.

38. E. H. Durfee. Blissful ignorance: Knowing just enough to coordinate well. In *Proceedings of the First International Conference on Multi-Agent Systems*, pages 406–413, San Francisco, CA, 1995.

39. E. H. Durfee and V. R. Lesser. Using partial global plans to coordinate distributed problem solvers. In *Proceedings of the Tenth International Joint Conference on Artificial Intelligence*, Milan, Italy, 1987.

40. E. A. Emerson and J. Y. Halpern. 'Sometimes' and 'not never' revisited: on branching time versus linear time temporal logic. *Journal of the ACM*, 33(1):151–178, 1986.

41. O. Etzioni, H. M. Levy, R. B. Segal, and C. A. Thekkath. The softbot approach to OS interfaces. *IEEE Software*, 12(4), 1995.

42. O. Etzioni and D. Weld. Intelligent agents on the internet: Fact, fiction and forecast. *IEEE Expert*, 10(4):44–49, 1995.

43. I. A. Ferguson. Integrated control and coordinated behaviour: A case for agent models. In M. Wooldridge and N. R. Jennings, editors, *Intelligent Agents: Theories, Architectures, and Languages, Lecture Notes in Artificial Intelligence*, volume 890, pages 203–218. Springer-Verlag, 1995.

44. K. Fischer, J. P. Müller, and M. Pischel. A model for cooperative transportation scheduling. In *Proceedings of the First International Conference on Multi-Agent Systems*, pages 109–116, San Francisco, CA, 1995.

45. K. Fischer, P. Müller, J, and M. Pischel. AGenDA — a general testbed for distributed artificial intelligence applications. In G. M. P. O'Hare and N. R. Jennings (eds), editors, *Foundations of Distributed Artificial Intelligence*, pages 401–428. John Wiley and Sons, 1996.

46. M. Fisher and M. Wooldridge. Specifying and executing protocols for cooperative action. In S. M. Deen, editor, *CKBS-94 — Proceedings of the Second International Working Conference on Cooperating Knowledge-Based Systems*. Springer-Verlag, 1994.

47. S. Franklin and A. Graesser. Is it an agent, or just a program?: A taxonomy for autonomous agents. In J. P. Müller, M. J. Wooldridge, and N.R. Jennings, editors, *Intelligent Agents III — Proceedings of the Third International Workshop on Agent Theories, Architectures, and Languages, Lecture Notes in Artificial Intelligence*, volume 1193, pages 21–35. Springer-Verlag, 1997.

48. D. Garlan. The role of reusable frameworks. *ACM SIGSOFT Software Engineering Notes*, 15(4):42–44, 1990.

49. D. Garlan and N. Delisle. Formal specifications as reusable frameworks. In D. Bjørner, C. A. R. Hoare, and H. Langmaack, editors, *VDM and Z – Formal Methods in Software Development, Lecture Notes in Computer Science*, volume 428, pages 150–163. VDM-Europe, Springer-Verlag, 1990.

50. D. Garlan and D. Notkin. Formalizing design spaces: Implicit invocation mechanisms. In S. Prehn and W. J. Toetenel, editors, *VDM'91: Formal Software Development Methods, Lecture Notes in Computer Science*, volume 551, pages 31–45. Springer-Verlag, 1991.

51. M. Genersereth and N. Nilsson. *Logical Foundations of Artificial Intelligence*. Morgan Kaufman, Palo Alto, CA, 1987.

52. M. R. Genesereth and S. P. Ketchpel. Software agents. *Communications of the ACM*, 37(7):48–53, 1994.

53. M. P. Georgeff and F. F. Ingrand. Decision-making in an embedded reasoning system. In *Proceedings of the Eleventh International Joint Conference on Artificial Intelligence*, pages 972–978, Detroit, MI, 1989.

54. M. P. Georgeff and A. L. Lansky. Reactive reasoning and planning. In *Proceedings of the Sixth National Conference on Artificial Intelligence*, pages 677–682, Menlo Park, 1987. AAAI Press / MIT Press.

55. R. Goodwin. A formal specification of agent properties. *Journal of Logic and Computation*, 5(6), 1995.

56. S. Grand and D. Cliff. Creatures: Entertainment software agents with artificial life. *Autonomous Agents and Multi-Agent Systems*, 1(1):39–57, 1998.

57. R. H. Guttman, A. G. Moukas, and P. Maes. Agent-mediated electronic commerce: a survey. *Knowledge Engineering Review*, 13(2):147–159, 1998.

58. I. J. Hayes(Editor). *Specification Case Studies*. Prentice Hall, Hemel Hempstead, second edition, 1993.

59. S. R. Hedberg. Intelligent agents: The first harvest of softbots looks promising. *IEEE Expert*, 10(4):6–9, 1995.

60. M. A. Hewitt, C. M. O'Halloran, and C. T. Sennet. Experiences with PiZA, an animator for Z. In J. P. Bowen, M. G. Hinchey, and D. Till, editors, *ZUM'97: 10th International Conference of Z Users, Lecture Notes in Computer Science*, volume 1212, pages 37–51, Springer-Verlag, 1997.

61. K. Hindriks, d'Inverno, and M. Luck. Architecture for agent programming languages. In *ECAI 2000 - Proceedings of the 15th European Conference on Artificial Intelligence*, pages 363–367. IOS Press, 2000.

62. K. Hirayama and J. Toyoda. Forming coalitions for breaking deadlocks. In *Proceedings of the First International Conference on Multi-Agent Systems*, pages 155–162, San Francisco, CA, 1995.

63. C. A. R. Hoare. Communicating sequential processes. *Communications of the ACM*, 21:666–677, 1978.

64. M. J. Huber and E. H. Durfee. Deciding when to commit to action during observation-based coordination. In *Proceedings of the First International Conference on Multi-Agent Systems*, pages 163–170, San Francisco, CA, 1995.

65. A. Ito and H. Yano. The emergence of cooperation in a society of autonomous agents. In *Proceedings of the First International Conference on Multi-Agent Systems*, San Francisco, CA, 1995.

66. N. Jennings, E. Mamdami, J. M. Corera, I. Laresgoiti, F. Perriollat, P. Skarek, and L. Z. Varga. Using Archon to develop real world DAI applications, part 1. *IEEE Expert (Intelligent Systems and Their Applications)*, 11(6):64–70, 1996.

67. N. R. Jennings, P. Faratin, M. J. Johnson, P. O'Brien, and M. E. Wiegand. Agent-based business process management. *International Journal of Cooperative Information Systems*, 5(2 & 3):105–130, 1996.

68. N. R. Jennings, K. Sycara, and M. Wooldridge. A roadmap of agent research and development. *Autonomous Agents and Multi-Agent Systems*, 1(1):7–38, 1998.

69. N. R. Jennings and T. Wittig. ARCHON: Theory and practice. In *Distributed Artificial Intelligence: Theory and Praxis*, pages 179–195. ECSC, EEC, EAEC, 1992.

70. W. L. Johnson and B. Hayes-Roth, editors. *Proceedings of the First International Conference on Autonomous Agents*. ACM Press, 1997.

71. C. B. Jones. *Systematic Software Development using VDM (second edition)*. Prentice Hall, 1990.

72. D. Kinny, M. Georgeff, and A. Rao. A methodology and modelling technique for systems of BDI agents. In Y. Demazeau and J.-P. Müller, editors, *Agents Breaking Away: Proceedings of the Seventh European Workshop on Modelling Autonomous Agents in a Multi-Agent World, Lecture Notes in Artificial Intelligence*, volume 1038, pages 56–71. Springer-Verlag, 1996.

73. C. Krogh. The rights of agents. In M. Wooldridge, J. P. Müller, and M. Tambe, editors, *Intelligent Agents II, Lecture Notes in Artificial Intelligence*, volume 1037, pages 1–16. Springer-Verlag, 1996.

74. Z. Kunda. The case for motivated reasoning. *Psychological Bulletin*, 108(3):480–498, 1990.

75. D. Kuokka and L. Harada. Matchmaking for information agents. In *Proceedings of the Fourteenth International Joint Conference on Artificial Intelligence (IJCAI-95)*, pages 672–679, Montréal, Québec, Canada, 1995.

76. Kevin Lano. *The B Language and Method: A guide to Practical Formal Development*. Springer-Verlag, 1996.

77. Y. Lashkari, M. Metral, and P. Maes. Collaborative interface agents. In *Proceedings of the Twelfth National Conference on Artificial Intelligence*, pages 444–449, 1994.

78. H. Lee, J. Tannock, and J. S. Williams. Logic based reasoning about actions and plans in artificial intelligence. *Knowledge Engineering Review*, 8(2):91–120, 1993.

79. M. Luck. From definition to deployment: What next for agent-based systems? *The Knowledge Engineering Review*, pages 119–124, 1999.

80. M. Luck and M. d'Inverno. A formal framework for agency and autonomy. In *Proceedings of the First International Conference on Multi-Agent Systems*, pages 254–260. AAAI Press / MIT Press, 1995.

81. M. Luck and M. d'Inverno. Structuring a Z specification to provide a formal framework for autonomous agent systems. In J. P. Bowen and M. G. Hinchey, editors, *ZUM'95: 9th International Conference of Z Users, Lecture Notes in Computer Science*, volume 967, pages 48–62. Springer-Verlag, 1995.

82. M. Luck and M. d'Inverno. Engagement and cooperation in motivated agent modelling. In C. Zhang and D. Lukose, editors, *Distributed Artificial Intelligence Architecture and Modelling: Proceedings of the First Australian Workshop on Distributed Artificial Intelligence, Lecture Notes in Artificial Intelligence*, volume 1087, pages 70–84. Springer-Verlag, 1996.

83. M. Luck and M. d'Inverno. Motivated behaviour for goal adoption. In C. Zhang and D. Lukose, editors, *Multi-Agent Systems: Theories, Languages and Applications — Proceedings of the Fourth Australian Workshop on Distributed Artificial Intelligence, Lecture Notes in Artificial Intelligence*, volume 1544, pages 58–73. Springer-Verlag, 1998.

84. M. Luck and M. d'Inverno. A conceptual framework for agent definition and development. *The Computer Journal*, 44(1), 2001.

85. M. Luck, N. Griffiths, and M. d'Inverno. From agent theory to agent construction: A case study. In *Intelligent Agents III: Proceedings of the Third International Workshop on Agent Theories, Architectures and Languages, Lecture Notes in Artificial Intelligence*, volume 1193, pages 49–63. Springer-Verlag, 1997.

86. A. Lux and D. Steiner. Understanding cooperation: an agent's perspective. In *Proceedings of the First International Conference on Multi-Agent Systems*, pages 261–268, San Francisco, CA, 1995.

87. P. Maes. The agent network architecture (ANA). *SIGART Bulletin*, 2(4):115–120, 1991.

88. T. Maruichi, M. Ichikawa, and M. Tokoro. Modelling autonomous agents and their groups. In Y. Demazeau and J.-P. Müller, editors, *Decentralized AI — Proceedings of the First European Workshop on Modelling Autonomous Agents in a Multi-Agent World*, pages 215–234. Elsevier Science Publishers B.V.: Amsterdam, The Netherlands, 1990.

89. F. G. McCabe and K. L. Clark. April — agent process interaction language. In M. Wooldridge and N. R. Jennings, editors, *Intelligent Agents: Theories, Architectures, and Languages, Lecture Notes in Artificial Intelligence*, volume 890, pages 324–340. Springer-Verlag, 1995.

90. R. Milner. *Communication and Concurrency*. Prentice Hall, 1989.

91. B. G. Milnes. A specification of the Soar architecture in Z. Technical Report CMU-CS-92-169, School of Computer Science, Carnegie Mellon University, 1992.

92. D. Moffat and N. H. Frijda. Where there's a will there's an agent. In M. Wooldridge and N. R. Jennings, editors, *Intelligent Agents: Theories, Architectures, and Languages, Lecture Notes in Artificial Intelligence*, volume 890, pages 245–260. Springer-Verlag, 1995.

93. B. Moulin and B. Chaib-draa. An overview of distributed artificial intelligence. In G. M. P. O'Hare and N. R. Jennings (eds), editors, *Foundations of Distributed Artificial Intelligence*, pages 3–56. John Wiley and Sons, 1996.

94. J. P. Müller. A cooperation model for autonomous agents. In J. P. Müller, M. J. Wooldridge, and N. R. Jennings, editors, *Intelligent Agents III — Proceedings of the Third International Workshop on Agent Theories, Architectures, and Language, Lecture Notes in Artificial Intelligence*, volume 1193, pages 245–260. Springer-Verlag, 1997.

95. J. P. Müller. Architectures and applications of intelligent agents: A survey. *The Knowledge Engineering Review*, 13(4):353–380, 1998.

96. A. Newell. The knowledge level. *Artificial Intelligence*, 18(1):87–127, 1982.

97. T. J. Norman and D. Long. Goal creation in motivated agents. In M. Wooldridge and N. R. Jennings, editors, *Intelligent Agents: Theories, Architectures, and Languages, Lecture Notes in Artificial Intelligence*, volume 890, pages 277–290. Springer-Verlag, 1995.

98. H. S. Nwana. Software agents: an overview. *The Knowledge Engineering Review*, 11(3):205–244, 1996.

99. R. Orfali and D. Harkey. *Client/Server Programming with Java and CORBA*. Wiley, second edition, 1998.

100. H. V. D. Parunak. Manufacturing experience with the contract net. In M. Huhns, editor, *Distributed Artificial Intelligence*, pages 285–310. Pitman Publishing: London and Morgan Kaufmann: San Mateo, CA, 1987.

101. H. Van Dyke Parunak. Applications of distributed artificial intelligence in industry. In G. M. P. O'Hare and N. R. Jennings, editors, *Foundations of Distributed Artificial Intelligence*, pages 139–164. Wiley, 1996.

102. H. Van Dyke Parunak. What can agents do in industry, and why? an overview of industrially-oriented R&D at CEC. In M. Klusch and G. Weiss, editors, *Cooperative Information Agents II, Lecture Notes in Artificial Intelligence*, volume 1435, pages 1–18. Springer-Verlag, 1998.

103. C. Petrie. What is an agent? In J. P. Müller, M. J. Wooldridge, and N. R. Jennings, editors, *Intelligent Agents III — Proceedings of the Third International Workshop on Agent Theories, Architectures, and Languages, Lecture Notes in Artificial Intelligence*, volume 1193, pages 41–43. Springer-Verlag, 1997.

104. A. S. Rao. AgentSpeak(L): BDI agents speak out in a logical computable language. In W. Van de Velde and J. W. Perram, editors, *Agents Breaking Away: Proceedings of the Seventh European Workshop on Modelling Autonomous Agents in a Multi-Agent World, Lecture Notes in Artificial Intelligence*, volume 1038, pages 42–55. Springer-Verlag, 1996.

105. D. Riecken. An architecture of integrated agents. *Communications of the ACM*, 37(7):107–116, 1994.

106. J. S. Rosenschein. Multiagent planning as a social process: Voting, privacy, and manipulation. In *Proceedings of the First International Conference on Multi-Agent Systems*, page 431, San Francisco, CA, 1995.

107. S. J. Russell, D. Subramanian, and R. Parr. Provably bounded optimal agents. In *Proceedings of the Thirteenth International Joint Conference on Artificial Intelligence*, pages 338–344, 1993.

108. M. Saaltink. The Z/EVES system. In J. P. Bowen, M. G. Hinchey, and D. Till, editors, *ZUM'97: 10th International Conference of Z Users, Lecture Notes in Computer Science*, volume 1212, pages 72–85, Springer-Verlag, 1997.

109. T. Sandholm. An implementation of the contract net protocol based on marginal cost calculations. In *Proceedings of the Eleventh National Conference on Artificial Intelligence*, pages 256–262, Menlo Park, 1993. AAAI Press / MIT Press.

110. T. Selker. A teaching agent that learns. *Communications of the ACM*, 37(7):92–99, 1994.

111. Y. Shoham. Agent-oriented programming. *Artificial Intelligence*, 60:51–92, 1993.

112. J. S. Sichman, R. Conte, C. Castelfranchi, and Y. Demazeau. A social reasoning mechanism based on dependence networks. In *Proceedings of the Eleventh European Conference on Artificial Intelligence*, pages 188–192, Amsterdam, The Netherlands, 1994.

113. H. A. Simon. Motivational and emotional controls of cognition. In *Models of Thought*, pages 29–38. Yale University Press, 1979.

114. A. Sloman. Motives, mechanisms, and emotions. *Cognition and Emotion*, 1(3):217–233, 1987.

115. A. Sloman and M. Croucher. Why robots will have emotions. In *Proceedings of the Seventh International Joint Conference on Artificial Intelligence*, pages 197–202, Vancouver, B.C., 1981.

116. D. C. Smith, A. Cypher, and J. Spohrer. Programming agents without a programming language. *Communications of the ACM*, 37(7):55–67, 1994.

117. R. G. Smith. The CONTRACT NET: A formalism for the control of distributed problem solving. In *Proceedings of the Fifth International Joint Conference on Artificial Intelligence*, Cambridge, MA, 1977.

118. R. G. Smith. The contract net protocol. *IEEE Transactions on Computers*, C-29(12), 1980.

119. R. G. Smith and R. Davis. Frameworks for cooperation in distributed problem solving. *IEEE Transactions on Systems, Man, and Cybernetics*, 11(1), 1980.

120. J. M. Spivey. *The fUZZ Manual*. Computing Science Consultancy, 2 Willow Close, Garsington, Oxford OX9 9AN, UK, 2nd edition, 1992.

121. J. M. Spivey. *The Z Notation: A Reference Manual*. Prentice Hall, Hemel Hempstead, 2nd edition, 1992.

122. D. Steiner, A. Burt, M. Kolb, and C. Leri. The conceptual framework of MAI^2L. In C. Castelfranchi and J.-P. Müller, editors, *From Reaction to Cognition — Fifth European Workshop on Modelling Autonomous Agents in a Multi-Agent World, MAAMAW-93, Lecture Notes in Artificial Intelligence*, volume 957, pages 217–230. Springer-Verlag, 1995.

123. T. Sugawara. Reusing past plans in distributed planning. In *Proceedings of the First International Conference on Multi-Agent Systems*, pages 360–367, San Francisco, CA, 1995.

124. M. Tambe. Recursive agent and agent-group tracking in a real-time dynamic environment. In *Proceedings of the First International Conference on Multi-Agent Systems*, pages 368–375, San Francisco, CA, 1995.

125. M. Tokoro. The society of objects. Technical Report SCSL-TR-93-018, Sony CSL, 1993.

126. C. Toomey and W. Mark. Satellite image dissemination via software agents. *IEEE Expert*, 10(5):44–51, 1995.

127. J. M. Vidal and E. H. Durfee. Recursive agent modeling using limited rationality. In *Proceedings of the First International Conference on Multi-Agent Systems*, pages 376–383, San Francisco, CA, 1995.

128. M. Weber. Combining Statecharts and Z for the design of safety-critical control systems. In M.-C. Gaudel and J. C. P. Woodcock, editors, *FME'96: Industrial Benefit and Advances in Formal Methods, Lecture Notes in Computer Science*, volume 1051, pages 307–326. Formal Methods Europe, Springer-Verlag, 1996.

129. E. Werner. Cooperating agents: A unified theory of communication and social structure. In L. Gasser and M. Huhns, editors, *Distributed Artificial Intelligence Volume II*, pages 3–36. Pitman Publishing: London and Morgan Kaufmann: San Mateo, CA, 1989.

130. C. D. Wezeman. Using Z for network modelling: An industrial experience report. *Computer Standards & Interfaces*, 17(5–6):631–638, 1995.

131. D. Wong, N. Paciorek, and D. Moore. Java-based mobile agents. *Communications of the ACM*, 42(3):92–102, 1999.

132. K. R. Wood. A practical approach to software engineering using Z and the refinement calculus. *ACM Software Engineering Notes*, 18(5):79–88, 1995.

133. M. Wooldridge. *The Logical Modelling of Computational Multi-Agent Systems*. PhD thesis, Department of Computation, UMIST, Manchester, UK, 1992.

134. M. Wooldridge. This is MYWORLD: The logic of an agent-oriented testbed for DAI. In M. Wooldridge and N. R. Jennings, editors, *Intelligent Agents: Theories, Architectures, and Languages, Lecture Notes in Artificial Intelligence*, volume 890, pages 160–178. Springer-Verlag, 1995.

135. M. Wooldridge. Agents as a Rorschach test: A response to franklin and graesser. In J. P. Müller, M. J. Wooldridge, and N.R. Jennings, editors, *Intelligent Agents III — Proceedings of the Third International Workshop on Agent Theories, Architectures, and Languages, Lecture Notes in Artificial Intelligence*, volume 1193, pages 47–48. Springer-Verlag, 1997.

136. M. Wooldridge and N. R. Jennings. Agent theories, architectures, and languages: A survey. In M. Wooldridge and N. R. Jennings, editors, *Intelligent Agents: Theories, Architectures, and Languages, Lecture Notes in Artificial Intelligence*, volume 890, pages 1–39. Springer-Verlag, 1995.

137. M. J. Wooldridge and N. R. Jennings. Intelligent agents: Theory and practice. *Knowledge Engineering Review*, 10(2), 1995.

Index

Printing: Saladruck, Berlin
Binding: H. Stürtz AG, Würzburg